Praise for *Ten Years to Save the West*

"Anyone paying attention knows that we are in the midst of an existential fight for our values and way of life. Liz Truss has been on the front lines of that fight, standing firm against dictators abroad and woke establishment tyranny at home. The odds are stacked against us, but Truss knows what's worth fighting for, and she reminds us in this remarkable book."

    —**Ted Cruz,** United States senator from Texas and bestselling author of *One Vote Away, Justice Corrupted*, and *Unwoke: How to Defeat Cultural Marxism in America*

"Liz Truss is right about one big thing—the old establishment economic models are failing. That's bad news for the entire Western world. And she is right that the last thing any of us now needs is more socialism, more taxes, and more regulation. We need to reject that tiresome refrain of the Global Left and instead pursue an agenda that unleashes enterprise and boosts economic growth. I commend this invigorating tract!"

    —**The Right Honorable Boris Johnson,** Prime Minister of Great Britain, 2019–2022

"By the time former heads of government get around to writing their memoirs, they usually look exclusively backward, focused only on legacy. This is not the case with former prime minister Liz Truss, and we are very fortunate that this is so. Truss is a true movement conservative who has served at the highest levels on the world stage, and in *Ten Years to Save the West* she diagnoses clearly and vividly the problems she found there. Western conservatism is under attack from inside and out, and this book is required reading for those all over the world who want to defend it. Liz Truss will be a leader in this fight for years to come, and her book pulls no punches in describing the stakes of today and the challenges of tomorrow."

    —**Mike Lee,** senior United States senator from Utah

"Liz Truss is that rare figure in the political arena today—a genuine leader of principle and conviction, who is willing to stand up and fight for policies that actually advance freedom and defend national sovereignty and self-determination. *Ten Years to Save the West* is vital and urgent reading for policymakers on both sides of the Atlantic. The West faces an era of dangerous, even irreversible decline unless we are willing to take action now to defend the very ideals that have driven its greatness. Like Margaret Thatcher before her, Liz is a true friend of the American people, and her spirited message in this book should be heeded on Capitol Hill and in the White House."

—**Kevin Roberts,** president of The Heritage Foundation

"Agree or disagree with Liz's politics, she asks the right questions with an intellectual boldness rarely seen in modern politics. This book is a call to action against a resurgent authoritarian axis threatening freedom around the world and a reminder to keep faith with the values that have led to the greatest rise in prosperity in human history."

—**Garry Kasparov,** World Chess Champion, 1985–2000, and
activist for freedom and human rights in Russia and the world

"There are those who watch and those who do. Those who commentate and those who get their hands dirty. The cold and timid critics, and those actually in the arena. Liz Truss was in the fiercest arena of all, fighting for free-market principles against entrenched interests, fashionable pundits, and hostile officials. In the end, her opponents got the better of her. Now she has had a year to mull over what went wrong, and what conservatives need to do differently. So when she, of all people, tells us how the West can overcome its enemies, foreign and domestic, we should listen."

—**Daniel Hannan,** Conservative member of the House of
Lords, where he sits as Lord Hannan of Kingsclere, and
former Member of the European Parliament

Ten Years to Save the West

Ten Years
to Save the
West

Leading the Revolution Against Globalism, Socialism, and the Liberal Establishment

Liz Truss

former Prime Minister of Great Britain

Since 1947
REGNERY
An Imprint of Skyhorse Publishing, Inc.

Regnery books may be purchased in bulk at special discounts for sales promotion, corporate gifts, fund-raising, or educational purposes. Special editions can also be created to specifications. For details, contact the Special Sales Department, Regnery, 307 West 36th Street, 11th Floor, New York, NY 10018 or info@skyhorsepublishing.com.

Published in the United States by Regnery, an imprint of Skyhorse Publishing, Inc.

Regnery® is a registered trademark and its colophon is a trademark of Skyhorse Publishing, Inc.®, a Delaware corporation.

Visit our website at www.regnery.com.
Please follow our publisher Tony Lyons on Instagram: @tonylyonsisuncertain.

10 9 8 7 6 5 4 3 2 1

Library of Congress Cataloging-in-Publication Data are available on file.

Cover design by John Caruso
Cover photograph by Getty

Print ISBN: 978-1-68451-551-6
eBook ISBN: 978-1-68451-562-2

Printed in the United States of America

To Hugh, Frances, and Liberty, who are my lodestars

CONTENTS

Introduction

I was impatient to get going. Plans had been made. I knew what needed to be done, but the weather was against us. From the window of the Royal Air Force jet, all I could see were the heavy clouds beneath us as we circled over Scotland. Thick fog had rolled in around the airport in Aberdeen, preventing planes from landing, so for the moment I was stranded in mid-air. As a woman in a hurry, the delay was frustrating.

My mind was already turning over the huge number of things I needed to do back in London once I took over as the prime minister of the United Kingdom. But before all that, I had an appointment with Her Majesty the Queen, and we were now at risk of being late or not getting there at all. At last, a gap in the skies appeared and the pilot managed to get us down on the ground. Another bumpy landing.

Boris Johnson, my predecessor, had flown up ahead of me on a different plane to see the Queen and officially tender his resignation as prime minister. His idea that we should fly together had been vetoed by the government's Cabinet Office. I guess it was too much of a security risk to have the outgoing and incoming prime ministers on the same plane.

On arrival in Aberdeen, the plan was for me, my husband Hugh, and my principal private secretary Nick Catsaras to transfer to a helicopter for a short flight to Balmoral Castle, said to be the Queen's favorite residence. The fog made this impossible, so instead we set out by road, adding yet more time to our journey. Our small convoy eventually arrived at the castle, where we were welcomed by the Queen's private secretary, Edward Young, and shown inside. Then, alone, I was shown into Her Majesty's drawing room.

The Queen, at the age of ninety-six, seemed to have grown frailer over the previous year, but she was evidently determined to carry out her constitutional duty of appointing the prime minister in person, as she had for each of my thirteen predecessors. This is how it works in the United Kingdom: the monarch invites the leader of the party able to command a majority in the House of Commons to become prime minister and form a government. I was told in advance that she had made a special effort to be standing to greet me, and she gave no hint of discomfort. She was as resolute, determined, and charming as ever.

Although I'd seen her at various Privy Council meetings and events, this was only my second one-on-one audience with her. On the previous occasion, after I had been removed from a different job in the government, she had remarked that being a woman in politics was tough.

After I had accepted Her Majesty's invitation to form a new government, we spent around twenty minutes discussing politics. She was completely attuned to everything that was happening, as well as being typically sharp and witty. Towards the end of our discussion, she warned me that being prime minister is incredibly aging. She also gave me two words of advice: "Pace yourself." Maybe I should have listened.

Once we'd finished our conversation, Hugh joined us for a few minutes. She asked about our daughters and then made some jokey observations about our new living quarters at Downing Street. We left with Her Majesty telling me she looked forward to our speaking again next week. I had no idea this meeting would be our last—and her final formal engagement as monarch.

I left Balmoral as prime minister and we began the trip back to London. Once again, the weather frustrated our plans as torrential rain poured down. I was amazed by the number of people who showed up to film the car and watch my every move. I was due to give my first speech outside Number 10 Downing Street, the official residence of the British prime minister, before going inside, but my people prepared an indoor option as the skies darkened. Convinced that fate was on my side and the weather would clear, I insisted on circling round in the car. Eventually the moment came.

I went straight from the car to speak at the lectern in front of my new home, telling the country: "Together we can ride out the storm." Having delivered this optimistic forecast and posed with Hugh for the obligatory photographs, I went inside to begin work. There was a lot to do: I had the Cabinet to appoint, my first Prime Minister's Questions the next day to prepare for, and then a major announcement on our support for people's energy bills the day after that. We had prepared a plan for the first hundred days in office—and there was no time to lose.

There was also no time to stop and reflect. Some people have asked how it felt to win the leadership election of the Conservative Party and thus become prime minister, and to step over the threshold of Number 10. What was going through my mind? The truth is the whole experience, from the moment Boris resigned, had felt like a rollercoaster, during which I was constantly in performance mode. I was moving from event to event, meeting to meeting, knowing that at this early stage I had to get everything right.

What actually came next, of course, was a profound shock that would reverberate around the world.

The Civil Service and Royal officials had been quietly making plans for the Queen's funeral and the accession of the new monarch for decades. "Operation London Bridge," as these plans were called, had been worked out in immense detail and tweaked over the years by successive governments in readiness for just this moment. But on a more human level, we were utterly unprepared. As I had just seen for myself, the Queen had remained robust, mentally sharp, and determined to do her duty. There simply wasn't any sense that the end would come as quickly as it did.

The first real indication I had of the gravity of the situation was on Wednesday night, the day after I had become prime minister. Having appointed my new Cabinet, my new ministers were set to be formally sworn into office, with the Queen joining remotely by video link from Balmoral. As we assembled in the Cabinet Office just before 6:00 p.m. for the meeting, word reached us that Her Majesty would not be available, as she had been advised to rest. That was when the machine kicked into action. My black mourning dress was fetched from my house in Greenwich. Frantic phone calls took place with Buckingham Palace. I started to think about what on earth I was going to say if the unthinkable happened.

The following morning, I was given an update that there were ongoing concerns for Her Majesty's health and contingency plans were starting to be stepped up, but with no further public comment from the Palace and no clear idea how quickly things would develop, we had to press ahead with the day's business. I went mid-morning to Parliament, where we were scheduled to have a debate at 11:40 a.m.

The House of Commons was full of the usual political squabbling. I was set to speak about my government's plans to tackle energy prices, though I had begun to think about a completely different speech that it would be my duty to give. Not long after I sat down after giving my speech, Nadhim Zahawi, the Cabinet Office minister, entered the House of Commons Chamber and came to sit next to me. I had spoken to him earlier about his role in coordinating some of the necessary arrangements if and when Operation London Bridge kicked in, so this was clearly not a good sign. He told me we had received word that things were very grave indeed. The Palace was about to issue a statement to the media that the Queen was "under medical supervision" and her doctors were "concerned for Her Majesty's health."

Up to this moment, I had believed concerns might mount over a period of days and weeks, a drama unfolding in slow motion, but I now realized with dread that the news could come in a matter of hours. Members of the Royal Family were rushing to Balmoral, and the media had recognized the significance of that. I left the House of Commons and headed back to Downing Street.

Later that afternoon we received the solemn news: Her Majesty Queen Elizabeth II had died peacefully at Balmoral at the age of ninety-six. Despite the preparations over the previous twenty-four hours, the confirmation came as a profound shock. After the frenzy of the leadership election and on only my second full day as prime minister, it seemed utterly unreal. Amid profound sadness, I found myself thinking, *Why me? Why now?*

Leading the nation in mourning after the death of our beloved monarch of seventy years was not something I had ever expected to do. I had come into office determined to focus on the British economy, which was heading for a downturn, and to take the tough decisions necessary to stimulate growth and put the country back on the right track. These were challenges I instinctively relished. But coping with the death of the Queen was something altogether different. I had experienced a fair amount of state ceremony and protocol during my time in politics, but in truth it was a long way from my natural comfort zone. Some prime ministers might have been better suited to the soaring rhetoric and performative statesmanship necessary in this historic moment, but I just felt a profound sense of sadness.

Queen Elizabeth had been a constant in the lives of British people for seventy years. There were few in the country who could remember a time without her. Everything from postage stamps to banknotes were a perpetual reminder of her presence. She had touched the lives of millions. Her calm reassurance and stability had given succor during hard times for the nation. Even until the last, people could appreciate her sense of duty above all else. No other British monarch had been on the throne so long.

At 6:30 p.m., the news was announced to the world, and shortly afterwards, having changed into my black dress, I spoke in Downing Street. My statement tried to express the sense of loss I knew the whole country and the world were feeling. Queen Elizabeth was, I said, "the rock on which modern Britain was built." I expressed how much of an inspiration Her Majesty had been to me, as she had been to so many who grew up knowing no other monarch. Finally, I urged the whole country to give its loyalty and goodwill to our new sovereign, King Charles III. I ended with words that had not been heard in public for over seventy years: "God Save the King."

The following day, I had my first audience with His Majesty at Buckingham Palace. On a human level, he was obviously deeply affected by the passing of his mother and touched by the public reaction to the news. I also felt a slightly bizarre camaraderie between us, with both of us starting out in our new roles and having to navigate unfamiliar territory. The big difference, of course, was that he had a lifetime's preparation, with decades of public service already under his belt. He certainly provided a reassuring presence to the nation in those early days of his reign in the wake of the Queen's passing.

The next ten days were a somber succession of ceremonies and public engagements as Hugh and I traveled with the King and Queen Camilla to memorial services around the United Kingdom. Politics was put on hold as we focused on a successful transition and handling what was a massive global event.

My first weekend as prime minister was spent with my family, watching on television as the Queen's coffin was brought from Balmoral in procession towards Edinburgh. I was suddenly overwhelmed by the emotion of it all, and I broke down into floods of tears on the sofa. Once again, the grief was mixed with a feeling of awe over the sheer weight of the event, and the fact that it was happening on my watch.

On the eve of the funeral, the King hosted a reception at Buckingham Palace for the many visiting heads of state and government who had come to London. It was an unprecedented gathering of world leaders, with hundreds of presidents, prime ministers, and diplomats filling the state apartments. As I went from room to room greeting them, it was as though the United Nations General Assembly had come to town. It was a striking demonstration of the great respect the late Queen had commanded across the world. I thought of the huge changes that had taken place over the seventy years of her reign.

When Elizabeth II first took the throne, the United Kingdom was just ceasing to be an imperial power. The United States had taken on the mantle of leading the West, and Britain was still dealing with the impact of the Second World War on its economy, foreign policy, and sense of identity. Over the course of the Queen's reign, there were profound changes on all these fronts. At home, the scale of the government's role in the economy had grown, then been tempered, before starting to grow again. Overseas, decolonization had continued, the Cold War had ended, and Britain's relationship with Europe had undergone fundamental changes.

In recent years, after a period of post–Cold War stability, we have seen the rise of China and renewed aggression from Russia, Iran, and their proxies. These regimes are now trying to challenge American leadership. This is wholly different from the situation when the Queen came to the throne. When sterling was replaced by the dollar as the world's reserve currency, we knew we were passing the baton to another free democratic nation. One that shared our values. Now there is a real risk of ceding leadership to totalitarian China.

In the first room at the Buckingham Palace reception most of the G7 leaders were gathered. As I looked around—seeing leaders like U.S. president Joe Biden, Canadian prime minister Justin Trudeau, and French president Emmanuel Macron—I asked myself: Has the fact that the Global Left has been in charge emboldened our adversaries? Does the West have the leadership required to face down these challenges and prevail? And why am I the only conservative in the room?

* * *

This book is not a traditional political memoir. I do not see it as just a chance to tell the detailed inside story of my time in government and justify every decision I made while I was there. There are huge problems in the world today, and major challenges for those of us who believe in freedom at home and abroad. Yet our political discourse is often fundamentally unserious, obsessing over trivialities and more concerned with personalities than with ideas. It is often the media that gets blamed for that, but the bigger problem is with the many politicians who buy into that agenda and willingly play the game. The result is a political establishment driven by short-term popularity, drifting on the prevailing winds of fashionable commentary. The real, deep-rooted issues in our society and our world are considered too intractable to be tackled.

The reason I got into politics was because I believe in the battle of ideas and in pursuing the policies that will make things better. I have strong views about the bold changes required to ensure that freedom and democracy win. I am not one of those who think the job of politicians is to manage whatever consensus they find when they take office and go with the flow. I think it is the job of political leaders to lead. That means challenging consensus and making very clear what you believe in and what you think is going wrong. It also means making genuinely tough decisions despite the ingrained hostility of others.

I was in government for exactly a decade, beginning as a junior education minister and ending as prime minister. Throughout that time, I sought to challenge accepted orthodoxy and push a conservative agenda against entrenched vested interests. My scope for doing so was, however, limited most of the time by the fact that I was serving under or alongside others whose priorities did not always match my own, and who had the power to hold me back.

When I stood for the leadership of the Conservative Party, I had the opportunity to make clear to party members what I believed. Whether you call me a Thatcherite or a committed limited-government conservative, it was pretty clear where I stood. I argued we needed to take bold action at once to turn the country around and get the economy moving. Having secured a strong mandate from the party membership for that agenda, I was ready to take it into government and deliver what I had promised. I knew it would be controversial and difficult, but with only two years until the next general election, there was no time to waste if we were to get the results we needed.

Things did not work out as I had hoped. My time in Downing Street was brief, and I did not have the chance to deliver the policies I had planned. We made mistakes, and I take my share of responsibility for that. I could write a whole book identifying what went wrong, complaining about the unfairness of it all, and justifying the choices I made. Maybe I will write that book one day, but for now I believe the situation is so urgent that there is no time for finger-pointing. We need to start winning the argument.

This isn't just a British problem. The conservative movement across the West has been faltering for almost a generation. Once it seemed like Margaret Thatcher and Ronald Reagan had shifted the landscape permanently. Now that work has been undone.

Just as there were urgent economic challenges in the United Kingdom at the time I stood for the leadership, there were also urgent international challenges to the West. These are becoming ever more pressing. The rise of China and the increased hostility of Russia and Iran are part of the biggest concerted threat to our established freedoms that we have seen for nearly a century. My deep concern is that we are seeing far too much complacency in response.

Genuine conservatism has come under attack, not least from those who should be its main advocates. We have high-taxing, interventionist governments expanding the role of the state while professing to be conservative. We have conservative politicians accepting extreme environmentalist dogma and wokeism. Time and again, left-wing arguments are indulged by those who should be fighting them, enabling the political agenda to move progressively to the left and away from the values that have defined and forged the freedoms for which we have previously fought.

The West has lost its way. We need to wake up and meet the challenges before us, or we will lose. Having fought and won an ideological battle in the Cold War against authoritarian communism, we have allowed ourselves in the years since to become decadent and complacent. We believed we had secured permanent victory, whereas what we really had was more like a temporary truce.

There was a time when the United States and her allies had a clear mission to spread freedom and saw that as a moral responsibility. But too often in recent decades we have failed to stand up to aggression from authoritarian regimes, which has only emboldened them. It is clear now that had we acted earlier, Russia would not have invaded Ukraine. China and other anti-Western powers will take their cue from how they see us acting and from the things they hear Western politicians saying. Weakness and disengagement will only heighten the threats we face.

On economics, there has been a tacit assumption that conservatives won the case for free markets, limited government, and low taxes, and that these arguments no longer needed to be made. But in practice, by not continuing to fight these battles, we have seen the role and size of the state increase. In the United Kingdom, government spending is now up to 46 percent of GDP, even higher than it was before the reforms of the Thatcher years, while in the United States it is 35 percent of GDP and getting higher under Bidenomics. Just as then, we are going in the wrong direction.

As I discovered, the political atmosphere is not conducive to those of us who genuinely believe in small government and low taxes. Even suggesting that a Conservative government should keep its election promises not to raise taxes was somehow presented as an extremist position. If that mindset continues to prevail even on parts of the Right, we are going to continue getting bigger and bigger government, more entitlements, and a tax burden rising to unsustainable levels. We saw in the 1970s how that ends, when the UK had to go to the International Monetary Fund (IMF) for a bailout thanks to massive inflation and spending under a Labour government. It is not unrealistic to imagine that something similar could happen again.

This book is a warning that we have to change our ways if we are to avoid that fate. I believe it is essential for conservatives everywhere to understand the challenges before them. That is what I tried to do, and while I was not sufficiently prepared for the institutional backlash and lacked enough support from my colleagues to win the argument, I remain convinced it needed to be done. It was in the best interests of my country, and of the Conservative Party's chances at the next election, to act quickly. I fear that opportunity has waned.

Another reason why change is so urgent is the need to refashion the United Kingdom's economy in the wake of Brexit. Arguments about whether Brexit was a good or bad thing are irrelevant if we don't answer the question of what we want to make of it afterwards. I have been a firm believer since the British people gave their verdict in the 2016 referendum that we have to reduce regulatory burdens and red tape, put in place more trade deals, control immigration, and boost our economy. That to me is the clear logic of Brexit. What I cannot understand are those supporters of Brexit who then want to behave in an anti-growth way and retain or add to business regulations. They are essentially condemning the country to be poorer.

The UK has not yet decided if we want to be Norway on Valium or Singapore on steroids. We are still in a halfway house, with virtually all the EU laws still sitting on our statute book. Contrast that with Australia and New Zealand in the 1970s, which implemented major reforms to make their agricultural sectors competitive and are now very successful. That is the sort of model we should be looking at, instead of continuing to argue about what happened in 2016.

It would not be the first time we have missed an opportunity to make some necessary and fundamental changes to the way our economy works. After the financial crash of 2008, countries responded in different ways, some of which have turned out to be more successful than others. In the UK, we rightly sought to curb government spending, which had grown too high under Labour. But we did so through a lot of salami-slicing, making cuts that would later come back to bite us, rather than taking the opportunity for a fundamental reshaping of the state in the way others did.

We saw during the so-called New Labour years under Prime Ministers Tony Blair and Gordon Brown a lot of supposedly progressive legislation that embedded a left-wing worldview into our institutions. These range from the Human Rights Act, which has implanted a particular concept of rights rather than freedoms, to the Equality Act, which enshrined the left-wing obsession with identity politics. These are all things with which conservatives instinctively disagree, but we failed to push back against them for fear of being labeled as illiberal or worse.

This brings me to the crux of why I wanted to write this book now. In 2024, both the United Kingdom and the United States will be having elections, while elections are due in Canada and Australia by 2025. Similar conversations are taking place among conservatives in all these countries about what they stand for, how to diagnose their national ills, and how they can best shape their arguments to their electorates. Our nations face many of the same challenges, and I believe the only way for us to present an attractive and credible program for the future is to see the issues I have described as part of a wider need to rediscover genuine conservatism at home and to reinvigorate the power of the West to defend freedom abroad. These two objectives are inextricably linked.

The book goes through my experience in government department by department. In many cases, reforms I wanted fell victim to vested interests and the leftward drift of our national institutions and political culture. Some have accused me of being a willful disruptor, setting out to upset political orthodoxies for the sake of it. I dispute that characterization. While it is true that I see myself as an instinctively anti-establishment figure, I have never wanted to disrupt things for the sake of it. I am, after all, a conservative, and I have had plenty of jobs in government that have required me to be a capable technocrat, dealing with problems from prison riots to floods.

When I see a failure to tackle long-standing issues, I want to break through the orthodoxy to solve it. When something has not happened for forty years, it's not because you have the wrong person heading the government this month; it's because something more fundamental is stopping it from happening. Too much of politics has become a cult of the leader, and a belief that changing the front person will in itself achieve some miraculous overnight transformation. In truth, it requires years of effort and hard work by a team committed to the same objective over a prolonged period of time.

For that reason, politics has to be about ideas. The conservative values of patriotism, freedom, and family. We know instinctively why they are better than those of our opponents. Political philosophy and ideology have become unfashionable in recent years. But trying to grip intractable policy issues without them is like trying to navigate a hazardous mountain range in the dark without a compass. Politics is ideological—you either believe in big government running everything or you don't; you either believe in low taxes stimulating economic growth or you don't. In order to mount a sustained campaign to fix the problems that need fixing, there has to be a unifying ideology around which a party can rally, and which it can fight for. Without that, well-meaning technocrats will continue to be pulled along on the tide of events.

Western nations have allowed themselves to become weakened abroad and subjected to creeping left-wing notions at home that have caused damage to their economies and harmed growth. If this is allowed to continue, the free world, which has taken its dominance for granted for decades, will be overtaken by its opponents. The West will be defeated by China, and authoritarian regimes will defeat liberal democracies. The prospect is now closer than ever, and it requires firm action to counter the threat.

It is not too late to do something about it. There are fundamental weaknesses in these authoritarian regimes, but to tackle them properly we need to wrest back control of the West from the Left, whose ideas have placed increasing burdens on our economies and undermined our values. There needs to be a positive movement on the conservative side to take back the agenda. The West is in danger, and conservatives need to step up and save it.

CHAPTER 1

A Leftist Education

I sat at the back of the math class watching Li-Mei, age eleven, stride up to the front and demonstrate a piece of algebra. It was something that children in Britain and the United States might only get around to learning at the age of sixteen, if they ever did at all. The Department for Education officials with me were shocked. This was just another high school in a humdrum city: Wuhan, China, in 2014.

It was a visible manifestation of how the West was falling behind. We were turning out children who struggled to read and write, while we spent vast sums of taxpayer money on their education and made life harder for working families in the process. Despite Britain's being the home of the Enlightenment, many British children are not being taught the most basic scientific and historic facts. Our results in English and math have been slipping for years. And England has some of the most expensive childcare in Europe.

I was in my first ministerial role, as a junior minister in the Department for Education. In 2012, then prime minister David Cameron had given me a dual mission: improve educational standards and make childcare easier and cheaper for parents. Before being asked to join the government, I had set out in a series of think-tank pamphlets how, by removing regulations and upping our standards, we could transform the system. This only showed the danger of writing pamphlets: real life is much messier. Even on an issue where the solutions seemed obvious, the resistance was huge. At this stage, I was just delighted to get my first government job. Little did I know what I was up against.

Progressive ideas were dominant in all areas of education—even at the heart of government. The previous Labour government had gone so far as to remove the very word "education" from the title of the department, instead rebranding it the "Department for Children, Schools and Families," complete with a childish rainbow logo. While we had restored the name upon taking office, the place still had rainbow decorations hanging from the ceiling. It was indicative of the culture we found.

High taxes on families and a squeeze on wages meant it was hard for parents to afford to have children or to stay at home to look after them. The progressive Left had both lobbied for more childcare and at the same time made it so exorbitantly expensive that parents couldn't afford it. For young children, the so-called experts favored "child-centered play" over counting and learning the alphabet. This approach was more labor-intensive, with the result that it required higher numbers of staff, hugely increasing costs. Regulations on childcare ratios set out the number of children that each member of a nursery staff was allowed to look after. Staff could only look after a maximum of four two-year-old children at a time. Even in nominally more socialist countries like

France and Spain, the regulations were much looser, with half or even a third as many staff being needed.

In the 1980s and 1990s, things had been much looser. Britain had a boom of women entering the workplace as well as of family incomes—our maternal employment outstripped France and Germany. But thanks to lots of state regulation by the Blair government, the number of childminders had halved to be replaced with government Sure Start centers, four hundred new childcare qualifications, and more state subsidy.

The result was that parents lost their choice as to how to look after their children. Instead we had a highly expensive, state-subsidized, prescriptive, bureaucratic model.

I wanted the opposite. I wanted parents to decide and to keep more of their own money. I arrived at the department determined to change this, but from the very first hour I could see there would be resistance. My officials had done their homework and were holding copies of my childcare pamphlet. Though trained to be courteous and respectful to whichever ministers they were sent, the looks on their faces made clear they did not like what they had read.

The position of a minister is akin to that of a child emperor. Your every whim about how you would like your coffee served or your papers stacked is pandered to. But when it comes to challenging the way the system operates or deeply embedded orthodoxies, there seemed endless ways requests could be evaded. I took this on in my usual style—full frontal.

I was very clear to my officials what I wanted to achieve. I set a deadline for them to put together initial proposals and was persistent in keeping up the pressure for progress. This was a culture shock for some of the civil servants, who seemed to want to take their time and were not impressed when I began telephoning them directly to ask why the deadline had not been met. Apparently this was not the correct protocol, and I should instead have restricted myself to asking staff in my private office to pass on a gentle reminder.

I soon found friends of mine across government having quiet words with me suggesting I might approach things differently. Articles appeared in the press describing me as a "strutting martinet." I received an award from *The Spectator* with the walk-on tune at the ceremony being "Little Miss Dynamite." This was the department where I first earned the sobriquet "Human Hand Grenade." And all for just asking officials to do things and adhere to deadlines. Having worked for Shell and Cable & Wireless at various rungs of the ladder, I was shocked by the slowness and bureaucracy of it all.

It was a particularly frustrating introduction to the way government works. None of the officials had objected to the deadline or suggested it was impossible to meet. The paper simply didn't arrive. The senior officials clearly regarded me as a naïve junior minister of little consequence and paid lip service to my demands while hoping I would eventually lose interest and move on to something else, or be reshuffled out of the department.

I also had to deal with the fact that back then we Conservatives were serving in a coalition government with the center-left Liberal Democrats. Each government department had a Liberal Democrat minister working alongside the Conservatives (known to us as spies), and in Education this was David Laws, a close ally of the Liberal Democrat leader, Nick Clegg. Although the Liberal Democrats claimed to be in favor of school standards, they were unable to resist the temptation of scoring political points with the progressive Left.

Getting round the Liberal Democrats, the officials in the department, and the rather squishy Conservatives in Number 10 was a way of life for the ministerial team at the Department for Education. Michael Gove, the secretary of state leading the department, was in his radical phase before he became a champion of Net Zero and anti-growth policies. He was constantly trying to pursue policies that Number 10 thought were too bold. His special adviser (SpAd) Dominic Cummings was his agent in the department, causing trouble and chaos. There was an element of the pirates having taken over the ship.

Cummings gave me useful advice about how to avoid unnecessary Number 10 interference in my activities. If I did a press release announcing a new policy, then that would have to be cleared by Number 10. However, if it was a "media script," that would avoid scrutiny. A lot of scripts were issued.

When it came to my childcare proposals, the institutional inertia from officials was compounded by the Liberal Democrat desire to play to the gallery. I drew up my plans, which proposed a modest loosening of regulations, allowing nursery staff to look after six two-year-olds instead of four, and four one-year-olds instead of three. They would also introduce more competition by permitting schools to expand their provision and reducing the number of regulations associated with setting up as a childminder. None of this would be compulsory, but it would allow parents greater choice and help reduce the costs they faced.

As far as the progressive Left was concerned, I might as well have proposed arming toddlers with handguns. I was accused by Polly Toynbee, a columnist at the left-leaning newspaper *The Guardian*, of wanting to establish "cut-price baby farming,"[1] while the Pre-school Learning Alliance launched a campaign saying the proposals were "a real risk" to children's "physical wellbeing."[2] Justine Roberts, the head of Mumsnet, a website for middle-class mothers in Britain, also came out against the proposals.

This orchestrated opposition came predominantly from vested interests in the nursery industry, which were keen to preserve their existing business model, with its high staff numbers and significant government subsidy. They told the world that the high costs of childcare were inevitable, and that they should therefore receive even more government money (that is, taxpayer money) to help pay staffing costs. They did not like being challenged as to whether they thought the high costs were in fact the result of their having to recruit twice as many staff as their equivalent nurseries in France to look after the same number of children. To me, the basic arithmetic was obvious. I could not understand why some seemed unable to grasp the point.

I also saw how this alliance was able to silence those who worked in childcare and agreed with me, gradually undermining support for my ideas. It was an early lesson in the ruthless power of progressive organizing and how the media prefers to report on personalities rather than truth and substance. Much of the reporting on me was highly personal, with even female columnists asking whether as a mother I would myself be able to cope with looking after multiple children.

Seeing the way the wind was blowing, despite not having previously voiced concerns about my plans (and having formally signed off on them), Clegg now turned hostile to them. In June 2013, he announced publicly that he would be blocking changes to the childcare staffing ratios. This was largely about pandering to various lobby groups and media commentators, but it was also widely seen as an act of political spite, attempting to defeat a prominent Conservative policy in retaliation for the failures of some of his own flagship proposals.

Clegg, I found, was one of those politicians who, despite fully understanding the logic and sense of a policy, nevertheless backs off as soon as there is any suggestion it might attract criticism from progressives. He would rather be popular than do the right thing. He has now found a much more appropriate home in California and is working for Facebook.

After my plans had been torpedoed, I was called in for a meeting with Prime Minister David Cameron. He wanted to reassure me. He said it was a huge surprise that I had gone into the job and tried to deliver on what I'd said I would do. Most ministers, he'd found, got sidetracked or gave up because it was too difficult. Indeed.

I remain frustrated that we were defeated on childcare. Ten years after this battle was lost, British parents still face immense costs, and government subsidies have gone up further.

We were more successful on school standards—another battle against the ingrained "progressive" education philosophy championed for decades by the Left. Ever since the revival of America's "progressive education" movement in the 1960s, and the publication in the United Kingdom of the Plowden Report around the same time, there has been a persistent and damaging idea in both countries that education should be "child-centered." Though this sounds warm and fluffy, what it has meant in practice has been a belief that children should be left to somehow discover ideas for themselves, instead of being rigorously and effectively taught the body of knowledge they will need to survive in a tough and competitive world.

This remains the heart of the debate over education. The reason children in Japan and China know their letters and numbers by the age of three is that they have been taught them. They haven't been left to "discover through play" on the off chance they might stumble upon the basics of literacy and numeracy. A lot of nonsense has been talked by "progressive" educationalists, and the result has been that too many children end up not being able to read, write, and add properly.

To my mind, there is nothing remotely "progressive" about leaving poor kids unable to get on in life and compete in the employment market while those from privileged backgrounds have access to a decent education that teaches them what they need to know. It is a tragic irony that left-wing ideologues have been embedding privilege in our society for decades.

The progressive movement in education arose out of trends in postmodernist philosophy, pioneered by the thinker Michel Foucault, which led to the notion that truth and morality are relative, and there is therefore no space for evidence and objective truth.[3] Instead, we should all celebrate finding our "own truth," whatever that is. Foucault also pioneered the crazy thinking about sex and gender ideology that now permeates the educational debate.[4]

The age-old resistance of young people to taking on the values handed down from older generations has become baked into an educational philosophy that says such generational transmission is somehow regressive and wrong. This sort of attitude has an instinctive appeal to a lot of people, who see it as being about overthrowing hierarchies and rejecting tradition in favor of free-thinking discovery. But taken to its full extent, as it has been in some quarters, it involves the undermining of historical and scientific facts.

The prevalence of this worldview reveals a deeper unease about our culture and values. We can see it in the obsession with condemning our history and promoting collective guilt through campaigns to "decolonize the curriculum." This is portrayed in the United Kingdom as a progressive movement to contextualize our imperial past, but it is in fact an ideological attack on that past that promotes a new narrative in which Western countries are always the villains. The scientific, industrial, and technological advances that made the West and now most of the world prosperous are turned into parables on the evils of capitalism and racism. This repudiation of the Enlightenment is astonishingly self-defeating. There is a distinct air of self-loathing about it that is characteristic of the Left.

The most pernicious part of this ideology is the suggestion that in the modern world, there is no need for children to be taught facts. After all, they can look things up on the internet, so we are far better off teaching them skills and encouraging their creativity. We need them to become free spirits with inquiring minds, not an army of drones reciting lists of dates and facts, right? You can see how this might be a superficially attractive argument. But it is utterly wrong.

Of course children should view the world with a critical eye, challenge accepted ideas, and be free to develop strong political views. But to do so they need to be taught the basics, warts and all, without having the facts conditioned and censored by left-wing ideology. As Martin Robinson has argued, we need to rediscover the basis of a classical education: the trivium of grammar, logic, and rhetoric. Under this curriculum, students are first taught the facts (grammar), before learning how to analyze them critically (logic), and then they acquire the skills to craft and present a convincing argument (rhetoric). This approach does far more to encourage their intellectual and creative development than bombarding them with precooked ideological interpretations from the very beginning of their schooldays.

My conviction that there is something profoundly wrong in my country's education system was formed to a large extent by my own experiences. I come from a middle-class family with well-educated parents who surrounded me with books and ideas, so I did fine at school. But there were too many kids who left without being able to read and write properly, while too much time was spent on supposedly "progressive" teaching practices and subjects. When I have spoken about this at various times during my career, it's often upset former teachers and classmates who find it uncomfortable. I guess they will just have to accept that this is "my truth."

I went to primary school in Scotland, which was still a very traditional experience—math in the morning, comprehension in the afternoon, every single day. "The belt" was still in use, a rarity in the early 1980s. When I moved to Leeds back in England at the age of ten, the teachers turned up their noses at my traditional Scottish education. I was told my new teachers were "modern" and did "projects" and had new subjects like "environmental studies." Even at the age of ten, I reacted viscerally to being informed that the education I had received was somehow backward, and that my current one was better and more enlightened. That wasn't my impression, particularly when I found that "environmental studies" was an awkward fusion of history and geography in which a lesson on Richard III's killing of the Princes in the Tower one day would be followed by something totally unrelated about the Consett Steelworks the next, devoid of any context.

Then it was on to Roundhay School, a state comprehensive in Leeds, where these progressive approaches were firmly embedded. I should be clear that there were some good teachers and good teaching there, and I have never sought to portray it as some dreadful sink school. It was a mid-table state school that was not particularly bad, but not particularly good either. What wound me up was the political correctness that pervaded everything it did, and the sense that lessons on unconscious racism seemed more of a priority than ensuring that everyone could read and write properly.

Lots of children did perfectly fine at Roundhay, but it was too often despite the prevailing ethos there than because of it. I had the benefit of my father being a math professor who helped me with extra tuition at home, but others were not so lucky. There was a general lack of discipline, and among most students it was seen as acceptable to mess around and rather uncool to do any work. I lived in fear of being beaten up in the lunch queue or stabbed with a pair of scissors in my media studies class. Attempts to "engage" children ended up with us, at age thirteen, being asked to stand on our desks to pretend we were on Sir Francis Drake's ship, *The Golden Hind*. These experiences were certainly not unique to my schooling, but I found the lack of challenge and the acceptance of mediocrity very depressing. When we talk about the "soft bigotry of low expectations," this is what I think of.

Having seen how pervasive the progressive orthodoxy had become, my experience when I became a schools minister showed how far it had spread into the bloodstream of the whole education system. The shared assumptions and outlook of those involved at all levels of education constitute what some have taken to calling the blob—a permanent, immovable mass of resolutely left-wing prejudices and vested interests. My attempts to reform the nursery provision had given me my first direct experience of it, as I quickly discovered that "the sector" would close ranks against any attempt to alter their established way of operating and would mount a highly emotive and quite effective PR campaign to push back against change.

In the aftermath of the nursery reforms being blocked, it was said that I should have approached it more gently—"rolled the pitch" better—and tried to bring people with me. But I believe there is very little that can be done to change hearts and minds when the blob is so implacably opposed to being challenged. They are never going to agree, so it is pointless to try to persuade them. The choice for a genuinely reforming politician is either to have the fight and face them down, or to accept that you simply cannot make changes if they are opposed to them. The latter was not an attractive option for me.

I chose to fight. My other significant battle was over reform of the math curriculum. Here I faced constant pushback and attempts to dumb it down, with concerns expressed that what I wanted to do was too challenging for children to cope with. But I had seen evidence from East Asia that proper rigorous teaching could achieve excellent results. My visit to China confirmed what I had read and cemented my impression that we needed a similar level of focus on excellence if we were ever to match their world-leading performance in math.

It has become fashionable in progressive circles to stereotype East Asian teaching methods as crude and rote learning that crushes pupils' creativity and turns them into joyless automatons. But what I found in the classrooms we visited in China was quite different. Teachers explained mathematical concepts clearly and gave students swift and encouraging feedback. Children were excited to be there, answering questions enthusiastically and taking pride in explaining the solutions to the rest of the class.

What made those Chinese classrooms stand out was the level of focus on the subject. Concepts and techniques were dissected and discussed in great detail, with examples then worked through with increasing levels of difficulty. Children sat facing the front, allowing the teacher to spot anyone not paying attention or struggling. Those teachers also specialized earlier than in the UK, with separate math teachers in primary school as well as at a secondary level. Math was taught every day from primary school onwards, while teachers provided swift feedback to individual students on their class exercises and homework to ensure none of them fell behind.

After this and other such visits, my view was that if children in China could manage it, why could British children not do the same? I used what I had seen to inform my proposals for reform of the math curriculum. It might seem a little odd that I should be so evangelical about Chinese teaching methods when so many of my wider arguments in this book focus on the threat posed by China to the West. But it is essential that we recognize the nature of that threat and understand how the challenge has been manifested. China's increased economic power comes in significant part from its advances in science and technology, and this is built on educational excellence. The story of how they came to do this is a revealing one. Many of the improvements arose out of Japanese teaching methods, which the Chinese system then perfected and rolled out on an industrial scale. What has characterized the Chinese approach to education, as in their attitude to so much in the post-war period, has been a simple desire to win. I felt we needed to match that determination.

I championed the adoption of the "math mastery" model, which was associated with countries like Singapore, and which the Ark chain of Academy schools in the United Kingdom had successfully introduced. I made other changes to embed rigor in the system, such as banning the use of calculators in tests at the age of eleven to improve mental and written arithmetic, and ensuring that long division was a required skill. Even this provoked a massive row from critics who said it was "old-fashioned." Those who might have been expected to be in favor were not always very helpful. The Royal Society's Advisory Committee on Mathematics Education, whose objective is to promote the take-up of the subject, seemed to think that the way to do this was just to make it easier. I found that utterly self-defeating.

Every day at the department was whack-a-mole in the battle for rigor and standards: combatting the anti-textbook attitude, where rather than having a tried-and-tested script, the progressives preferred teachers to invent every lesson; getting rid of coursework, which had led to widespread cheating; creating new tougher grades and cracking down on grade inflation; and teaching proper grammar, which led to a widespread debate in the media about whether anyone really knew what a fronted adverbial was.

There were hazards in being the minister responsible for all of this. It meant constantly being tested on my spelling and arithmetic live on television and radio. On one occasion, I remember an Eton-educated press officer desperately holding up a sign behind the interviewer's head, on which he had scribbled the word "rhythm" to assist me during an impromptu spelling quiz. The scene would not have been out of place on *Yes, Minister*'s contemporary equivalent, *The Thick of It*. This showed the triviality of our media, which is more interested in gotcha moments than a serious discussion of the issues. But it also highlighted a deeper problem with its implicit suggestion that knowledge of the basics was somehow an irrelevant obsession rather than a key component of a successful education.

Our efforts to improve literacy centered on the use of synthetic phonics, which has been conclusively proven to be the most effective method of teaching children to read. Despite this, some in the educational establishment refuse to accept the weight of evidence and continue to advocate a return to the progressive "whole language" approach that became fashionable in the 1960s. It is clearly less effective and has been shown to leave children unable to read properly, but because it stands in opposition to traditional teaching methods, it continues to have a vocal fanbase on the left.

The same goes for the use of setting in schools. The evidence shows that teaching children according to their ability in different subjects enables lessons to be pitched at the right level, with appropriate support given to those who are struggling while the more able can be stretched to achieve their full potential. It makes perfect sense, and it works. But again, "progressive" thinking considers it inegalitarian and elitist, so they would rather lump all children together. This attitude demonstrates the left-wing worldview, which would rather see us all fail together than accept any suggestion of inequality of outcome.

Time and again, battles we thought had been won had to be refought. We worked hard to embed rigor in our educational system and provide evidence that doing so improved results. But as soon as we turned our attention away to address other challenges, the progress we made risked being undone. It was like weeds in a garden—if you didn't constantly keep clearing them away, they would eventually take over and strangle all the other plants.

All across the West, these progressive notions remain embedded in school systems. Not only does the dominance of left-wing ideology pose a problem for conservatives, but, by eroding academic rigor and lowering educational standards, it has also created serious problems for future competitiveness. International league tables show the extent of the challenge. China and Singapore sit at the top of the Organization for Economic Co-operation and Development's (OECD) PISA rankings of math, science, and reading scores, while the United Kingdom, the United States, and most western European countries languish mid-table. This has been the case for many years now.

It should be no surprise that we are suffering the consequences of taking our foot off the accelerator when it comes to educational attainment. There is in some quarters a fatalistic acceptance of this relative decline, as though it were inevitable that we should lose our preeminence and be overtaken by others. But we are not passive actors. Conservatives should be pointing out that we have done this to ourselves by changing our behavior and indulging damaging ideas that have proven regressive to our international standing.

How has this happened? Why have we, the most technologically advanced and prosperous countries on Earth, given in to politically correct virtue-signaling while allowing others to outpace us in educational standards? I believe it comes down to complacency. When a society becomes rich enough, there is a risk that it becomes decadent and stops trying so hard. The sense of entitlement built up by dominating the world stage for so long can lead to an implicit assumption that our children don't have to be as good or educated as children from East Asia in order to succeed.

This, I believe, goes a long way toward explaining why some of the post-1960s progressive notions managed to take root. While other countries focused relentlessly on teaching in order to get the best results they could, we indulged the idea that we could diverge from those proven methods without suffering any adverse consequences.

The West's decline in education can be reversed, but only if we consciously address the root of the problem and get serious about fixing it. When we are resolute, we can win. When we have done so, it has yielded results. In the case of math teaching in England, the PISA study showed a dramatic increase in the scores of English students between 2015 and 2018, the first time any such improvement had been recorded since the study had first been conducted in 2000. The number of countries significantly outperforming English students fell from nineteen to twelve. This marked improvement was in contrast to the situation in Scotland, where the government run by the left-wing Scottish National Party has squandered the country's previous excellence in education and seen its math scores drop to the lowest level ever.

England's jump in the league tables showed what a focused and rigorous approach to math teaching can achieve. We have also made some progress in encouraging more students in the UK to study math.

There is a similar story of progress in literacy. We have seen significant improvements to England's reading scores in recent years thanks to the phonics approach championed by Nick Gibb, the UK's long-serving schools minister. He has been evangelical on the subject since before the Conservatives were in government and has made it his mission to fight the battles needed to get phonics firmly embedded in our schools. We also managed to get grade inflation under control, though this ballooned again during the COVID-19 pandemic as a result of having to rely on teacher assessments instead of independent testing.

So my message is not a pessimistic one. Experience has shown we can make progress to improve results when we put our minds to it. It is undoubtedly difficult and involves fighting tough battles against persistent opposition, but it can be done. We have to view this as an existential challenge and go back to promoting the core values we know to be right. Truth. Science. Rigor.

This means being prepared to attack progressive ideas head-on and say they are wrong. We have to fight as hard as the Left and stop conceding ground to them. Too often, conservatives are either passive observers who fail to make their case or naïve enablers who support progressive nonsense out of a misplaced belief that doing so is the only politically possible course of action.

The latest examples of this are the ludicrous claims being made about gender in schools. We should be clear about the scientific facts about biological sex and not allow any under-eighteens to make irreversible decisions about their own bodies. That includes not allowing social transitioning, which is a pathway to this. Too many conservatives fear being seen as "on the wrong side of history," but fail to recognize that the only way to be on the right side of history is by fighting for what they know to be right and winning the argument.

The battle must continue to be waged against the educational blob, because doing anything else means the Left will win by default. Here we should take note of O'Sullivan's Law, which states, "All organizations that are not explicitly right-wing will over time become left-wing." This is what has happened in education. It is not just the university teacher-training departments, teachers' unions, and professional bodies, where we might expect such capture to have taken place. It is also the plethora of regulators, independent bodies, and even some academy school chains that have failed to challenge progressive ideas and have thus become their enablers.

The best bulwark against this is the power of parents. This has been a consistent theme of the Conservative Party's reform of education, which has tried to give parents greater control and choice over their children's education. The free school movement we have pursued in the UK is built on lessons from the charter schools in the United States and is meant to turbocharge our own existing Academies program. It's been a success in opening up choice and improving failing schools. But we cannot allow ourselves to get complacent.

The fact is that the left-wing state has taken too much power and responsibility away from parents. As we've seen in the field of healthcare in the United States with Medicare and Medicaid, and in the reach of tax credits in the UK, the encroaching power of the welfare state seeks to bring ever more people into its controlling orbit. Welfare should not go so far up the income scale. Parents should be able to make decisions about how to look after their children with less government interference. The same applies to looking after elderly parents. Parental rights and responsibilities should also be clear on trans issues.

The bureaucracy that has grown up around the new mix of schools in Britain is already under threat of capture. Giving parents more power is the answer. Parents know what they want from their children's schools—and can see when they are not getting it. We should let their clear and simple interest in demanding high standards for their children override the ideological indulgences of the teaching and education establishment. Cutting the power of the central bureaucracy is necessary to do this.

We should learn from the U.S. school choice movement and institute a full voucher system in the United Kingdom. Conservatives have been on the back foot in education for too many years, and the results of allowing the Left to experiment on generations of children have been plain to see. Too many children in Britain and the United States lack a knowledge of our history, our values, and even basic English and math. China and other countries in the Far East have overtaken the West by focusing relentlessly on effective teaching while we have indulged in ideological fads. To remain competitive in the global knowledge economy, we in the West have to face up to the challenge and match the determination of our competitors to win. The only way we can do that is if conservatives step up the fight to wrest back control of education from the failed left-wing ideas that have done so much damage.

CHAPTER 2

A Hostile Environment

"Liz is the Grinch who wants to stop Christmas!" That was the response in Cabinet from Michael Gove, the environment secretary, to my eleventh-hour attempts to ditch COP26, the UN climate change conference that the UK was poised to host in 2020. It was late 2018, and I was by that time chief secretary to the Treasury, charged with keeping a tight grip on public spending across government. With an estimated price tag of over £200 million ($250 million), I strongly questioned whether organizing this jamboree should be a priority for the government.

I was in a minority of one yet again. It was in the midst of the fraught Brexit negotiations, and I thought the last thing the UK needed was to host tens of thousands of delegates at an international shindig that was bound to create more hot air than genuine environmental solutions. From the reaction of my colleagues, you would have thought I had just suggested napalming the Brazilian rainforest.

As a former environment secretary, I was more than familiar with the global challenge of climate change and the need to reduce carbon emissions. But I also knew there were no quick wins to be had on the issue. Had I believed the conference was likely to make any difference, I might have been more sympathetic. But I could see no prospect of that. World leaders would fly in on private jets to bloviate about the environment and reaffirm their aspirations to reduce emissions, while the biggest culprits would continue to do nothing.

More than anything, bidding for COP26 was about appeasing the green lobby by making a grand gesture aimed at gaining short-term popularity without changing the fundamentals. It was environmental virtue-signaling, with the taxpayer picking up the hefty bill. We had seen too much of this in government over the years.

But the rest of the Cabinet was in the grip of climate fever. When they weren't posing for selfies with Greta Thunberg, they were busy trying to ban wood-burning stoves and plastic straws.

After David Cameron's "hug a husky" phase, during which he literally went to the Arctic and hugged a dog for the cameras before zealously courting the green lobby, we'd done nothing to reverse Labour's statist climate change policies. One of my campaigns as a constituency MP was a major expansion of a trunk road, the A11, which got built in 2015. The project had been hugely delayed and the price massively hiked by all the environmental objections and works. In particular, the road builders had been forced to install "bat bridges" where bats could travel safely across the highway. Needless to say, no bat has ever been seen on these bridges. Anyway, bats fly!

When Cameron came to see the new highway being built, he bemoaned all the nonsense that had led to increased costs. It was just another example of how no one—not even the prime minister—could stop this juggernaut. In turn, by the end of Prime Minister Theresa May's government in 2019, we had committed ourselves to binding climate change targets with very little discussion of the consequences.

The environmental debate is the single greatest example over the last three decades of conservatives losing the argument to the Left.

We have dumped costs on families with no regard for whether they can afford them, and we have failed to plan for the long term—while having little discernible impact on overall environmental outcomes. Many programs, such as the switch from gasoline to diesel in cars or the use of electric vehicles, have either harmed the environment in other ways or empowered our polluting adversaries elsewhere in the world.

Big corporations, central bankers, and other cynical actors in the global establishment have latched on to tackling climate change as a way of seeking subsidies as well as buffing up their image. This is not just harmless virtue-signaling. It has provided an excuse for not taking a tougher stance on global aggressors like China. It has also damaged our economic competitiveness and hit people on the lowest incomes hardest with all manner of environmental taxes and costs incurred from regulations.

This is all out of step with what the public want. Environmental measures have often disproportionately put burdens on the poorest. The backlash against the Ultra-Low Emission Zone (ULEZ) implemented by London mayor Sadiq Khan—under which older cars are subject to a punitive daily charge for being driven anywhere in Greater London—demonstrates what happens when highfalutin objectives come into contact with the reality of hard-pressed people who have to drive to work or take the kids to school.

Whilst there are serious issues with the environment, the level of alarmism and ever-increasing rhetoric is not enabling a healthy and proportionate debate to take place.

There are also ludicrous claims that pursuing a Net Zero agenda—defined as seeking a 100 percent reduction of greenhouse gas emissions by 2050 compared with 1990 levels—will boost the economy and drive growth. This is patently not true and wishful thinking. Additional environmental regulations have already hampered growth.

For example, the National Grid estimates a cost of £3 trillion ($4 trillion) for decarbonizing the electricity system. And the opportunity cost of not fracking, and not fully using our North Sea gas reserves, is immense. According to some estimates, the United Kingdom could be fully self-sufficient in gas—which would allow us to bring our prices down to U.S. levels.

Yet the adoption of new global objectives has allowed local resistance to schemes such as London's ULEZ to be circumvented. More decisions have been outsourced to international authorities and courts that are fundamentally anti-democratic. This unstoppable bandwagon has continued regardless of who has been in office. Much of this was still going on while that noted skeptic of the eco-agenda, Donald Trump, was leader of the free world.

President Trump withdrew the United States from the 2015 Paris Climate Accords, which committed all 195 signed-up nations to reducing emissions of greenhouse gases—although the lengthy process of withdrawal spanned most of his presidency before it came into effect. His decision found little international support, with British prime minister Theresa May even publicizing that she had telephoned him to express her disappointment. Needless to say, President Biden reversed the decision the very day he took office.

In the United Kingdom, the Climate Change Committee was established by the 2008 Climate Change Act passed by the Labour Government, legislation that has not been reversed or reformed by Conservatives. This committee advises the government on achieving Net Zero emissions through all manner of methods, including limiting the eating of meat and stopping new airports.

We have adopted an approach of unilateral economic disarmament—as dangerous to our strategic interests as unilateral nuclear disarmament would have been in the 1980s. A focus solely on climate change at the expense of other issues has meant vital national interests like food security and energy security have been ignored. It's a situation that is belatedly and partly being righted only as a result of Vladimir Putin's invasion of Ukraine, which threatened our food and natural gas supplies.

In our haste to not be seen as on the wrong side of history, we failed to make conservative arguments for environmental improvement—arguments centered on property rights, individual and family endeavors, and the free market. Instead we empowered our ideological opponents and accepted much of their extremist agenda.

The environmental movement is fundamentally driven by the radical Left. I know who these people are. I literally grew up with them. My parents were members of the Campaign for Nuclear Disarmament in the 1980s and had friends who were in the Ecology Party, an early iteration of the UK Green Party. As a child, it seemed all about beetroot tarts, composting toilets, and talking about the dangers of overpopulation. The movement has its roots in the late 1960s, amid idealistic notions about rejecting the market economy, going back to nature, and living in self-sufficient communes. This fused with other trends on the New Left such as pacifism, nuclear disarmament, and militant feminism.

The "watermelon" tendency is green on the outside, red on the inside—a modern rebranding of socialism. It features the same instincts of collectivism and authoritarianism. This has traditionally been expressed by advocating the redistribution of wealth, the imposition of higher taxes, and bigger government. But environmentalism has provided a potent new outlet for these instincts, with anti-capitalist campaigners jumping on the bandwagon.

The New Left in both the UK and America evolved from trade unions representing organized labor into a cultural movement that represents so-called "progressive values." Environmental politics has now been shaped into an integral part of that agenda, which sets itself up as a fierce critic of conservative values, free-market economics, and pretty much the entire basis of capitalism.

It fits with the broader worldview that became prominent on the left during the Cold War: that the Soviet Union was somehow morally superior or at least equivalent to the United States and that all the evils of the world originated in the West. There's an element of self-loathing in this mindset that we can readily identify on the left. Capitalism, they believe, is the cause of all of our problems, and the industrialized West must therefore be punished for its success by adopting punitive measures as a form of retribution. The hand-wringing liberal guilt associated with this narrative has shaped the debate on green issues.

The environmentalist worldview has become mainstream. It is now the dominant ideology in major corporations, media on both sides of the Atlantic (including the UK's state-owned BBC), and the legal establishment. There are also cynical motivations for those who espouse it. Many have embraced it as a way of making money after politics or officialdom, whereby they can rake in cash and appear virtuous.

Of course, it was also loved and embraced by government employees. Although civil servants in the UK are supposed to be impartial, one can always sense the level of enthusiasm among them for particular policies. Tackling climate change was certainly pursued with a lot more fervor by officials than stopping the boats that have brought tens of thousands of illegal migrants to British shores.

Historically, there is no basis whatsoever for the belief that protecting the environment should be a left-wing cause. During the 1980s, it was none other than Margaret Thatcher who first raised climate change as a global priority and pushed for the Montreal Protocol, which banned chlorofluorocarbon chemicals to reverse damage to the ozone layer. And it was the Soviet Union that was one of the worst environmental polluters in the world and responsible for the Chernobyl disaster. Today, of course, the accolade for worst polluter goes to Communist China.

I believe it is wrong that a company can be responsible for pollution, have a negative impact on the health of other people and the nearby environment, and not have to pay for it. But I support a free-market approach to these issues, which in economic terms involves "internalizing externalities." If you're causing pollution, you should pay for it. Once a framework has been set with the right rules and prices, we can let companies get on with going about their business and making money.

When I was appointed environment secretary in 2014, my first Cabinet role, I saw it as an opportunity to address environmental concerns from a free-market perspective. This was easier said than done. The Environment Department and its officials had been hijacked by watermelon-oriented non-governmental organizations (NGOs). It became apparent that in order to be deemed up to the job, you had to pass an environmental purity test. The NGOs saw themselves as gatekeepers and arbiters at the department.

As a result, it was sometimes hard to tell where the officials on the payroll ended and the activists began. Many civil servants saw it as their job to work for the "sector," a word that always made me nervous. Usually it meant the department felt in hock to the particular vested interests with which they were dealing. This was either because they genuinely agreed with them, or just because serving them and getting along made for an easier life.

Similar relationships with external "stakeholders" mean that this is true in many government departments. The ministers who are supposed to run these departments often see their jobs as being representatives of their sectors in the Cabinet. The education secretary is expected to speak up for teachers, the health secretary to speak on behalf of the National Health Service (NHS), and so on. At the department responsible for the environment, it meant being expected to speak up for farmers and the environmental movement. By contrast, I was clear that my job was to speak up for the wider public interest, which was not always the same thing.

Campaign groups like Friends of the Earth, Greenpeace, and the Worldwide Fund for Nature are highly adept at lobbying and channeling public sympathy toward their agendas. Many of them have huge resources from their membership income and donations. Most of their supporters contribute their hard-earned cash under the innocent belief that they are merely supporting a cute animal charity. They have little idea just how much of their money is being channeled into lobbying the government on tangential issues.[1]

All these groups spend a lot of time not only with each other, but also with NGOs and sympathetic officials, meaning that groupthink becomes inevitable. The consensus that develops on what is and is not desirable then becomes difficult to oppose, particularly when you are dealing with organizations all too willing to mobilize their campaign machinery to whip up a firestorm of public protest to exert pressure on members of Parliament and ministers.

The campaigns are incessant, often highly misleading, and can lead to perverse and damaging outcomes. An example on my watch was the successful campaign to ban the use of neonicotinoids as a pesticide in farming. The chemical was considered harmful to bees, and the European Union consequently banned it from use on a number of crops in 2013. In 2015, I authorized an emergency application for the limited use of some neonicotinoids by farmers whose rapeseed crops were at risk of destruction by beetles. This prompted a huge outcry, including protesters dressed as bumblebees entering Downing Street. MPs' inboxes were inundated with emails. The panic resulted in the prime minister backing down. The result was that the ban remained in place while farmers ended up using more harmful chemicals and crops were lost.

The animal rights activists I encountered made the environmentalists look reasonable by comparison. These people sought to intimidate, bully, and do damage, pure and simple (tactics that, regrettably, the most aggressive eco-campaigners have also begun to adopt in recent years). It was no coincidence they wore the outfits of criminals, clad in balaclavas, when they sought to protest against and disrupt essential operations that the department had sanctioned.

There were thankfully at least some more robust officials who had been at the department longer and were informed by veterinary advisers and scientists. They were more practical and hard-nosed about the realities of farming and the countryside. It was on their advice that I found myself making slightly surreal life-and-death decisions about the natural world, such as ordering the gassing of five thousand ducks in Yorkshire during an outbreak of avian flu.

The most contentious animal rights issue was the badger cull, the necessary trapping and shooting of wild badgers that had been spreading bovine tuberculosis—a disease that was lethal for dairy and beef cattle. Distraught farmers had been losing herds for years because of this terrible disease. There were no other realistic options to grip the spread apart from culling the badgers. Yet it was hugely politically contentious, with a host of high-profile, well-funded objectors as well as some very wily saboteurs who had to be outwitted. I was condemned by Queen guitarist Brian May, and at one point the protesters traveled around Parliament Square with a mini-badger coffin with a toy badger inside. They were successful at influencing corporations, getting the coffee shop chain Caffè Nero to boycott milk from farms that were participating in the cull.

The objectors relentlessly used the tools created for open government to hound the people carrying out this important work. They pursued us through the courts. Transparency laws meant they could find out where the cull was taking place and intimidate the farmers. I was constantly consulting with lawyers, thereby adding to the taxpayer bill.

As well as dealing with the politics, there were the practical issues about getting the cull done during a limited time window. I got involved in everything from the bait being used—peanut butter and maize worked best—to motivating the shooters who had to go out late at night.

The start of the cull coincided with the annual Conservative Party Conference in Birmingham. Because I am a cheapskate, I had booked myself into a capsule hotel. Little did I know that I would be required to give a pep talk to Gloucestershire shooters over a walkie-talkie from there. I don't think the muscular ex-marine who was leading the cull quite believed it when he was asked to sit in this tiny room with me and two special advisers as I shouted bellicose rhetoric down the walkie-talkie: "Go out there and deliver, you can do it! This is important for the country! We need to foil the saboteurs and get this done!"

I later learned that the cull was, in fact, being followed in high places. At the Royal Garden Party at Buckingham Palace the following year, the then Duke of Edinburgh, Prince Philip, congratulated me on actually getting the job done. These animal culls were necessary to tackle very real threats from the spread of disease, but the animal rights activists were absolutists. They simply didn't care.

The excesses of the animal rights lobby can be hugely disruptive. While the majority of them care about animal welfare, most also accept there has to be a balance struck between the humane treatment of animals on the one hand and the need to support agriculture and give people the choice to eat meat on the other. In my own constituency in South West Norfolk, I had to intervene to help pig farmers who were being targeted by vegan campaigners. The farmers had been facing ongoing problems getting their pigs into Norfolk markets. We simply cannot allow this kind of obstruction to be normalized: farmers have a right to go about their business, and conservatives need to be firm in pushing back against this kind of activism. Every time a conservative appeases this lobby, for example by saying we should eat less meat or switch to non-dairy alternatives, they are giving succor to our opponents.

Representing one of the best farming areas in Britain with pigs, poultry, and arable land, I was determined that the agriculture industry—vital for food security and also our economy—should thrive. Yet it was clear that farming was seen by too many as a "nice to have," meaning it was subordinate to environmental goals.

Coming into the job as environment secretary, I was frustrated that as a country we weren't prouder of the food we produce and were not grasping its potential for growth. In nations like Ireland and New Zealand, dairy farms are a major contributor to the economy and have become serious industries that export their wares around the world. By contrast, in Britain, it seemed we no longer cared much about agriculture.

We have a lot to be proud of in terms of the quality of our food production. I felt we needed to do much better at promoting British food both at home and abroad. Food and farming in the UK contribute £127 billion ($160 billion) to the economy and employ over four million people, which is far from insignificant, but there is still a huge amount of untapped potential. In seizing the opportunities presented by Brexit, we should be looking to grow and maximize our exports into new world markets. Farming is a great part of Britain's heritage, but it should be a big part of our economic future too.

I am a big proponent of genetic modification, which enables farmers to achieve better yields using fewer pesticides and less water. Yet again, the green movement was against this technology, despite the fact that it enabled farmers to produce food in a way that has less impact on the planet.

They also objected to trade. I wanted trade deals to secure more opportunities for British farmers and business overseas. I visited the

United States to meet Tom Vilsack, secretary of agriculture in the Obama administration, to talk about the Transatlantic Trade and Investment Partnership (TTIP), the proposed Europe–U.S. trade deal. Yet the reaction in the UK was simply to slam the Americans for washing chicken with chlorine to protect against disease and injecting beef with hormones—despite the fact that hundreds of thousands of Britons visit the United States every year and merrily devour flavorsome steaks and chicken wings. In general, their attitude towards trade reflected the same mixture of snobbery and self-loathing at which the Left are specialists.

It is fitting that the left-wing activists who adopted a radical interpretation of environmentalism were often the same people campaigning for unilateral nuclear disarmament. In many ways, the manner in which the debate over climate change has developed over time has followed the same self-defeating logic.

Most people would agree that in an ideal world we would want to reduce the number of nuclear weapons. The divide is between a rational belief in working towards multilateral disarmament by agreement and the misguided naïveté of those who think that unilateral disarmament will magically prompt other countries to do the same. Of course, taking the unilateral route would leave us defenseless against enemies who have no intention of disarming.

In the same way, most people will agree with the objective of reducing carbon emissions to tackle climate change. But while the West has adopted stringent targets for reducing carbon emissions and pledged itself to Net Zero emissions over time, China has carried on building more and more coal-fired power stations. Nothing the West does can be effective while this is the case. Meanwhile, we are ourselves contributing to the problem by outsourcing more industrial production to Chinese factories, which in turn are causing more pollution while being subject to no penalties. We have also ended up dangerously dependent on Chinese solar panels amid our push for more renewable energy. Effectively, all we have done is to outsource our carbon emissions to China.

Having visited Chinese cities like Chongqing, Shanghai, and Beijing and seen the levels of pollution there, I know little of the rhetoric I heard from the Chinese environment minister was being enacted. We know their numbers can't be trusted because this is a totalitarian regime with little transparency.

The truth is that China, Russia, and Iran are prioritizing the expansion of their totalitarian regimes, not tackling climate change. What this means in practice is that we in the West are tying our hands behind our backs by not using our natural resources and accepting huge additional costs to move to lower-carbon technologies, while our rivals are busily exploiting the strategic advantage given to them by our unilateral disarmament.

There is another parallel to the Cold War. Just as the Soviet Union exploited the disruptive efforts of the Campaign for Nuclear Disarmament and other left-wing movements to destabilize Western governments, so too are China and Russia benefitting from the efforts of green activists. In the UK and Europe, Russia has funded anti-fracking campaigns and spread disinformation as a way of keeping Europeans hooked on Russian gas. They have also funded anti-fracking campaigns in the United States.

We cannot treat the issue of climate change as though it exists independently of the wider challenges we face and the geopolitical realities of the world. And until we take China seriously, we will not be taking climate change seriously. Instead of fighting shy and pretending the Chinese are our partners in this global endeavor, we should call it as it is and attack them as the world's leading polluter. Western countries should then use the levers we have at our disposal to penalize them economically. That means presenting a united front to give them worse terms of trade unless they change their behavior.

In the meantime, we need to be realistic about what we can achieve by unilateral action. We should benchmark ourselves against other G7 countries and be honest about the limits of that action and the costs of it. We need to focus squarely on the real culprits and stop with the nonsensical gesture politics, such as localities declaring "climate emergencies" without any plan to take meaningful action.

I support using a combination of nuclear energy, renewables, and exploiting our own oil and natural gas—including fracking, which is currently banned in the UK. This is not simply an environmental issue. It will have direct economic benefits, as well as both securing our supply and reducing our vulnerability to shocks such as we have seen in recent years.

My environmental credentials go back many years. I made a speech to the Liberal Democrat conference in 1993 when I was a member of that party in my youth attacking the then party leader, Paddy Ashdown, for being a hypocrite on the issue of wind farms. He had spoken of his support for them while simultaneously opposing a wind farm development near Yeovil in Somerset, his constituency in Parliament.

After the speech, he called me into a meeting and tried to pacify me by telling me we were on the same side. I gave him short shrift, and he later wrote me a letter telling me I was "utterly fearless" in not backing down. It was my first taste of how politicians would emote about the environment without being prepared to carry out the policy.

I feel the same about how Conservatives during the last days of Theresa May's premiership legislated for Net Zero carbon emissions by 2050 without any accompanying plan to achieve it. The switch to renewables is a huge undertaking for which our current national infrastructure is unprepared. The electricity grid is currently configured around former power stations, not offshore wind or places where small modular reactors might be sited. Nor can the intermittent—and expensive—nature of wind power be solved just by building more of it.

Changing that configuration is a massive challenge, but for politicians across the spectrum it's been a case of legislate first and worry about the consequences later. That is not a serious way of doing business.

Instead, Britain should aim to be energy independent by 2040 using oil and gas as well as nuclear and renewables. We are in an excellent position to become a net energy exporter, given the amount of sea by which we are surrounded where offshore wind farms can be located, as well as our expertise in nuclear power. The use of North Sea oil and gas is crucial, so there needs to be investment in that too. There also should be fracking in the UK. We are in the ludicrous position of importing fracked gas from the United States that has been liquified to –180 degrees Celsius (–292 degrees Fahrenheit) but refusing to frack ourselves. Meanwhile Brits are paying twice as much for their energy as Americans.

In order to cut costs for our citizens and boost our energy security, we must have the courage to do what is required for the long term, rather than chase virtue-signaling headlines. We need affordable energy to improve people's standards of living, make our businesses more competitive, and boost our economy.

As a conservative, I believe strongly in protecting our natural environment. Without action, we will harm our quality of life and the planet. A conservative agenda and economic growth are dependent on a healthy environment. But we should not be sidetracked into gesture politics for the sake of short-term kudos from the predominantly left-wing green lobby.

Just as in education, conservatives must remain on their guard against the left's persistent capturing of the agenda. It should not be a surprise to us that leftists believe that environmental policies must take the form of higher taxes, burdensome regulations, and industrial subsidies. Those are, after all, their responses to every policy challenge. In response, we on the right need to be equally assertive in highlighting alternatives that focus on maximizing the economic opportunities available, increasing our competitive advantage, and growing the economy.

We need to take on the pernicious degrowth ideology. This means challenging those who think population shrinkage and the limiting of human ambition are the answers. All these people are doing is damaging the future of the West and aiding our opponents. The best way to protect the environment is through property rights, not collectivism.

We should have no tolerance for anti-capitalist activists exploiting legitimate environmental concerns to pursue their leftist agenda. It's time conservatives fought back against the watermelons and called them out for the damage they're doing. It is not just the eco-warriors gluing themselves to the road and blocking traffic who need to be quashed. It is also the more respectable-sounding advocates of damaging economic policies who have glued themselves to the political agenda and need to be prised off.

In the geopolitics of today, we should also be alive to the fact that our obsession with environmental virtue-signaling on the world stage risks putting us at a further disadvantage in the economic battle with our opponents. China, Russia, and other authoritarian regimes will not be shamed into going green, and still less will they be somehow inspired by our example into an altruistic conversion. They will merely take full advantage of the economic restrictions we are placing on ourselves to grow even stronger.

In order to make ourselves more competitive after Brexit, we in the UK should have streamlined our regulations—but instead governments here and all across the West have been adding to the burden. And in the case of environmental regulations, the result has been that we have merely pushed pollution elsewhere while inflicting damage on ourselves.

We should recognize that this is not just about preserving the planet. It is also about saving and improving the lives of the people who live on it. We cannot do that if we lose sight of the wider challenges and fail to tackle the other real threats to people's freedom and well-being. The number one threat to the environment and our freedom and security is the rise of authoritarian regimes and the decline of democracy. Therefore, we need to cancel failed multilateral structures and work with allies that share our values.

We should cancel the COP gravy train, which simply provides an arena for lobbyists to make money and countries to try to greenwash their reputations. If there is a global agreement on carbon emissions to be had, it can only work if every country agrees. There is no chance of this with the bad actors we have today. It's much better these policies are managed at a nation-state level.

We should abolish the Climate Change Act and instead adopt a new Climate Freedom Act that enables rather than dictates technology. The United States should reverse the Inflation Reduction Act, and the EU should abandon its equivalent measures. Instead of subsidizing that which makes us less competitive and hurts our allies, we should be competing to achieve the best technological advances.

The United States, along with its allies like the UK, the G7, and other leading nations, should work together through an economic NATO to agree on a coordinated approach to the polluters like China. This should be done in conjunction with tackling other problems such as the use of slave labor, intellectual property violations, and the undermining of freedom and democracy.

In the UK, we should protect our environment by protecting property rights, allowing enterprise to develop new green technologies, protecting existing technologies like genetic modification, and removing bans on imports provided the food supply is kept safe.

We should call out the green lobby's brazen anti-capitalist agenda. They are the extremists in today's politics and should be labeled as such. They say they want to reduce carbon but oppose nuclear power. They say they want less pesticide use but oppose genetic modification. They organize their protests on iPhones, devices that came into existence through free markets.

We also have to wrest back control of environment policy from the legions of bureaucrats. Ultimately these decisions should be made by politicians who have to answer to the people.

CHAPTER 3

2016

By the spring of 2016, I'd been making steady progress at the Environment Department, dealing with the worst floods since the 1950s and trying to tame the environmental lobby. I was getting my feet under the table in Cabinet. The calm was superficial. In short succession we had a Brexit referendum campaign with a shock result, a brutal Conservative Party leadership election, and a seismic U.S. poll. Whatever the powers that be might have felt—people wanted change.

My Brexit referendum campaign started with a hurried and unplanned departure from Europe. It was February 2016, and we were on a half-term family holiday in Paris. The tiny Airbnb I'd found on the top floor of an apartment block near the Arc de Triomphe looked much more attractive in the photos than it turned out to be in real life. We had only been there a few days when the call came from London: Prime Minister David Cameron had completed negotiations on his new deal with the European Union. He was convening an urgent Cabinet meeting the following day to showcase it and fire the starting gun on the promised referendum on the UK's continued membership of the EU.

Not for the first time, a family holiday was kiboshed by political events outside my control. Remaining in Europe was not an option for me. Hugh, Frances, and Liberty would have to tour the catacombs of Paris in my absence. The sudden recall was an unwelcome disruption. As I organized my hasty retreat back to London, I had a call with the chancellor, George Osborne, who would go on to be a key cheerleader for the Remain campaign. While he read out numbers from a PowerPoint presentation over the phone, I paced the top floor of that tiny apartment and my heart sank.

On the specific question of our EU membership, I had been on the fence for some time and would rather have put the whole thing in the "too difficult" pile. I was no fan of the EU and had strongly opposed the UK's ever joining the euro, the European single currency. In fact, it was my fundamental opposition to adopting the euro that had finally prompted me to leave the blindly Europhile Liberal Democrats in the mid-1990s. Joining the euro would have tied our hands and accelerated political union, because if monetary policy were controlled at an EU level it would have been hard to retain our control over matters of taxing and spending. That was a thick red line for me.

But I hadn't yet made the journey to back a complete departure from the EU. First, I was loyal to David Cameron and George Osborne. They had put me where I was. They'd supported me through various trials and tribulations. I was also just not bold enough at this point. I still believed in the system and working my way up through it. Despite my skirmishes in education, I did not yet realize how broken it was.

With the UK not in the euro, I believed a deeper split would eventually come, but for us to have precipitated it at that juncture would not have put us in a strong negotiating position. Frankly, I also wasn't convinced the Leave campaign could win. In referendums, people tend to vote for the status quo. I failed to sense the public appetite for a big change. After all, they had just reelected the Conservatives in the 2015 election.

When I got back to London, there was a palpably tense atmosphere at the special Cabinet meeting that Saturday afternoon. Clearly the deal Cameron had negotiated with the EU was lame. And I could tell from the speeches around the table that this was going to turn into a massive psychodrama.

For my part, while I said I thought the UK's long-term future did not lie within the EU, I questioned whether this was the right time for our departure. Having unexpectedly secured a Conservative government with a parliamentary majority in the 2015 general election, I felt these were our "golden years" to sort out Britain. I feared that extricating ourselves from the EU would require ten years of government time and bandwidth that could otherwise be devoted to domestic reform.

My personal political obsessions were addressing Britain's lack of competitiveness, high taxes, and bloated and lethargic public sector. We had yet to make any serious effort to begin taking apart Tony Blair and Gordon Brown's legacy of red tape, legal constraints, and redistributionism.

I was completely blindsided by the growing extent of the Brexit movement, both among Conservative MPs and in the country. By 2010, Euroskepticism was very much the mainstream attitude in the party, and I shared that outlook. But wanting to leave the EU entirely was then considered quite a far-out, fringe position. Had I spent more of my time thinking about it during those years, I might have come to share that view. But I had been busy as a minister, knee-deep in floods and other distractions, with not much time for thinking.

Clearly the EU was distant and undemocratic. I had seen and felt that for myself at the regular gatherings of EU agriculture ministers in airless Brussels meeting rooms. Every major decision was stitched up in advance by the French and the Germans, and bureaucracy was an end in itself. The air of smugness and complacency was difficult to take. But I also thought the same about the Civil Service back home and many of the unaccountable quangos that operate in Britain. (Quangos is short for "quasi-autonomous non-governmental organizations." These are public bodies that operate at arm's length from ministers but are still funded by taxpayer money and wield significant power.)

It would certainly have been in character for me to throw my weight behind the Leave campaign. I am someone who instinctively wants to shake things up, and part of me would have relished joining the side of the disruptors. Some of my colleagues put pressure on me to do so, pointing out that most of my friends and natural allies on the right of the party would be backing Brexit.

That gave me pause for thought. But while it was true that many people I liked and admired were fervent Brexiteers, there were also a number of people in that camp whose views troubled me. I was not seeing a vision from the Brexiteers predicated on a clear free-market prospectus to use the opportunity of Brexit to ease regulation and increase global trade. Some of my friends who were leading lights in the Vote Leave campaign—notably Matthew Elliott and Dan Hannan—certainly were making that case. But others seemed to consider Brexit a charter for protectionism and anti-growth policies. That contradiction was never quite resolved during the campaign, as attention focused on rows about NHS funding, immigration, and short-term economic effects.

I therefore decided, reluctantly, to back the prime minister and join the Remain campaign. Once I had taken that decision, my instincts as a campaigner kicked in and I got on with it. But I soon discovered that all was not well inside the Remain campaign, branded as it was under the banner "Britain Stronger in Europe." It seemed badly organized, and it was quite clear that despite officially backing the campaign, the Labour Party under Jeremy Corbyn's leadership didn't have their heart in the fight. It's fair to say the campaign was a mess.

And while I was happy making arguments about free trade, I hated the uncritical celebration of the EU from some of the devout Europhiles on the campaign. I also didn't like their negativity about Britain, their sense that there was something vulgar about the idea of Brexit.

So I found myself caught in the middle, approving of neither side's arguments. I did not believe the UK was doomed outside the EU, as the Remain campaign tried to suggest. But Vote Leave's main campaign message—infamously painted on the side of a bus—was simply a pledge to increase public spending on the NHS. This seemed an odd rallying cry for free-market conservatives. There were good arguments for Brexit, but that wasn't one I found particularly convincing. The anti-growth rhetoric emanating from elements of the Leave coalition didn't help either.

That colleagues were fighting each other so brutally also poisoned the well inside the Conservative Party. I hated that people—friends— with whom I had worked so closely (including most of my fellow authors of *Britannia Unchained*, a book I co-wrote with other Conservative MPs) were on the other side.

One of the legacies of the referendum campaign was the protracted "blue on blue" fighting between fellow Conservatives (unlike America with its red states, Conservatives in the UK fly the color blue). Once such discord has entered the bloodstream of a party, it is almost impossible to get rid of it, as we were to discover painfully over the ensuing years.

The result, when it came, was a political earthquake.

That dull June night, I was in the Blue Boar pub in Westminster with some of the Remain campaign team, having done a few interviews for the world's media on London's South Bank. Somebody was there with a spreadsheet plugging in the results as they came in. Sunderland, the city in the Northeast of England known, among other things, for the speed at which they count ballot papers, had plumped for Leave in far greater numbers than we had expected. I could see the faces getting more and more anxious. I decided to leave the event and ended up wandering around central London in the middle of the night.

As the results continued coming through and it became clear Leave had won, I felt a sense of disorientation.

British politics had been changed forever. Not only had David Cameron been crushed, but his electoral coalition had been dissolved—a coalition that had combined the affluent middle classes in the suburbs with more traditional rural voters. There was now a whole new swath of people in play: working-class voters from former mining areas in the North and Midlands, many of whom had never voted before, and among those who had voted, it certainly had never been for a Conservative. At the same time, much of the self-assured South found themselves out of kilter with the national decision.

The next morning, just after 8:00 a.m., I tweeted my reaction: "The British people have spoken. We must now put our shoulder to the wheel and ensure we leave the EU in the best way for Britain."

A few minutes later, David Cameron emerged to announce his resignation as prime minister, kicking off a leadership election in the Conservative Party. Some said he shouldn't have quit, but I don't think he had a choice. His point of view had been roundly rejected, and on a voter turnout that was far higher than in any normal election campaign.

I feel personal affection for David, who gave me my first opportunities on the national political stage. He was a very plausible prime minister and handled the media well. He was intelligent and sharp-witted.

Yet I never really sensed a drive to transform the country. And the bottom line is he was not prepared to do the bold things that Britain needed and indeed demanded after the financial crisis, whether it was leaving the EU or much of anything else.

There was a lack of clarity about what he wanted to achieve. There was too much wishy-washy flannel about "the big society" and "general well-being." I don't believe he truly understood the scale of change required. With a bolder prospectus, I believe we could have won an overall majority in 2010, negating the need for a coalition with the Liberal Democrats. We could have done much more, and earlier, to reverse the energy-sapping legacy of Tony Blair and Gordon Brown. Cameron and Osborne were good tacticians, but you can't have long-term leadership without a central vision. The tactical dice were rolled once too often.

Having said that—and having in time made my own mistakes in the role—I do appreciate how hard it is to fulfill the office of prime minister. You are expected to be a front man or woman and a visionary—as well as an adept manager and implementer. Margaret Thatcher managed this by working night and day, but that was in an era with far fewer media demands and with the public generally expecting less of the government. Saddled with a twenty-four-hour news cycle and the perils of social media, the challenges these days are immense.

In any event, it was clear that Cameron's time was over. The country had voted for a big change, and we needed a leader, a team, and a plan to deliver it. Here was a new opportunity to move forward with a clear agenda. The obvious logic was that the party and country should be run by someone who had played a leading role in the Brexit campaign. Michael Gove and Boris Johnson stood out above all others. Yet they themselves didn't seem to have planned for this eventuality!

I had worked with Gove in the Department for Education. We had many rows, most of which he ended by reminding me he was the boss. But we agreed on the fundamentals of education policy. I did not know Boris as well, so my first call that weekend was to Gove, telling him I thought he should run. He immediately declined, saying he was backing Boris and that I should join his campaign. After a friendly meeting with Boris, I did so, and decided to announce my support in an article in the *Daily Telegraph*. That article duly appeared the following Thursday—the same morning Boris was due to launch his campaign formally.

Early that morning, however, I received a phone call from Gove. "Liz, you need to sit down for what I'm about to say. . . . I've decided to run." My initial reaction was incredulity: I asked him what on earth he was talking about. Having declined to run when I suggested it to him over the weekend, he had spent virtually every waking hour since getting others to back Boris. Now, on the very morning of the campaign launch, he was asking "Will you back me?" It was extraordinary. I muttered something about needing to think about it and hung up.

It was a shocking development, and I was honestly devastated by it. Having initially favored Gove, I had been entirely persuaded that Boris and he would make a winning combination—the showman and the fixer. There was also a strong democratic argument for it, the *de facto* leaders of the Leave campaign working together to deliver their mandate for Brexit.

I had bought into the whole concept, and now he was telling me the partnership was off. I was due to be at Boris's launch event in several hours and I had no idea what to do. As the news spread and chaos descended on Westminster, I decided I had to get out of the madhouse. That morning my then seven-year-old daughter Liberty was performing in *Mr. Sandman*, a school play that I had been due to miss, so I went along to that instead and enjoyed the temporary distraction of normal life. Meanwhile, at his planned launch event, Boris made a shock statement withdrawing from the contest.

Around lunchtime, I headed into my office at the Environment Department to try to make sense of what had happened. My Special Adviser says he had never seen me so depressed. I just looked at him and said what we were both thinking: "What the actual f***?"

That afternoon Gove called me again, still seeking my support. By this time my shock had given way to anger. I told him bluntly I could not back him. Whatever regard I previously had for him, his actions in stabbing Boris in the back were unforgivable. I simply did not understand how someone could do that. Gove had been in charge of whipping other Conservatives to support Boris until that very morning.

I then received a call from Home Secretary Theresa May, who was keen to sign me up to her campaign. I had found her difficult to deal with in the past, but I was prepared to give her the benefit of the doubt, given the situation in which the party now found itself. Had Boris stayed in the race, I would have continued to honor my support for him, but after he dropped out, Theresa seemed to be the only viable candidate left.

Funnily enough, this all brought back memories of a lunch I'd had with Boris in 2014 when I was an education minister and he was mayor of London. Always on the make, he tried tapping me up as to whether I would back him to be leader in the future. I said I couldn't guarantee it, but I would back him if he were up against Theresa May. . . .

There was yet more drama to come. Exhaustive ballots finally narrowed the contest down to two candidates to be put to party members across the country. Theresa was set to be on the ballot paper alongside energy minister Andrea Leadsom, but within days Andrea pulled out after a media storm over an interview she'd given in which she said being a mother had granted her a larger stake in society than May. From the reaction of my party members in Norfolk, I believe Andrea actually would have won if she had stayed in the race. But as it was,

Theresa May was declared the winner unopposed and became prime minister within days.

Under Cameron, no planning had been done for the eventuality of a Leave vote. He and Osborne had—somewhat recklessly, you might argue in retrospect—banned civil servants from undertaking any such work, so the plan for Brexit right now amounted to nothing more than a blank sheet of paper.

Theresa, to her credit, had been an effective home secretary, but she was not someone who obviously had a great vision for the future of the country. As far as Brexit was concerned, this left lots of room for internecine warfare about what should actually happen, including the prospect of reversing the result, as some of my democracy-denying erstwhile colleagues from the Remain campaign would try and have it.

It also surprised me that some on the pro-Brexit side seemed to want to pursue a so-called "Norway-style solution." This would have entailed remaining in the single market but having to make contributions to the EU budget and being subject to laws and regulations from Brussels over which we had no say.

Having crossed the Rubicon after accepting the democratic decision of the people, I was very much in the camp of doing Brexit properly. The EU wasn't going to play nice. And the worst thing Britain could have done would have been to end up as a supplicant to the EU. I believed we had to get on with the legal divorce and urgently be looking for new partners like the United States with which to do trade deals. It was also imperative that we take back control of our borders: we could not be half in and half out.

Had Boris Johnson (with or without Michael Gove) been a candidate in the leadership election, he would have been tested on this point, and the contest would have provided an opportunity for him to lay out a post-Brexit vision. Having been the face of Vote Leave, he would have then had the authority to strike a deal to leave on the terms he set.

As it was, we were left with Theresa May, whose views on the matter were largely unknown and whose principal proclamation on the subject was the rather meaningless slogan "Brexit means Brexit." With Andrea having quit the race, we were denied a leadership contest in which Theresa's views could be tested over several months. She thus became leader without a mandate from either the Conservative Party membership or the referendum. Combined with a narrow parliamentary majority, this put her in a weakened position from the get-go.

It was in this context that the next three and a half tortuous years of Brexit negotiations began. Initially, Theresa benefited from the post-referendum civil war inside the Labour Party, which arose mainly because the party's enthusiastic Remainers blamed left-wing leader Jeremy Corbyn's reluctance to embrace the pro-EU cause for the referendum result. While Corbyn won the support of his members in the country (if not his MPs), the turmoil helped propel the Conservative Party to large opinion poll leads of up to twenty points, and it seemed Theresa was well placed to deliver the change the British people had demanded. I remained hopeful that we would be able to seize that opportunity to make some fundamental changes at home too. But before too long my optimism was to be sorely tested.

* * *

By the summer of 2016, a buzz was developing around the upcoming American presidential election. As an early fan of the TV show *The Apprentice*, I enjoyed the Donald's catchphrases and sassy business advice. In the Smoking Room in Parliament, various colleagues had reveled in doing competing Trump imitations. We were going to win so much we were going to get tired of winning . . .

Wandering through Swaffham, one of the market towns in my constituency, I was struck by the number of elderly ladies who were Trump fans: traditional Norfolk Conservative voters who probably also voted for Brexit, they seemed genuinely animated by the disruptive Republican candidate. It gave me pause for thought, as I realized that if he could have that sort of effect on traditionally minded middle-class conservatives on this side of the Atlantic, he perhaps had more of a chance in the United States than was being predicted.

Yet I was taken in by the establishment hype that Hillary Clinton would win. It was a case of déjà vu at the American Embassy party on Election Night—although this time I had absolutely no skin in the game. The embassy, at that time still housed in a rather utilitarian building in London's Grosvenor Square compared to the expansive Winfield House, the official residence of the ambassador, was full of complacent Clinton supporters. As the night wore on and the early results came in, it seemed the American establishment was prevailing. Exhausted by the ongoing demands of my role as justice secretary and bored with the party, Hugh and I decided to head home.

The following morning I awoke to the radio with the news that Trump had won. Wow.

What really struck me was that he had won the same types of areas in the United States that had voted for Brexit in the UK, working-class strongholds like Ohio and Wisconsin. We were seeing a shake-up of American politics with cities and suburbs being dominated by Democrats, while rural areas and small towns were taken by the Republicans. Working-class people were no longer automatically attached to the Left. Your vote reflected the kind of country you wanted to live in.

Those who had supported Trump or Brexit were not happy with the political menu they had been served. Living standards were not increasing, with blue-collar areas in particular feeling they had been left behind. All the while, they were being subjected to increasingly pious lectures on green issues and served up a feast of political correctness, regardless of which party was in power.

Although we had a Conservative government in Britain, the Blair legacy very much remained in place. And in the United States, Obama had shifted the policy dial to the left. Trump's rallying cry to "Make America Great Again" resonated with voters who agreed that America was not as great as it had been. The driving force behind Brexit had arguably been about Making Britain Great Again.

Of course, all this was hated by the establishment in Britain. And you almost have to feel sorry for the poor Foreign Office. They were only just beginning to compute that they would have to get on with delivering Brexit when it emerged that they would have to deal with an unreconstructed right-wing tycoon in the White House. This was a man who had very much made his reputation as a businessman.

I was glad to see the back of the anti-British, condescending Obama, whose failures in Syria and on Russia would come back to haunt us. He had also presided over the slowest economic recovery since the Great Depression.

Trump's election had, of course, upset all the usual suspects on the British liberal left. I genuinely thought his election would be good for Britain—and might even give the Conservative Party a much-needed kick up the backside to become more conservative. He was instinctively low-tax and deregulatory. He was also at heart a deal-maker, and we were now in a situation post-Brexit where we had the opportunity to strike new trade deals.

I concluded that voters on both sides of the Atlantic had seen things that I had missed about the way our respective countries were run: the vested interests that had held us back, along with the groupthink and caution that had led to our declining economic positions.

I knew what the problems were already. After all, I'd co-written two books about them, set up the Free Enterprise Group, and already had a series of battles with the "blob." What 2016 showed me was how big this was, both the scale of the change that was needed and the level of resistance that would be encountered.

I believe voters have an instinct about things that often surpasses that of those of us involved in politics. We struggle to see the wood for the trees. The way I got bogged down at the Environment Department was a case in point. The Brexit referendum and Trump's election saw many people participate in the electoral process who had previously felt marginalized and unrepresented. Brexit and Trump caught their imaginations. That should not be ignored.

This was all brought home to me when I heard a constituent of mine in Norfolk after the referendum proudly proclaim, "We stuck two fingers up at London!" It was a very revealing comment. They hadn't stuck two fingers up to Brussels but *London*. This attitude, which I found to be widely shared, showed the real disconnect between what the British governing classes were up to and what people actually wanted. The referendum result had been a protest vote against the status quo and the establishment in Westminster and Whitehall just as much as it was against the unelected bureaucrats in Brussels.

They were registering a protest against decline in their communities, a result of decades of poor economic policy, but they were also taking a stand against what they saw as people talking Britain down.

I had some prior experience with this attitude some years earlier in 2001 when I was standing as a parliamentary candidate in Hemsworth, West Yorkshire. It was a solidly Labour seat in a mining community and I was destined to lose, so I got little to no support from my party HQ. But the one thing that really motivated people was my "Keep the Pound" stand, which we set up in various locations to advertise the

Conservative Party's campaign against UK entry into the European single currency.

As we campaigned in the streets and markets of Hemsworth and Featherstone, we found this message had a real resonance. Lifelong Labour voters came up to talk to us and said they would never vote Conservative but were attracted to our patriotic appeal. It was more of a cultural statement than a political one, and I found that very interesting.

That was what I thought of again as we saw the appeal of Brexit to many of the same people a decade and a half later. There would also be much talk during the UK's 2019 general election about the voting habits of those in the so-called "Red Wall," former Labour working-class strongholds in the Midlands and North of England that cast aside their traditional allegiances to vote for Boris Johnson's Conservatives. But it has been a more long-term trend, with Conservatives starting to do progressively better in traditionally Labour areas over several decades. The same story can be seen in the Rust Belt of America, with similarly disruptive political consequences.

The disdain for Brexit and Trump was universal among the British intellectual commentariat and left-leaning elites, who could neither understand nor accept what had happened. I hate that attitude. Sneering at people for voting for change and dismissing it as "populism" is not only disrespectful but self-defeating.

The truth is that political parties do need to be popular. If we cannot present our policies and ideas in a way that attracts mass electoral support, we will never prevail. When people feel alienated from politics, it is our job to reconnect and win their trust. That doesn't mean offering them instant gratification or jumping on every passing trend. It means having a clear view of what people actually want and showing how our policies will help them obtain it.

Too many politicians think they know best and spend their time trying to curtail people's ability to choose for themselves. I fundamentally object to that arrogant paternalism, and challenging it is at the heart of what I believe.

As we saw in 2016, the instinct to rebel against an out-of-touch political establishment is a potent electoral force. A clear message was delivered in the United States and the United Kingdom. I fear that eight years on, the changes our countries wanted and needed have still not happened.

Ultimately an even bigger earthquake may yet come before the message hits home.

CHAPTER 4

Rough Justice

"There is going to be some in-flight turbulence." That was the warning I gave to Theresa May once I had found my feet as Lord Chancellor and secretary of state for justice in her Cabinet.

Theresa became prime minister after David Cameron resigned following the referendum vote in favor of Brexit. She arrived with a mandate to get Brexit done, but I was preparing for a different fight: taking on the British judiciary over their appointment practices. I had a premonition it would end in tears—my tears. But what's the point of being in government if you're not going to push for what you believe in?

I had become increasingly concerned that Britain's judiciary had become a self-perpetuating oligarchy. Here was a group of similarly minded people from similar backgrounds who had a particular world-view and were resolute in protecting their own interests.

Then there was the fact that we were saddled with an increasingly left-wing legal establishment that had successfully tied successive British governments up in knots through judicial reviews, in particular challenging policies on welfare and immigration, and most recently the entire Brexit process.

Courts and lawyers had been accruing power during the 1980s and 1990s through the judicial review process—and the European Union's promotion of statute law over common law only added to the problem. But it was Tony Blair who had made a bad state of affairs a whole lot worse. The policies he pursued as prime minister had made it considerably harder for elected politicians to get things done and put far more power in the hands of the unelected.

Until 2005, the Lord Chancellor held a special constitutional position not only as a Cabinet minister but also as the head of the judiciary and the Speaker of the House of Lords. These were historic duties dating back to before Magna Carta.

In other words, he (and until my appointment it always had been a man) was a very powerful figure, playing a role in the executive, judicial, and legislative branches of government. He sat in the House of Lords and was a practicing judge, with many of his responsibilities involving the direct administration of the judicial system and the selection of judges.

Parliament is sovereign. The independent judiciary maintained the common law principles of the rule of law. Ultimately they were subordinate to the executive in Parliament.

The Constitutional Reform Act 2005 changed this by denuding the Lord Chancellor of much of this power. These changes were devised by Charlie Falconer, Lord Falconer of Thoroton—a one-time flatmate of Tony Blair's.

One of the justifications for this constitutional vandalism was a desire to fit in with the rights-based philosophy of continental Europe. The UK's ratifying of the European Convention on Human Rights

(ECHR) in 1951 ultimately gave rise to individual petitions being accepted in the United Kingdom. This created an alternative source of power to the sovereign Parliament. Eventually Blair incorporated the ECHR into British law in 1998 through the Human Rights Act.

Under this approach, it was thought no longer right for a Cabinet minister to be a judge and head of the judiciary, so Blair stripped the Lord Chancellor of these active judicial roles. But in removing the power of the executive to appoint senior judges, the Blair government did not move instead to an elected system, as exists in other countries. Rather, a new judicial appointments quango was created, as was a Supreme Court in place of the Law Lords. Judges were also given partial responsibility for running the courts service. The Lord Chancellor would still have to swear an oath to protect the independence of the judiciary, but all the associated powers were removed and handed to the administrative bureaucracy. The net impact was to make the judiciary more of a self-appointing oligarchy and reduce levels of accountability. As we were to see in everything from welfare policy to immigration to legal aid, this made it harder for democratically elected governments to deliver policies the public had voted for.

The legacy legislation from the Blair and Brown administrations that we had failed to repeal—including the Human Rights Act and the Equality Act—tied up the government in red tape and gave more powers to the courts and lawyers.

All this meant a key part of the apparatus of the government had become further removed from any sense of accountability.

I looked enviously across the Atlantic, where there were elected judges and prosecutors and a constitutionally appointed Supreme Court. Of course, the U.S. system is not perfect. The activities of increasingly activist lawyers, funded by deep-pocketed left-wingers, were cause for concern. But the Supreme Court's recent rightward tilt, the result of

Republicans winning elections rather than any oligarchic preference, gave me hope.

I felt instinctively that major reform was needed in Britain to reverse Blair's disastrous legal takeover and return to the system that had successfully been tried and tested for virtually one thousand years.

Yet when I was appointed Lord Chancellor and secretary of state for justice, I had limited time to think grand thoughts about the constitution. As with other reshuffles, I'd had no prior notice that I would be getting the job. And the minute I arrived at the department, it was clear there was a whole series of fires that needed to be put out.

Blair had created the Orwellian-sounding Ministry of Justice in 2007 as one of his final acts before leaving office and handing the reins of power to Gordon Brown. It was an awkward amalgam of ceremony and *Prisoner: Cell Block H*—and contained yet more hard-to-manage quangos dealing with everything from prisons and probation to the Child Support Agency.

The Ministry of Justice was housed in the old Home Office headquarters overlooking St. James's Park. This 1970s concrete office block was a brutalist monstrosity. I quickly discovered that the department was in a mess and short on cash to fix the justice system, which was both overcrowded and the guardian of a dilapidated estate of buildings around the country.

Back in 2010, Ken Clarke, the former chancellor who made a surprise comeback to frontline politics as a justice secretary, wanted to cut the budget by letting people out of prison earlier.

Liberal-minded people often think it should be easy to reduce prison numbers, as though our jails are full of shoplifters and other minor criminals. The reality is that by far the largest number of inmates—over 60 percent—are in prison for serious sexual or violent crimes or drug offenses. Unless you are prepared to make their sentences shorter—which I was certainly not—there is not much leeway to reduce numbers.

In fact, by international standards, the UK has a fairly modest rate of imprisonment, with around 144 prisoners per 100,000 people in England and Wales. This is mid-table as far as OECD countries are concerned, and vastly lower than the United States, which has seen rates of up to 755 prisoners per 100,000 people in the last decade.

Whether you agree with cutting prisoner numbers or not, the fact is that it didn't happen, with David Cameron rowing back on his support for Ken Clarke's proposals. There was no reduction in the prison population in England and Wales, which passed 85,000 for the first time in June 2010 and peaked at just over 88,000 in November 2011 (a point that was reached once again in late 2023). The spending cuts went ahead regardless, however, leading to huge pressure on the prisons budget. This was obvious as soon as I arrived, with prison violence on an upward trend and the system stretched to the breaking point. My predecessors had tried to paper over the cracks by talking about big ideas—there was allegedly a white paper laying out proposals on prison reform ready to go. I soon found out it didn't exist.

I was horrified by the state that our prisons were in, many of which dated back to Victorian times. They were rodent-infested. It was remarkably easy to get phones, drugs, and other paraphernalia inside. Not enough work and training was taking place. There were some beacons of hope, like the Norwich Prison café and the Bad Boys' Bakery in Brixton, but they often relied on heroic individuals rather than systemic improvements.

It was the frontline staff who had to deal with all of this. Prison officers were some of the most impressive and least appreciated public servants I came across during my ten years in government. They were massively underpaid, given the difficult and dangerous job they had to do. Their lives were on the line, and they were facing significant increases in violence from inmates. Many of them were on salaries of under £30,000 ($40,500)—no wonder so many were leaving the service. Combined with the overall cut in prison officer numbers as a result of budget reductions, many prisons were dangerously understaffed, while unreformed working practices were leading to further problems. It was an appalling situation.

One of the few things that did once keep me up at night was the fate of a prison officer who was left severely injured by an inmate and whose life was hanging by a thread. Mercifully he survived.

To make our prisons safe and secure, we needed to recruit more prison officers and pay them better. This would require 2,500 prison officers, at a cost of some £100 million ($135 million) per year. We set to work on drawing up a white paper on more comprehensive reform to the prisons system that included this commitment.

I am an instinctive hawk on spending, but I was determined to spend more in this area and reverse the cuts that my predecessors had made. I've always believed that the state should do less, but what it does do, it should do better. Incarcerating criminals to keep the public safe is a core function of government, and pursuing cuts to the system without considering the consequences had been an example of the worst sort of short-termism. We were paying the price for that in terms of the safety of prison officers, and I had no hesitation in doing what was necessary to fix the problem. It was a moral duty.

To get it done, I first had to secure the necessary additional funds. I went to see the chief secretary to the Treasury, David Gauke, who thankfully understood at once the scale of the problem. He agreed to the increase in the prisons budget I was seeking and we were able to finalize the white paper on that basis. I announced it at the start of November 2016.

The need to take urgent action on prisons was becoming ever more apparent. Overcrowding and a shortage of staff was leading to dangerous conditions and outbreaks of violence. Days after my announcement, two hundred inmates rioted at Bedford Prison, and on the same day two prisoners escaped from Pentonville, where weeks earlier an inmate had been murdered. The Prison Officers' Association (POA) organized protests outside prisons and encouraged a walkout by officers that amounted to an unlawful strike. This was not just against the law; it was highly dangerous. It meant staffing in prisons was stretched even further, requiring prisoners to be kept in their cells for prolonged periods, stoking resentment and the potential for more violence.

After frantic phone calls that morning, we took the POA to court and officers were ordered to end the protest and return to work. The situation was still highly volatile. Frazzled prison officers, overcrowded prisons awash with drugs like "spice" (a type of synthetic marijuana), and rising levels of violence made for a tinderbox at constant risk of igniting.

The spark came in Birmingham the following month. On Friday, December 16, I had gotten in the car with Hugh, Frances, and Liberty to drive to Norfolk for Christmas when I took a call from the junior prisons minister, Sam Gyimah. He told me there was a serious riot underway at HM Prison Birmingham and the situation was spiraling out of control. We hadn't gotten much farther than a few streets from home when we had to turn the car around and head back. I hurried straight into the office to get to grips with the situation.

That morning, an inmate in the prison's N wing had climbed onto some safety netting between floors. When prison officers tried to intervene, one of them had his keys snatched. The staff had to withdraw for their own safety and the prisoners soon gained control of the wing—and then the neighboring P wing. Offices were looted and mattresses were set on fire. A "Tornado Team" of specialists was dispatched, but by lunchtime prisoners had gained control of a further two wings. We learned later that just one padlock on a single gate separating the other wings had prevented the entire prison from being overwhelmed.

As further reinforcements were summoned and police secured the perimeter, Gyimah and I spent a tense afternoon on the phone to senior Prison Service staff and prison governors around the country. The danger was that once word spread to other prisons of what was going on at Birmingham, it would trigger a wave of similar violence across the country. We authorized extra resources to try to ward off trouble elsewhere, as officials put together a plan to retake the rioting wings. That evening, ten Tornado Teams swept through and had taken back control by 10:00 p.m.

It was the most serious prison disturbance since the Strangeways riot of 1990 in Manchester, England, which lasted twenty-five days and injured close to two hundred people. On investigation it seemed the trigger had been a mix of complaints about cold showers, the food, gym time being canceled, and prisoners being locked in their cells all day because of a lack of staff. In the immediate aftermath of the riot, we made it a priority to fix some of these basic problems. I found myself on a daily phone call with prison governors authorizing extra budget for chips and the like to keep the prisons calm. Ministers ended up having to personally direct the service and take responsibility for the problems—many of which were decades in the making.

The state of the prisons was the most severe problem, but it was clear that serious reform was needed across the board from youth justice to family courts to probation.

In the end, I only had eleven months in the job at the Ministry of Justice. It would take more like eleven years of serious reform to make the system functional. It is very hard to see how this will ever be achieved. There is frankly limited public and media interest.

I'd announced the extra funds to recruit thousands of prison officers in a speech on November 3, 2016, which had received some coverage. Yet that very evening, the *Daily Mail* published a story that would completely obliterate any of the achievements we'd made on prisons.

The UK's High Court had earlier that day handed down judgment in a case brought by pro-EU activist Gina Miller over whether the government was required to win a vote in Parliament before it could trigger the start of Brexit negotiations. The court found the government did require parliamentary approval, a decision that provoked intense criticism from ardent Brexiteers. The following day's *Daily Mail* carried the front-page headline "Enemies of the People" below pictures of the three senior judges who had given the judgment.

As it happened, on the night that front page appeared, I was at a dinner at Middle Temple, a professional association for lawyers at the heart of the British legal establishment. There seemed to be no outrage or demands for me to intervene—just an acceptance with an air of resignation that this was the *Daily Mail* being the *Daily Mail*. Some of those present later jumped on the bandwagon of criticism, but it was clear that night that they saw it as nothing more than the Euroskeptic press having its say, albeit in a rather forceful way.

The story was whipped into a scandal because of the febrile politics of Brexit. Those on the Leave side felt outraged at what they saw as the legal establishment seeking to block the democratic will of the people. The Remain side saw the headline as an outrageous attack on the independence of the judiciary and, it seemed, the beginning of the end of civilization as we knew it. The calls for me to wade in and condemn the *Mail* grew ever louder, with social media campaigns demanding I issue a statement alongside pious commentary about how I had sworn an oath to defend judges and how it was my duty to do so now.

I found the outrage completely mystifying. Of course I supported and do support the independence of the judiciary, and had indeed sworn an oath to uphold the rule of law. But this was a headline in the *Daily Mail*, not an attempted coup. I also believe passionately in the freedom of the press and in the right of people to criticize those in positions of authority. In my view, the *Daily Mail* was perfectly entitled to criticize judges, and judges were perfectly at liberty to ignore the newspaper. That is the essence of a free society. Judicial independence is important, but that isn't the same as being entirely immune from criticism.

Those were my instincts when the row over the headline began to escalate. A narrative began to develop that I had been ordered by the prime minister not to say anything and that I was too weak to push back. The truth was that I needed no encouragement to stay out of the media storm. I had no interest in providing fuel to the fire when I was in the middle of trying to tackle a near-crisis in the prison service. And at that point the judiciary and the Lord Chief Justice, Lord Thomas of Cwmgiedd (one of those pictured on the *Mail* front page that day), weren't asking me to get involved.

But the hysteria spread like wildfire. More and more lawyers and commentators demanded I say something, and of course whatever I did say didn't satisfy them—because I thought it was completely wrong for a government minister to be interfering with what the press had printed.

Civil servants at the Ministry of Justice seemed more interested in appeasing a wounded judiciary than doing what was right. They were beholden to this vested interest and their own ideological leanings rather than reflecting the will of the democratically elected government. I held a town hall meeting in the foyer of the Ministry of Justice building and one staffer asked why I had not condemned the attacks on the judiciary. There was a large outburst of applause, leaving me in no doubt about what people's views were on what was a policy question.

In retrospect, maybe I should have been more front-footed before the row escalated to absurd levels. But had I done so, it would have merely been to say that I believed fundamentally not just in the independence of the judiciary but also in the freedom of the press, and that both must be respected. I was never going to join those who wanted the *Daily Mail* pilloried for daring to criticize a judicial decision.

Yet again, the British media would rather have had a witch hunt over what someone had or hadn't "condemned" than deal with the very serious underlying issues with our democracy and the parlous state of the criminal and civil justice system.

Looking back at the "Enemies of the People" row, I should not have been surprised that it blew up with such vehemence. While it had properly exploded, appropriately enough, on Guy Fawkes' Day, November 5, the issue of my relationship with the judiciary had been a slow-burning fuse that had been lit months before.

It is fair to say the judicial establishment had not welcomed my appointment as Lord Chancellor in July 2016. Lord Faulks, a lawyer who had been minister of state for justice for two years, resigned immediately in protest. He questioned my ability to do the job and whether I would have sufficient "clout" to stand up to the prime minister.

The former Lord Chancellor Charlie Falconer joined the attack, writing a withering article for *The Times* arguing that I had failed to meet the criteria laid down in law of being "qualified by experience" and calling me an "ambitious middle-ranking cabinet minister." This was absolute cheek from the man who had vandalized the constitution and denigrated the role of Lord Chancellor by devising the Constitutional Reform Act 2005. But it set the tone for much of the commentary during my first days in office.

All the lawyers who attacked me were keen to stress that their remarks were nothing personal. But it seemed odd that such a fierce backlash had not accompanied the appointment of my two immediate predecessors, Chris Grayling and Michael Gove. Neither of them had a background as a lawyer, but they seemed to have been given the benefit of the doubt.

The root of the problem, I soon realized, was that the judiciary and wider legal profession are special interest groups that have been used to having their own people in positions of power for centuries and don't take kindly to outsiders, particularly transient politicians. They wanted a Lord Chancellor who was from their background and comfortable in their world. Failing that, they wanted someone who would champion their interests and not challenge their fundamentals.

I was clearly not this. Politicians are there to represent the public, not professional interests. Although special pleading is common across departments, the judiciary had become used to being a particularly special case.

In part, this is because many politicians have been too scared to take on the judiciary. Senior judges can indeed be quite intimidating. They have a unique ability to make life extremely difficult for a government should they be so minded. The legal profession is also strongly represented in Parliament and public life more generally, and they form a strong and effective lobbying network to resist any change they don't like. Advocacy is what they do, after all.

I hadn't realized quite how the legal establishment works. They operate by briefing the press—particularly *The Times*—as well as using their many connections in the House of Lords. They tried to both charm me and shame me into going along with what they wanted: lots of cozy breakfasts and dinners on the one hand while not clapping loudly enough when they "welcomed" me on the other. As somebody who has never aspired to be part of the establishment, this didn't impress me very much. I am, after all, a contrarian. I was more interested in changing things to make them better.

I view respect for the rule of law and an acceptance of the importance of independent court judgments as cornerstones of our freedom. But the independence of the judiciary has begun to be interpreted as meaning they should be immune to any challenge to how they operate or the way they are appointed. Making independent and impartial judgments does not mean carte blanche.

This was most obvious in the field of recruitment. Since the Blair vandalism of 2005, the judiciary had become a self-appointed oligarchy, choosing and promoting those who shared their values. I was particularly concerned by the lack of meritocracy in the selection of judges. The system of promotions was biased entirely towards traditional lawyers, called barristers in the UK, and against solicitors, a different type of lawyer who tend to spend their time helping clients navigate the legal system rather than in the courtroom.

The first step in the process of being appointed as a judge is a requirement to first sit part-time for a year, which is far easier to do if you are a barrister and more difficult if you are a high-flying solicitor with a global firm. I wanted to make it easier for solicitors to progress up the ranks by merit, but this was hugely resisted by the snobby senior barristers. Likewise, good women seemed to have been overlooked because they didn't fit the profile. It struck me at the time as a cozy old boys' club, and they considered it a gross impertinence that I should even be questioning them on such matters.

Things came to a head over the process for the recruitment of the next Lord Chief Justice, with Lord Thomas due to retire in the autumn of 2017. It seemed clear to me that a classic establishment stitch-up was in progress to appoint a particular candidate favored by the incumbent and other senior judges, the then chief of the criminal court Brian Leveson. The problem, however, was that he was approaching the mandatory retirement age (then seventy) and would only be able to serve for about eighteen months. With so much going on, not least with regard to

Brexit, I thought we needed a bit more stability in the judiciary. Given that U.S. Supreme Court justices receive lifetime appointments, surely the UK could offer a bit more tenure without upsetting the apple cart too much?

I therefore exercised what limited influence I had over the process to insist that candidates must be able to serve for at least four years. This is what Lord Thomas would have served by the time of his retirement and has in fact been the average term served by each Lord Chief Justice over the last thirty years. Had we ended up with an appointee serving less than two years, it would have been the shortest tenure in the role since 1921, when an exceptional decision was taken to make a temporary appointment, which was hugely controversial at the time.

Despite my request being entirely reasonable in terms of the expected tenure of the appointment, it sparked another huge backlash from the judicial powers that be. The idea that I, a non-lawyer politician, should have a role in the appointment process was painted as an outrageous attack on judicial independence—and the press were briefed accordingly.

The fact that prior to 2005 such appointments were routinely made by the Lord Chancellor, who sat in the Cabinet, was conveniently ignored. Under the current system, I had no role in the actual choice, which was entirely run by the Judicial Appointments Commission. They conducted the interviews and made a recommendation of a single name. Rejecting that name was technically possible, but I was left in no doubt that doing so would have been seen as tantamount to declaring war.

In any event, the backlash came in the form of a quite extraordinary diatribe from the outgoing Lord Chief Justice, Lord Thomas. Giving evidence to a House of Lords committee in March 2017, he belatedly attacked me over the "Enemies of the People" saga, saying I was "utterly wrong" not to have condemned the *Daily Mail*. Having expressed no concerns whatsoever at the time, he only chose to turn his fire on me when I blocked his plan to handpick his successor.

By this time, I was also getting some resistance to changes I wanted to make to the courts administration, and Lord Thomas also took a swipe at some of those in his remarks. One of the most prominent changes I was advocating was to extend the use of video evidence by women in rape cases. This seemed to me an obviously humane way of reducing the psychological impact on those victims who would otherwise have to appear in front of their alleged attackers. I had a lot of support on that from victims' organizations and even Labour MPs, but the judicial establishment had been airily dismissive. I'd had to have several arguments with them even to get a pilot program up and running.

Yet again, the judiciary had been allowed to exempt themselves from political accountability and scrutiny. It is all very well to respect the independence of learned judges to interpret and apply the law, but why should they also be left to run the whole administration of the justice system?

As a result, we have a situation where judges are in charge of everything from the upkeep of court buildings to the daily listing of cases, deciding where and when cases are heard and how many court sitting days there will be per year. Administrative matters that have a huge impact on people going through the legal system are also left to them to oversee, and they resist any attempt from ministers to rationalize and improve the system. There doesn't seem to be any huge constitutional principle at stake in ensuring that the delivery of a vital public service that costs millions of pounds of taxpayer money is subject to proper accountability and direction from politically accountable ministers.

We see this most clearly in the case of illegal immigration. Time and time again attempts to get tough on migration have been thwarted when lawyers have been able to take on immigrants' cases, paid for through taxpayer-funded legal aid, usually after citing some article or other from the European Convention on Human Rights.

I am all for the UK's asserting its sovereignty and leaving the convention. But I don't believe that alone will solve the problem. We will not fully be able to sort out our borders and illegal immigration until we have reformed the appointments and governance process of the British judiciary.

My eleven months as justice secretary were an eye-opener. Although I no doubt went about it in a clumsy fashion, I tried to deliver what I thought most people in Britain would want from their justice system: fixing the very serious problem of violence in prisons, making life better for victims, and trying to introduce more meritocracy into the judicial system.

The sheer level of snobbery, the power of vested interests, and the disdain for the democratically decided will of the British people—whether it was over Brexit or immigration policy—shocked me. The public-sector quangos put in charge after 2005 have allowed the legal establishment to run the whole system themselves. This is part of a wider culture of increased technocracy, with politicians lacking the self-confidence to assert their democratic right to exercise responsibility and take decisions on behalf of the public. From the Bank of England and the Office for Budget Responsibility (OBR) to the Judicial Appointments Commission, the message is that politicians are not to be trusted and we should leave things to "independent" experts.

The truth is that none of these bodies is truly independent. Too often that word has come to mean merely a lack of accountability to the public. This becomes a serious problem when, as is inevitable, the vested interests begin to develop a worldview and set of priorities that is out of step with the wishes of the people.

In order to change Britain and deal with these long-standing issues, political accountability must be restored to the justice system.

In the United States, there is a much more democratic debate over the appointment of judges and political input into the process. At the federal level, the president nominates Supreme Court justices and other federal judges who are then subject to confirmation by the Senate. At the state level, a similar process exists whereby governors nominate some candidates while others are directly elected.

It is vital that we restore democratic accountability to the judicial system in the UK. This means parliamentary sovereignty, which is at the core of the British Constitution, and reinstating the proper role of the Lord Chancellor.

CHAPTER 5

Brexit Gridlock

A s I walked up Downing Street on the Sunday after the 2017 general election, I was extremely nervous. The press standing outside Number 10 shouted questions at me as I knocked on the door to see the prime minister. They must have noticed I looked on edge, no doubt assuming I was dreading my fate in the Cabinet reshuffle that was sure to follow. But I had something more immediate on my mind: I was trying not to throw up.

Whether it was the grueling pace of an election campaign or a combination of stress and exhaustion, I had found myself falling quite badly ill by polling day. I felt so bad at the election count that my agent had to read my speech for me onstage after I was declared the winner in my constituency. Meanwhile I was throwing up in one of the gyms at Lynnsport, the King's Lynn leisure center where this exercise in democracy for my voters in South West Norfolk was reaching its conclusion. I then continued to be sick all the way from Norfolk to London.

Thus the traditional parade in front of the waiting cameras on Downing Street was even worse than usual. Usually during a reshuffle, the prime minister invites you into the Cabinet Room to be told of your appointment. But on this occasion, I was led upstairs to the Margaret Thatcher Study on the first floor to wait. I correctly interpreted this as a bad sign.

Theresa May joined me in the study and told me she was moving me to be chief secretary to the Treasury, a more junior post and technically outside the Cabinet, albeit with an entitlement to attend Cabinet meetings. It was a significant demotion. While this was not a complete surprise—given that it had been briefed to the press for weeks—I told her I was not happy about it. I reminded her of my warning of turbulence over my reforms at Justice and her pledge to back me on them. She said that was not the only reason, and I realized there was no point in prolonging the awkward conversation.

Before I left Downing Street, I had to see the Cabinet Office official responsible for the mechanics of ministerial appointments, Sue Gray. To my surprise, she took it upon herself to commiserate with me by giving me a hug, before telling me that as a result of my demotion, my salary was being cut. I didn't welcome her unsolicited embrace—I am not a hugger—but given how delicate I was feeling, she got off lightly.

I was frustrated that my time at the Ministry of Justice was being cut short. All the things I had done, from sorting out prisons to trying to get a handle on judicial appointments, had been predicated on my being in the job for a while. The idea was to do the difficult tasks first, after which things would start to get better. I didn't think I would be removed after less than a year, but as is so often the case in government, the game of musical chairs propels you elsewhere before you have a chance to do all you wanted to do.

In fact, I had known my days as Lord Chancellor were numbered for several weeks. As we sat around the Cabinet table on April 17, 2017, Theresa May had taken most of us by surprise by announcing she had decided to call an early general election to secure a renewed mandate and stronger majority ahead of the Brexit negotiations that lay ahead. I felt a wrench in my gut the moment she announced it. Something felt wrong, even though we were leading Labour by over twenty points in the opinion polls and Theresa's own satisfaction ratings dwarfed those of Opposition Leader Jeremy Corbyn.

I knew in that moment that I was toast as justice secretary. The controversies over appointments and the constant briefing against me by the judiciary made me an obvious candidate for the sack when, as was expected, Theresa stormed to a landslide victory in the election. Number 10 had not exactly given me unqualified support, and it was clear what that meant. This made it a pretty miserable campaign for me, as I found myself totally frozen out by the powers that be. I was relegated to the back row in Cabinet appearances and kept away from the media. My special advisers kept telling me not to worry, that it was nothing personal. But I knew it was.

As it happened, I wasn't the only one having a bad time. At the start of the campaign, Theresa May was in a commanding position, but as it got underway she was shown to be increasingly ill at ease in public, with stilted campaign events and awkward media appearances. An embarrassing U-turn over a pledge made in the Conservative Party manifesto on social care exemplified the confusion, and our poll lead shrank.

This culminated in a shock result, with Jeremy Corbyn's Labour Party capitalizing on its status as the underdog to perform much better than expected. Instead of the landslide predicted at the start, we lost our overall majority, leaving us dependent on the votes of the Democratic Unionist Party's ten MPs to stay in power. Given the object of the election had been to strengthen our position in Parliament, it was little short of a disaster.

In these circumstances, Theresa was in a much-weakened position, and it was unclear whether she would be able to remain as leader for much longer. Her planned major Cabinet reshuffle, in which it was rumored she would have sacked her chancellor, was shelved. For my part, I was told by someone close to her that had she won the expected victory, I too would have been fired altogether. Instead, she only felt able to demote me, in one of the few changes she made.

The irony was that I had always wanted to be in the Treasury, and although this was not the role I had envisaged, I did at least have a strong interest in the subject. Environment and Justice were interesting briefs, but I hadn't gone into politics to deal with floods or fix prisons. Now I was able to get stuck into something I was driven by—economic policy—which was a silver lining.

The experience of being demoted, after a bruising period in a senior job, changed my outlook on politics. Up to that point, I had tried to behave myself, play the game, and do the right thing. Now, having only just avoided being sacked outright, I had nothing much to lose. I decided I was going to say what I thought and stop worrying so much about the consequences. I adopted a more irreverent style on social media, moving away from the slavish retweeting of government slogans and instead having some fun with it. I was more honest about what I believed—perhaps a bit too honest at times.

I upset my Cabinet colleagues by publicly criticizing their un-Conservative policies of generally banning and taxing things. At this point, my colleagues seemed to be in overdrive to make Britain uncompetitive. They introduced new environmental regulations, banning plastic straws and woodburning stoves. I was surprised much of this was coming from Brexiteers. I couldn't understand the logic of freeing ourselves from the shackles of Europe only to impose more regulations in Britain.

But my new era wasn't just a change in style. My experience in the Ministry of Justice had radicalized me. I saw how the establishment operated to freeze out change. It didn't seem possible to get the right things done through the system. It was a case of go along with the status quo or get crushed.

My new boss at the Treasury, the chancellor, Philip Hammond, was the archetype of an ultra-cautious, risk-averse establishment figure. His main preoccupation was stopping the prime minister and others from spending too much money. On this, we agreed. But while we rubbed along, we had differing views on the dominant issue of the moment, Brexit.

As he put it to me on one occasion, he disagreed with my *Weltanschauung* (worldview). Despite having made Euroskeptic noises earlier in his career, he was now a signed-up member of the Treasury's EU exit damage-limitation exercise. Pretty much the entire Treasury was working to keep the UK closely aligned with the EU, maintaining similar regulations and approaches. In all his public utterances, Philip gave the impression he thought Brexit was a terrible idea and needed to be mitigated by all means possible.

I thought the opposite. We had crossed the Rubicon. There was no option of being half in and half out that didn't make us subservient to Brussels. We needed to use the opportunities of Brexit to revitalize Britain's economy and democracy. And there were lots of opportunities, as the EU was sclerotic. The British people had voted for it, and we needed to get on with it. I favored a clean break. Our differences reflected a split right down the middle of the Conservative Party. A further twenty or so MPs didn't want Brexit to happen at all.

I looked across the Atlantic for inspiration as to how Britain's prospects could be transformed by removing the shackles of EU laws and trade rules. I visited Washington, D.C.; Cleveland, Ohio; and Detroit, Michigan, to see how President Trump was delivering tax cuts and a regulatory rollback that was spurring the American economy (alas, my attempts to include Green Bay, Wisconsin, on the itinerary were thwarted by Treasury officials and the British Embassy in Washington).

I liked the go-getting, self-reliant nature of the vision. I met Neomi Rao, Trump's regulatory czar, who told me about how they were rolling back all of the Obama-era regulations. I saw opportunity zones and free ports that were bringing in new investment and business. I saw the manufacturing industry getting ahead on cheap fracked gas. The rollbacks of Obama-era regulations were clearly working. Patronizing people was over. This was exactly what we needed in Britain to win over the new voters who had supported Brexit and wanted their towns and cities to be great again.

But back at home, the Treasury and Whitehall were intent on trying to manage the fallout and patch things up with Europe rather than looking for new opportunities—even though their own analysis suggested the biggest opportunity of Brexit was a trade deal with the United States (alongside abolishing the EU's Working Time Directive, which told people how long they were allowed to work). I was packed off to Luxembourg to deputize for Philip at a meeting of European finance ministers.

I felt like I was at a wake, as the corpse. All of them were so sad that Britain was leaving the club. All, that is, except for the French finance minister, who pointedly ignored me. I gave full vent to my vision of Britain as Singapore-on-Thames and suggested the entire continent needed to become more competitive. This seemed to come as a shock to the Treasury officials with me, although I think the local representative had some sympathy. I was not asked to deputize for the chancellor again.

In the Treasury, as across the rest of government, Brexit was a fault line that was constantly having to be papered over to maintain the pretense that the government was united on the way ahead. No one really believed that. Instead, following the 2017 general election debacle, we were set on a course for two years of increasing chaos and parliamentary gridlock.

My Cabinet colleague Andrea Leadsom, the Leader of the House of Commons, formed the "Pizza Club," a group of us who favored a clean break from the EU. We would get together in her office—sometimes with actual pizzas—and talk about how we could get Brexit done. It was more like a therapy session than anything else.

At one point during the interminable Brexit negotiations, Theresa May opened a meeting of the Cabinet by informing us that our discussion on the topic was not intended to reach firm conclusions that day.

"This is not a decision-making Cabinet," she announced.

How right she was. Reaching agreement with the EU was one thing, but keeping together an increasingly fractious Conservative Party and securing a majority in Parliament was quite another. Her tentative attitude made for slow progress, and it was never really clear what her own views were on where the deal should land. At one of the biggest moments in our country's history, when we needed a firm vision and bold leadership, we had an ultra-cautious prime minister and an ultra-cautious chancellor. At a time when bold decisions were needed, we had a government that seemed averse to making any.

I had to some extent been insulated from the wider Brexit psychodrama while I had been at Justice because of the all-consuming nature of the job. But as chief secretary, I was under less intense pressure, and the work of stewarding the public finances and resisting public spending demands was more in my comfort zone. I therefore had more time to involve myself in the wider politics of the moment.

As time went on, I became more and more frustrated at the lack of boldness. Brexit was always going to be a tough negotiation, and we needed to approach it from a position of strength. In any negotiation, you have to be willing to walk away. That meant having the credible threat that we would even be willing to go for no deal with the European Union. But just as with David Cameron in his under-whelming renegotiation before the referendum, that threat simply was not there. Theresa May clearly was not going to walk away from the talks, and the EU knew it.

It was hard to discern what Theresa's view of Brexit was. She had campaigned somewhat half-heartedly for Remain. She gave the impres-sion of not being an enthusiast one way or the other. Her focus was always on mitigating downside risk, not looking at the opportunities.

She was a cautious and technocratic manager, not one for making bold political gambles. Even if she were, the 2017 general election had boxed her into a corner. The party was in a fractious state and she did not command a united view in Cabinet, let alone in the parliamentary party. This left us negotiating among ourselves rather than negotiating with the EU.

My own view was that we should have been much more hard-headed about the negotiations from the outset. The UK's decision to leave was always going to be seen by the EU as an act of war. That being the case, you have to proceed on that basis. The only thing they understand is pain. We should have told them we were prepared to go for no deal, put tariffs on their agricultural imports, and pursue a trade agreement with the United States. The truth is we potentially had a lot of leverage, but we never used it. That was a persistent frustration for me. When you have a prime minister and a chancellor both keen to listen to cautious civil servants, that sort of bold, bellicose approach was never going to fly.

Once again, it is hard not to conclude that the logical and best outcome in 2016 would have been for Boris Johnson to have become prime minister and forced through Brexit with a combination of aggres-sive brinksmanship and political chutzpah. This he eventually did in 2019, but only after we had endured three painful years of gridlock under May. There was no shortage of grandstanding and tough talking during that time, but without a robust position to back it up it was just hollow words. The old political maxim is to speak softly and carry a big stick. Between 2016 and 2019, the government was often shouting while waving a twig.

In July 2018, the Cabinet was summoned to the prime minister's country house, Chequers, where we were asked to endorse the outline of a deal that May would seek to agree on with the EU. The room was set up with round tables as if we were attending a wedding. At the time, this was seen as a make-or-break meeting at which a united position would finally be reached. In any event, it was something of a damp squib. I recall a barbeque with some rather undercooked chicken.

The Chequers proposal was an attempt at a compromise, aligning with EU rules in the short term while ensuring a future government would be able to diverge. It was clear this later divergence "would have consequences," possibly in the form of tariffs or additional friction at the border. Needless to say, this compromise pleased nobody. A "Chuck Chequers" campaign immediately started. And in the days afterward, a succession of ministers resigned from the government, firstly Brexit secretary David Davis and then Foreign Secretary Boris Johnson.

I was willing to back this very messy agreement because I feared the alternative of not leaving at all. The noises from squishy Conservative MPs and their friends in the media and the establishment were getting louder. Not leaving would have been a disaster. As well as being completely undemocratic and a national humiliation, it would also have resulted in severe electoral punishment for Conservatives at the ballot box.

From then on, it was a slow and painful descent into even worse division and gridlock. There were interminable Cabinet meetings. Some of my colleagues were placing bets on how long another would speak for. Normally no one leaves a Cabinet meeting during proceedings. Yet during this time one colleague's regular lengthy monologues became the cue for other ministers to leave the room for comfort breaks.

In the months that followed, the government completely lost control of the parliamentary agenda. That December, Theresa survived a no confidence vote on her leadership by MPs, but the writing was on the wall.

As we entered 2019, a number of colleagues joined me in again making the case for no deal. By that point, it was the only roll of the dice left to play, and in my view the only way we could get a successful outcome. As the March 31 deadline approached, I was clear with the prime minister that the only option she had for the sake of the country, the party, and herself (in that order) was to go for a no-deal Brexit. Others piled on. It was very clear that Nigel Farage's Brexit Party would make mincemeat of us if the UK ended up participating in the European Parliament elections due to take place that May because we hadn't managed to leave the EU in time.

Faced with the prospect of no deal, the Opposition parties and Tory Remainers united to thwart that option, and the prime minister in any case was not prepared to entertain the idea herself. Again, the EU could see every faltering footstep of our internal wrangling and knew we were playing with a broken bat.

In late 2018, Theresa had struck a deal with the EU that was not dissimilar to the flawed Chequers deal: it left the UK as a "rule taker" over large areas of EU law, locked us in a Customs Union without the ability to leave, undermined the integrity of the union by creating internal borders within the UK, and left the European Court of Justice with the whip hand over the agreement.

Again, it was far from optimal, but I was swayed by Attorney General Geoffrey Cox's argument that we should do the deal in order to at least get the raft into the open sea, as he put it. We could always revisit it in due course. It was kicking the can down the road, but at least the can would be moving.

Three times the deal was put to MPs and three times it was rejected—in no small part because Labour refused to back it. I had found it especially galling to see Cabinet colleagues going cap in hand to Labour Leader Jeremy Corbyn and Sir Keir Starmer, his Brexit spokesman, begging them to back the government. It was a mistaken strategy that I strongly opposed, but Cabinet ministers like Michael Gove and Philip Hammond were determined to pursue this course of action. Whole books can and have been written about the chaos of this unhappy period, marked by all sorts of parliamentary shenanigans and infighting. But the basic point was simple: a broad coalition of Remainers in the Conservative Party, the Opposition, and the bureaucratic establishment tried their hardest to water down Brexit, while ultra-Brexiteers on the other side rejected every deal on the table and refused to give an inch. To my mind, the issue *was* black or white—we could either be in the EU or be completely out of it. The worst position would have been to remain in a semidetached state, unable to gain any of the benefits of leaving while the EU made things as hard for us as possible. That was where we risked ending up.

Yet for the Conservative Party, it had been a lucky escape. If a deal had been done with Labour, it would have split our party down the middle and caused a potentially fatal schism. I would have had to rebel at that point. I was not willing to defy the will of the country and my constituents.

Theresa May was a competent administrator and, in a quieter time in politics, she might have been seen as a strong and stable leader, to coin a phrase. But amid a fundamental change for the country when bold decisions needed to be made, she simply did not have the instincts to play hardball with her party or the EU. The decision to hold an election in 2017 was logical on its own terms, but the poor result crippled the party and put her government at the mercy of others. She did not have the strength she needed, and the EU was calling the shots. By the time we found ourselves in the ludicrous position of having to run candidates in a European Parliament election because we hadn't succeeded in leaving by the deadline, her position was untenable. In retrospect (and I feel qualified to say this), she did well to cling to office for as long as she did, but for what purpose?

Ever since Boris resigned from the Cabinet in the wake of the Chequers meeting, it was inevitable that he would at some point mount a leadership challenge. Having backed him in 2016, I was sympathetic to him and was increasingly of the view that he was the only person who could provide the necessary shock to the system to break the deadlock and actually deliver Brexit. As the government went into meltdown in the early months of 2019, his phone calls to me and other colleagues got more frequent, and he was soon joined by other contenders as they jockeyed for position for what looked like an inevitable leadership election.

The trickle of ministerial resignations became a flood, but I was not seriously tempted to join them. Rightly or wrongly, I had thought it was better to stay on the inside and try to force progress from there. By the time the wheels really came off, it was clear the government was doomed and my joining the exodus would not have made a material difference.

When Theresa eventually bowed to the inevitable on the eve of the disastrous European election results—the Brexit Party triumphed—the leadership race began in earnest. Bizarrely, as it all kicked off, I was sitting in a field in Hay-on-Wye attending a slightly lefty philosophy festival where I had been booked to give a speech. A flood of phone calls came in from the likes of Dominic Raab, Michael Gove, and Andrea Leadsom as they sought my support for their leadership ambitions. There was no way I was going to support Gove after his betrayal of

Boris last time round. I had also since grown appalled over his maneuvering to thwart a hard Brexit.

Some intriguing offers were floated to entice me to support one candidate or another, but I had pretty much decided to back Boris. As I spoke to other colleagues, including Rishi Sunak, it became clear they were coming to the same conclusion. When I spoke to Boris himself, he was as charming and animated as ever, and I agreed to join his team. After my public declaration, I got stuck into helping thrash out his platform, and I was encouraged to see signs of a bold approach that had been so lacking over the previous few years.

After the usual soap opera of Westminster politics during the MPs' voting rounds, the contest went to the Conservative membership across the country. It became clear that Boris would prevail over Jeremy Hunt (his successor as foreign secretary), who was effectively the continuity candidate of the political establishment. To my mind, we had tested the idea of overly cautious compromise to destruction, and I had no appetite for more of the same.

As for my own prospects, it was no great secret that my ambition at this time was to be chancellor, but I knew there was little chance I would be offered the job, which was pretty much nailed on for Sajid Javid. I thought, however, that I might be given a strong economic brief, and had been expecting business secretary. So when Boris called me to Number 10 after his victory, I walked up Downing Street with rather more of a spring in my step than in 2017 (and without the fear that I might vomit).

I was surprised to be offered the job of international trade secretary, and I was initially slightly worried. Was it a real job? The previous incumbent, Liam Fox, had frankly little to do while the Brexit talks dragged on and had not been allowed to start negotiating trade deals until the Withdrawal Agreement with the EU was in place. I had always thought this was a massive missed opportunity, and I was keen not to be in a similar position of sitting on the sidelines, twiddling my thumbs.

Would I be allowed to get on with it? Boris assured me I would. I was also worried about being away from home a lot and actually burst into tears the minute I got back to my house that evening and saw my daughters.

But in truth, I loved the job. There was a dynamic permanent secretary in Antonia Romeo, and the second permanent secretary, Crawford Falconer, was a sardonic Kiwi who had been hired for trade negotiations. I was pleased to be back as a full Cabinet minister after two years of sitting on the naughty step at the far end of the Cabinet table. But most of all, I was excited by the prospect that we would now, to quote Boris's campaign slogan, "Get Brexit Done." The government had been paralyzed for months, after more than two years of infighting and painfully slow progress. Now, three years after the British people had voted for a dramatic shift away from the EU, it was well past time for that mandate to be delivered.

Boris was the ideal person to do it. He was a great showman, charismatic and engaging, and had shown during the referendum campaign that he could connect brilliantly with those who felt left behind by the political establishment in Westminster and Brussels. They recognized in him a maverick who would shake things up and cut through the diplomatic niceties to call it as he saw it. Comparisons with Donald Trump are overly simplistic, but just as in the United States, we saw an unconventional and often controversial leader appealing to disengaged voters in a way that others struggled to match—and whom opponents failed to understand.

In retrospect, and with the benefit of my subsequent experience in Number 10, the painful experience of the Theresa May years provided a portent. The lesson I took from it at the time was that a lack of boldness in seizing the moment left a government directionless and at the mercy of events. This was certainly true. But beneath the surface, there were signs about how powerful the resistance to a serious shake-up in Britain was. The establishment did not like disruptive political initiatives that did not accord with their worldview. Brexit had crashed through the cozy centrist consensus of the British establishment—and the establishment pushed back.

From the opposition parties in Parliament to parts of the Conservative Party, there was outright defiance of the expressed will of the British people. But just as significant was the more subtle opposition from within the government and the official machine itself, aided and abetted by their friends in the financial markets and the legal world. The foreign policy establishment had ignored the rise of Trump and failed to make any progress with our main alternative trading partner. These interests made concerted efforts to water down Brexit, urging caution about playing hardball with the EU, pushing for closer alignment, and trying to rule out no deal at all costs. This fatally undercut the government's negotiating position from the outset.

What I should have learned from this was how these powerful interests can work together to frame the choices available to the government, embedding groupthink at all levels and making radical action seem unthinkable.

In the months after he entered Number 10, Boris Johnson's bold attempts to break from this approach met with huge resistance and were nearly derailed. Europhile MPs from both sides of the House conspired to take control of the Order Paper (the House of Commons agenda) to stop Brexit. Boris then prorogued Parliament (suspended it) to stop them from doing this. He was then challenged in court by a group of Europhiles—and the Supreme Court ruled in their favor.

It was only by calling a general election and winning an unequivocal mandate that he was finally able to prevail, and it is a testament to his political skills that he was able to do so. But his success should not erase the memory of just how hard others fought to thwart him, both inside and outside the government.

The other relic of this period was a fractious and febrile Conservative parliamentary party. The Brexit referendum had unleashed and normalized infighting. Factions openly attacked one another in public and conspired and plotted behind the scenes. Once discipline is lost, it is very hard for it to be restored, if it even can be. I cannot help but think that the increased propensity of the party to dump its leaders in the years since 2016 has been a result of this ingrained disunity. Theresa May was its first victim. She would not be its last.

CHAPTER 6

Free Trade and Lockdowns

A snap general election was held in December 2019 on the promise we would "Get Brexit Done," and it resulted in a thumping eighty-seat Conservative majority in the House of Commons. The Withdrawal Agreement was signed, and the UK formally left the EU at the end of January 2020. The Brexit deadlock had been broken. Boris had brought a fresh pizzazz to Downing Street and a new optimism to the Conservative Party.

However, beneath the surface, the fractures among Conservatives had not gone away. Our majority proved illusory, as there was a lack of agreement about the right path to take. There were those who wanted to cleave as closely to the EU as possible, not allow concerns about China to damage domestic priorities, and carry on with business as usual. Then there were others, of whom I was one, who felt we owed it to the public to deliver on the promise of the 2019 manifesto and make Britain a truly independent, successful nation.

I saw trade as a key area where we could boost the economy, lay out Global Britain's stall, and lead the world in promoting free trade and free enterprise. As with the Corn Laws that divided the Conservative Party in the nineteenth century, not everyone agreed. There were those with anti-growth instincts who wanted the UK to simply replicate the trade policies of the EU—including their Meursing table (of commodity codes to calculate agricultural tariffs), which had 150 different classifications of biscuit!

These differences were not resolved up front by the prime minister. Instead, I had a series of battles to get the mandates for the UK's new free trade agreements I wanted to negotiate agreed to and done. And even once they were resolved, Cabinet ministers would relitigate decisions and stop progress.

There was a relentlessly negative backdrop from the leftist media about the UK's ability to do trade deals. Our competence was questioned. There were predictions that we wouldn't be able to get as good deals as the EU could. These points were all proved to be wrong. In fact, Department for International Trade officials did a heroic job. Yet it did not change any of the naysayers' minds.

The Brexit Withdrawal Agreement with the EU was largely out of my hands, but it occupied the full efforts of the first months of Boris's government, as he sought to succeed where Theresa had failed. Eventually, after some tough negotiations and bruising parliamentary battles, he had his deal. We then had effectively until the end of 2020 to secure the EU–UK future partnership, including trading arrangements. This negotiation was not one for which I had responsibility and was instead conducted by David (later Lord) Frost.

A fundamental mistake the government made early on was not treating the United States and the European Union as parallel deals and playing them off of each other. Europe's farmers, especially the Irish, were very dependent on the British market. Opening up to American agriculture would have been very damaging to them. As any negotiator knows, you need to build all the leverage you can during a negotiation, wherever you can find it. The threat of the UK being in the U.S. regulatory orbit would also have spooked the EU. I advocated a list of "pain" that we could inflict on them if we didn't get what we wanted.

Sadly it was not used. The government laid down our weapons in the EU negotiations by offering tariff-free access both ways for agricultural products, rather than negotiating hard line by line. This was a mistake. Every trade negotiator knows agriculture is the hardest part of any deal because all countries have a protectionist farming lobby. The balance of trade was in the EU's favor because they exported much more to us than we did to them. We should have traded off reducing tariffs for something else in turn. We may have ended up with a zero-tariff relationship, but we could have secured more in return. I found myself in alliance with the National Farmers' Union and the agriculture secretary, a rare moment of common cause.

Despite the pugnacious "Get Brexit Done" mantra of that time, Michael Gove, who was now minister for the Cabinet Office, and his close ally Dominic Cummings, the prime minister's chief adviser, were not keen to pursue an ambitious trade agenda. They wanted to focus on simply rolling over existing EU trade deals and play down the possibility of new agreements with other potential major trading partners. They had anti-growth instincts, and they also worried the EU could cause us major pain. The power of the Treasury and the wider establishment, which had spent more than forty years under the EU comfort blanket, was significant. It was a strategy for risk mitigation, not one that was going to drive economic growth.

I wanted to get on with what I saw as the biggest prize and what should have been our priority—a new trade deal with the United States. Even the Treasury's economists had deemed it the number one economic opportunity of Brexit! This would take time, and in order to achieve results before the next general election—and indeed the next U.S. presidential election—we would need to get going fast. My belief had always been that we should have started these talks years before, in parallel with negotiating the Withdrawal Agreement, using it as leverage to get a better deal from the EU. That hadn't happened, but I still believed we could make up for lost time.

This was an argument I had from the moment I was appointed international trade secretary in July 2019. At that time, we had in Donald Trump a U.S. president who had talked about a U.S.-UK Free Trade Agreement on many occasions and was evidently sincere in his desire to reach what he called "a very big trade deal." With a presidential election due the following year in which a less favorable candidate could be elected, there was a narrow window to get something done, and I was determined we should use it.

My first official meeting as international trade secretary was with the U.S. ambassador to London, Woody Johnson. I made clear to him that the deal was my top priority. Woody was beyond enthusiastic and determined to do all he could to assist. The following week, I traveled to Washington for talks with my counterparts, the U.S. trade representative Bob Lighthizer and the secretary of commerce Wilbur Ross. Lighthizer is a tough negotiator and not a free trader. One of his early roles was negotiating with the Soviet Union on grain quotas under President Reagan. But he was likeable, conservative, and I could work with him. You always knew where you stood with Bob. He said what he meant and meant what he said.

I wasted no time in getting down to business, and we had some substantive discussions, somewhat to the surprise of my officials, who had tried to play down expectations of anything more than a round of courtesy meetings. While in Washington, I made a speech at the Heritage Foundation in which I quoted Ronald Reagan's 1980 campaign slogan, declaring that as far as a trade agreement was concerned, "The Time Is Now." This got a negative reaction from Number 10 apparatchiks.

In September, I was back in the United States for the UN General Assembly, where I met ministers from around the world. I was not scheduled to attend Boris's meeting with Trump. This was despite the fact that Trump would be accompanied by a large delegation, including Lighthizer, Vice President Mike Pence, Secretary of State Mike Pompeo, and about half the U.S. Cabinet. As was the wont of the deep state, Boris was the only politician listed to attend from the British side, accompanied by Foreign Office officials.

I was keen to attend to talk about trade and was also concerned about U.S. threats to slap tariffs on Scotch (which they, alas, did do the following month). So after attending an early morning business reception with Boris at Hudson Yards, I chased him down a fire escape, grabbed him by the shoulders, and demanded to come. He agreed, and further official protests were duly elbowed aside.

At the meeting itself, which took place in the basement of the UN building, I sat alongside British officials on one side of the prime minister, while on the president's left sat Vice President Pence and Bob Lighthizer. With a large media presence recording the event, Trump opened the meeting by telling Boris:

> We're going to be discussing trade. We can quadruple our trade with the UK. And we can, I think, really do a big job. Bob Lighthizer is here, our trade representative. Your trade representative is here, and they're already scheduled today to continue negotiations. But we can have substantially more trade with the UK, and we look forward to doing that.

In his remarks, Boris also expressed his hope that we could make "a lot of progress quite fast on trade," before going on to talk briefly about other issues and field questions from journalists about events back in the UK. As usual, the British media were distracted by the latest turn in the Brexit drama. The UK Supreme Court had just ruled that the government's prorogation (suspension) of Parliament had been unlawful—news of which had woken us up at around 6:00 a.m. in New York.

Once the media had left, Trump was even more loquacious about the opportunities for a trade deal. He was enthusiastic and entertaining and clearly very enamored with Boris. He repeated that we could "quadruple" trade between the United States and the UK, that we would outdo Germany. He urged Lighthizer and me to get on with talks. Lighthizer made some hardball comments, as usual. I said we were ready to go.

Every time Trump talked trade, Boris kept trying to move the conversation to Iran and the Joint Comprehensive Plan of Action (JCPOA) nuclear deal. This clearly was not a ripe avenue, as there was a fundamental disagreement between him and Trump. I'm not sure if this focus on Iran was a result of the Foreign Office brief or whether it was because of the negativity in Downing Street towards the whole prospect of a trade deal.

I have no doubt that we could have done a trade deal with Trump. We missed that opportunity. As well as the anti-growthers in the Cabinet, many in Number 10 unfortunately seemed to want to hold Trump at arm's length for political reasons. The UK media provided universally negative coverage of Trump, and leftists in the Conservative Party were keen to insult him at every opportunity. My view was that he was the leader of the free world and an important ally.

I found it deeply frustrating. Here was a U.S. president who was keen to do a trade deal with the UK. No more "back of the queue," as President Obama infamously threatened while visiting the UK in the run-up to the 2016 referendum. At the margins of that very same UN meeting, Trump and the Japanese prime minister had signed a new trade agreement. In time we could have done that too. It might not have been perfect, but it would certainly have been beneficial to both our countries and would have strengthened our hand in negotiations with the EU and others around the world. Ultimately, we threw away that opportunity.

Boris, I believe, had instincts that were closer to my own. Whenever I pinned him down to give a clear direction on this issue, he backed my position. But (as I would discover for myself in due course) the prime minister has to deal with endless demands for meetings and calls with foreign leaders, public events, media appearances, and so on. It's impossible to give constant direction to every area of policy, however important.

When it came to trade, anti-growthers wanted to focus on the EU deal and change as little as possible. They actively sought to thwart me in my attempts to pursue a more ambitious policy with the United States and elsewhere. There were delaying tactics and bogus nonsense spouted in Cabinet subcommittees about Brazilian rainforests. I am all for saving rainforests, but it was nonsense to suggest that my proposed trade agreements were threatening them. I knew if I could get the prime minister in a room where he had to make a firm decision, he would make the right one. In Greenwich in February 2020, Boris made a powerful and unequivocal commitment to expanding free trade. But despite such pronouncements, it became a daily battle to stop the machine from sliding back into obstruction.

There was also a clear degree of reluctance on the part of our diplomats to push trade with the Americans. This was part of a wider systemic problem: our embassy in Washington and the Foreign Office were much more in tune with the leftist Democratic establishment than with the Republican Party and those on the right. And if they had to deal with Republicans, they would rather it was the Bushes than the Trumps.

I had seen this dynamic on my first ministerial visit to Washington as environment secretary back in 2015. I'd wanted to visit the Heritage

Foundation and see Nile Gardiner, who heads up its Thatcher Center for Freedom. Before I'd even left Britain, the British Embassy in Washington, via the Foreign Office, was raising concerns. This was because Gardiner had criticized the Obama administration as well as the British government.

I told them I wanted to go ahead with the visit. On arrival at the embassy, the then ambassador Kim Darroch tried again over welcome drinks to dissuade me from visiting the Heritage Foundation. I told him, "I'm a conservative politician, and this is a conservative think tank in America—I want to go to Heritage." They relented, but the official car dropped us off two blocks from our destination, as though the sight of the ambassadorial limousine outside the Heritage Foundation would trigger some sort of diplomatic incident.

Unsurprisingly, when Trump took office, the official British diplomatic establishment had developed no real links with him or his people. Instead they continued reaching out to their old friends at the Democrat-leaning think tanks and foreign policy organs, such as the Atlantic Council. There was apparently no concern then about offending the incumbent administration by speaking to the other side. Indeed, when I first proposed making my 2019 trade speech at the Heritage Foundation, there was almost the same reticence from the Foreign Office and the embassy as before.

I finally managed to get Boris to sign off on starting trade talks with the United States when he was holed up at St Thomas's Hospital in London while recovering from COVID in April 2020. I knew he would have his mobile phone on him and be free of nefarious Downing Street influences. We then kicked off negotiations by video in May, and these continued for the next few months. However, with the U.S. election looming, talks were paused after the fourth round of negotiations in October 2020. They never resumed. We had started too late.

Still working on getting the whisky tariff removed, I was on a phone call with Bob Lighthizer on January 6, 2021. Sitting in the Executive Office building, he remarked to me in passing that the street was full of people with huge American flags walking towards Congress. Little did I realize how seismic that event would turn out to be.

We did eventually get the whisky tariff removed in the summer of 2021, with my special adviser Sophie Jarvis in particular having pushed hard on a political level in talks with the new Democrat administration. Indeed, we secured a deal before the EU did, much to the annoyance of officials in the European Commission. But with Joe Biden as president, it was made quite clear that a trade deal with the United Kingdom was no longer a priority. We had missed the boat.

As well as working on the United States, I had to secure continuity trade deals with sixty-eight nations before the end of December 2021, when our EU exit would be implemented and our existing deals with those countries would end. Having not been an independent trading country for nearly fifty years, there was work to be done just to get the negotiators in place and build up the necessary capacity. This was particularly the case given that dozens of such agreements would have to be negotiated in parallel.

Many of these agreements were dismissed as "rolling over" the existing deals we had as an EU member, as though it were simply a matter of cutting and pasting them into a new document. It was ironic that the same Brexit skeptics who had previously said it would be impossible for the UK to get as good deals as the EU now took it for granted that we would.

It was not an easy matter to get countries to agree to the same terms of trade they already had with the EU. In particular, they could not reduce the size of the import quota for a particular product—for example, butter. Therefore, in any agreement with the UK, they were effectively having to give additional market access for that product.

Every country has its sensitive sectors it wants to protect—like Singapore's financial services or Canada's dairy industry. And lots of countries used the opportunity to seek new access to the UK for everything from strawberries to rice to chicken. The ministerial team, the negotiating teams, and I were involved in an unprecedented flurry of negotiations to secure these deals. Many of these came down to the wire, and there were tricky moments during each of them. But by December the finalized agreements had begun to pile up.

On December 3, we signed a deal with North Macedonia, followed by one with Egypt on December 5, and then a significant one with Norway and Iceland on December 8, the same day we signed an agreement with Kenya. The following day, we signed the UK–Canada deal, followed by Singapore the day after that, then Vietnam on the eleventh, Switzerland on the fourteenth, Mexico on the fifteenth, and Moldova on Christmas Eve. In the week after Christmas, it was perhaps appropriate that we had Turkey left over to sign, which we did on December 29. In total, we had concluded trade deals covering sixty-eight countries by the end of the year—a real Herculean achievement by the negotiators at the Department for International Trade.

The most important deal done that year was with Japan, the third-largest economy in the world and a key UK ally. In September 2019, I had kicked off the process in Tokyo with Foreign Minister Toshimitsu Motegi. We were both agreed that we wanted to go further than the existing EU deal and include more terms on digital trade and business visas to deepen our close economic relationship. The sticking point was on the issue of quotas, most specifically on blue cheese. When Motegi visited London for talks in August 2020, he told me it was impossible to keep the same level of access for British blue cheeses like Stilton. This is because the Japanese National Diet (parliament) had specifically ruled out expanding the quota. It's one of the ironies of trade negotiations that deals worth billions can potentially be blown off course by a single product. Eventually we managed to find a solution that guaranteed our exporters access.

The UK–Japan Comprehensive Economic Partnership Agreement (CEPA) was the first major trade deal signed by the United Kingdom as an independent trading nation. It pointed the way to other deals in the future and demonstrated that we were able to secure better and more bespoke terms for British exports than we had done as members of the EU. When I went to Tokyo to sign the final agreement in October 2020, I brought Motegi a pot of Stilton. It has now become a running joke. In celebration of the deal, I had the honor of feeding the carp at the Foreign Office building, a privilege that had most recently been extended to President Trump.

The deal was also the first step towards the UK's joining the Comprehensive and Progressive Trans-Pacific Partnership (CPTPP), a trade agreement among eleven nations. This was important in order to take on China and its unscrupulous trade practices. In order to get into the CPTPP, we needed to agree on trade deals from scratch with two of its existing members, Australia and New Zealand.

I had known Tony Abbott since he was Australian Leader of the Opposition, when he had consulted me about childcare reforms during my time at the Department for Education. I knew he would be the perfect person to sit on the revamped UK Board of Trade. He was positive about Global Britain and had negotiated trade deals as Australian prime minister. He was also a human dynamo with infectious optimism.

I went on my first visit to Australia in December 2019. It was love at first sight. Like Britain—but without the hand-wringing and declinism. I toured Sydney Harbour promoting British exports and met all the key political players in Canberra, including new prime minister Scott Morrison. There was clearly a massive desire in Australia to get a trade deal done. I gave a press conference with my Australian counterpart, Simon Birmingham (known universally as Birmo), during which I suggested that part of a trade deal could be making it easier for Brits and Aussies to travel and work in each other's countries.

It was the night of the Canberra political ball, an annual event that featured a Pacific Island theme, right down to the guests wearing garlands. That night it served as a victory lap for Morrison for recently winning the election he'd been expected to lose. After the ball, I headed back to the UK ambassador's residence where I was staying before heading off to board a flight for Tokyo at 4:30 a.m., during which I was able to sleep off the evening.

It was only when I arrived in Japan that I learned Number 10 was outraged that I had been promoting the free movement of people with Australia. I was duly slapped down for proposing to make it easier to live and work in Australia for young Britons, and in Britain for young Australians. This was completely different from free movement of people across the European Union, which put no checks or controls on people entering Britain from the EU when we had been members. (In fact, the final deal did enable young Brits under the age of thirty-five to travel freely to Australia and be able to work without having to labor on a farm.)

By the time negotiations formally started, the COVID pandemic had taken hold, so we did our kick-off video aboard the *Cutty Sark*, the historic tea clipper in Greenwich. There were months of talks and various sticking points, including whether there would eventually be tariff-free access to all products that included beef and lamb and the removal of the farm work requirement for Brits going to Australia. It quickly became clear that our biggest problem was not with Australia, but with anti-growth colleagues in the British government who didn't want us to diverge from the EU and didn't want to have free trade with Australia.

The arguments put about were ludicrous. All we were talking about was giving Australia the same access to the UK beef and lamb market that the EU enjoyed, but with a huge time delay of fifteen years. (This was the access that Australia had before Britain had joined the EU.) It was already the case that neither Australian nor New Zealand farmers used their lamb quotas, and given that meat prices were far higher in Asia than Europe it seemed unlikely that Australian producers would want to undercut themselves. I suspect some of the objection was from the Irish who exported a lot of beef to the UK and were probably concerned about Australian beef cutting into that.

Throughout the process, the agricultural lobby and their friends in the anti-growth environmental lobby tried to claim we shouldn't do a deal with Australia because they had low animal welfare standards. This wasn't true. Aside from that, Australia is a sovereign nation not subject to British law. But this didn't stop misinformation being spread. One adviser to the Department for Environment, Henry Dimbleby, had to apologize to me for emailing me graphic pictures of Australian veterinary practices that were designed to prevent parasitic disease.

There were many leaks about the arguments around animal welfare and the Australian trade deal in the press. I got a call from Boris, who asked me if I'd leaked anything. It was obviously not in my interests to do so. I told him it had been Gove, and what did he expect given that Gove was a serial offender? I asked him if he thought Gove had been leaking. He replied, "Do bears shit in the woods?"

Even at the last minute, Gove tried to stop the deal from happening in a Cabinet subcommittee meeting. I pointed out that we had given away quota-free access to the EU and he'd seemed perfectly happy with that. We were merely giving Australia the same terms but with a fifteen-year delay, which in any case was much less of a threat, what with Australia being on the other side of the world. Boris finally opined. Who had been on our side over the years? Who had fought alongside us to defend freedom? It certainly hadn't been some of the member states of the EU. After what Australia had done for us at Gallipoli, we should do the deal.

I believed that to get this deal done, I was going to have to force the pace because of all the internal opposition. The G7 Summit in June 2021 provided the perfect opportunity, as Scott Morrison, known in Australia as ScoMo, would be in the UK. I knew Boris would not be able to resist doing a deal. I just needed to get the ducks in a row. I saw ScoMo at a barbeque at Stoke Lodge, the official London residence of the Australian high commissioner, then George Brandis. Apart from telling me he was a descendent of a Cornish yarn thief, we discussed what would be needed to make the deal work. I was still holding regular video calls with Dan Tehan, my Australian counterpart.

The scene was set for Boris's dinner with ScoMo the next night. All they had to do was agree to the level of beef and lamb quotas over the transition period. This proved a confusing evening, and it was very hard to get a read-out of what had actually been agreed to. The team worked through the night to prepare the text of the Agreement in Principle.

In the morning, I had to go to breakfast with Boris and ScoMo and sort out a few things. Namely, the UK would not have to make any more concessions to get into the CPTPP. We also had to agree to the details of the quotas. The Cabinet meeting scheduled for that Tuesday morning was delayed while this haggling was going on, and there was a farcical scene where a Downing Street staffer got stuck in a double door as the protagonists roamed around the building. At several points, Scott Morrison threatened to get on his plane and leave London. Eventually it was all nailed down. We had agreement in principle.

The UK–Australia trade deal is an example of what can be achieved between two close allies with huge economic and social benefits to both. With young people able to travel freely between the two countries and services freely exchanged, from legal services to banking to tariff-free access to goods, this is what trade should be about. Once we had done the Australia deal, the Kiwis did not want to be left out, and we were able to get agreement in principle with New Zealand four months later in October.

The Japan, Australia, and New Zealand deals were all critical to the UK's accession to the CPTPP. With them done, all we had to do was get the text agreed on. I faced the usual barrage of Cabinet anti-growthers who did not want the deal to go ahead. But again we faced them down and got it through. I formally submitted the United Kingdom's membership application in February 2021 and began the negotiations that resulted in our successfully joining this major trading bloc in 2023. As well as being an important economic opportunity for the United Kingdom, the CPTPP was also an important alliance for taking on China.

At International Trade, I was unceasing in my pursuit of trade deals with countries around the world. But there was one country with which I had no desire to deepen our relationship. Despite constant pressure from Number 10, I was determined not to make China a priority.

In my early years in politics, I had subscribed to the conventional belief that free trade by itself would expand and entrench freedom, that if we traded more with China it would move in the right direction. My doubts over this grew over my time in government. I had already seen some evidence of restrictive trade practices while I was environment secretary, with shipments into China being blocked for arbitrary reasons that were clearly political.

I also remembered my rather surreal trip around that time to what I called the "Potemkin dairy" in China. I was taken to a massive dairy plant full of shiny steel machines, where I was shown around under the watchful eye of the ever-present Chinese Communist Party functionaries. They were very proud of this state-of-the-art facility, but there didn't seem to be anything happening. No actual production was taking place. It was very strange—and not exactly evidence of a normally functioning industrial sector.

It was in 2018 that the last remaining scales fell from my eyes. That was the year President Xi abolished his term limit and had himself effectively declared president for life. It gave the lie to the theory that increased engagement with the West and greater trading relations would automatically lead to greater democratization and political liberalization.

It was clear that the Chinese were subverting the international trading system to their own benefit, including through intellectual property violations and illegal subsidies for key commodities like steel. The stance taken by the Trump administration and my counterpart, Bob Lighthizer, was right. I was firmly against any moves to seek a closer trading relationship with Beijing. I kept being urged by Number 10 to set up a meeting of the Joint Economic Trade Commission with China, but I used every delaying tactic I could think of to keep this at the bottom of my in tray and avoid spending any time on it.

I also wanted Chinese telecom giant Huawei's equipment stripped out of the UK phone network. I had a row with Dominic Cummings about this. He said we wouldn't meet our 2025 target for broadband availability if we took their equipment out of the network. Yet again, the UK's long-term security was being trumped by short-term economic interests. Later on, under pressure from the U.S. security establishment, we ended up having to do it anyway.

A free market can only exist when there is trust. That means property rights and the freedom to work without facing coercion. Slavery has no place in a free market. If goods produced with slave labor are being flooded into a market where everyone else subscribes to basic human freedoms, that is not a fair system or a truly free market. We should always ask if a trading relationship enhances freedom and democracy or undermines it. In the case of countries whose entire system is built on exploitation of their people and hostility to Western ideas of freedom, the answer should be obvious.

Thus I believe it was a huge mistake for the West to have allowed China into the World Trade Organization and to have opened up ever greater economic ties. Not only has this failed to improve human rights and democracy for people in China, but it has hugely boosted the global power of a country that is actively hostile to us and our interests. Regrettably, the WTO has been powerless to change this.

China frequently levels hostile trade sanctions against supposed trading partners, as was shown in 2020 when Beijing imposed tariffs on a range of Australian imports in apparent retaliation for the Australian prime minister's call for an independent investigation into the origins of COVID.

In the absence of credible institutional restraints, we must accept that we cannot regulate the behavior of hostile economic actors. Instead we should seek to limit our trading relationships to those who share our values and our belief in economic and personal freedom. We need to develop a trading network of allies in the free world—and shut out our enemies.

This bloc can be an economic NATO. In the same way that Western countries have clubbed together to impose punitive sanctions on Russia, we should band together to push terms of trade on China.

During the Cold War, Western allies cooperated closely to decide how to deal with the Soviet Union. There was a sense of shared interest in the name of freedom against those who sought to undermine us. We would never have seen Western leaders flying to Moscow to ply their exports and toast new trade deals with members of the Politburo. Yet today we see this constantly, from President Macron of France to U.S. Treasury secretary Janet Yellen.

Of course, as I was getting my feet under the table at the Department for International Trade, China was about to create an even greater problem for the world. The prime minister's Greenwich speech on trade in February 2020 was one of the last big moments in politics before the COVID pandemic changed everything—both for the world and for him personally. A week earlier, on January 30, the World Health

Organization had declared the outbreak to be a "public health emergency of international concern." That same day, the first two cases in the United Kingdom were confirmed. More followed during February, and health authorities in the UK issued advice to the public to wash their hands regularly to limit transmission of the virus.

Despite these concerns rumbling in the background, there was no sense of just how massive an issue it was going to be. I was getting on with my job, including preparing for the World Trade Organization's General Council meeting in Geneva at the start of March, where I would retake the UK's independent seat and become the first British minister to represent our trade interests at such an international meeting since Peter Walker nearly half a century before.

When I arrived at the meeting on March 3, the impact of COVID was starting to be felt. Instead of shaking hands, ministers and officials bumped elbows, somewhat awkwardly and self-consciously. As I made my speech, proudly declaring that "Britain is back," the prime minister was speaking at a press conference in Downing Street alongside the UK's chief medical officer and chief scientific adviser to unveil the government's coronavirus action plan.

From then on, things moved rapidly. Pictures on the news showed chaotic scenes in Italy, which began to implement regional and then national lockdowns. Fears grew of similar measures being required in the UK. On March 16, Boris gave another press conference and advised people to avoid unnecessary social contact and to work from home if possible. A week later, the first national lockdown was announced, with people instructed to stay at home.

Like everyone else in the country, this had an immediate impact on me and my family. But the work of government carried on, with all of us becoming much more familiar with Zoom and other online video conferencing platforms. Cabinet meetings took place virtually, and after a while I was also able to resume trade meetings with my counterparts around the world. While I was not directly involved in the pandemic response, my main concern was to ensure that trade routes remained open for essential supplies, despite the imposition of emergency measures and restrictions at ports around the world. At one point early on, we were two weeks away from running out of paracetamol, and I had to lobby the Indian government to help us obtain vital supplies.

The whole pandemic was a grim experience, but one of the most shocking moments came on the evening of Sunday, April 5. Sitting on my sofa at home, I received a phone call from the Cabinet secretary, Simon Case, to tell me that the prime minister had been taken to the hospital. Boris had been ill with COVID during the previous week, and his symptoms had been getting steadily worse as he self-isolated in the Downing Street flat. There were a few Cabinet video calls in the preceding days where we could see he was not at all well.

Initially it was announced that he was going into St Thomas's Hospital as a precaution, but the following day we heard he had been taken into the intensive care unit. This was profoundly alarming, and it was made very clear that his condition was causing serious concern. For the next three days this remained the case, until thankfully he was judged to be out of danger and returned to a general ward where he remained until being allowed to go to his country residence of Chequers to continue his recovery.

I still find it shocking how close we came to the prime minister dying in the first weeks of the pandemic. The fact that this could happen was, to my mind, a major failing of the state. It demonstrated how shockingly unsupported and exposed our prime minister is when compared to other world leaders. As we watched Boris struggling through meetings on Zoom in the days before he was hospitalized, I simply couldn't understand why he was apparently being left to fend for himself. I could not imagine the U.S. president or German chancellor being similarly neglected and left without appropriate medical attention.

The contrast to what I saw in Washington, D.C., a few months later, once lockdown rules had eased enough for me to travel there for meetings, was stark. A comprehensive system was underway in which people were isolated in the Executive Office Building next door and tested for COVID before being allowed into the White House. The president and vice president had full medical teams looking after them. It was a world away from the frankly shambolic arrangements at the heart of the UK government.

The welfare of the country's chief executive at a time of national emergency is objectively important. Much attention has since been focused on evidence that staff in Downing Street broke lockdown rules by holding social events, and I can well understand the public anger, given the huge personal sacrifices people across the country were forced to make.

But the other implications of such failures have largely escaped attention. In the first weeks of the pandemic, the health secretary, the prime minister's chief adviser, the chief medical officer, and the prime minister himself all caught COVID. As a result, the government's entire senior leadership was at risk of being incapacitated at a moment of extreme national peril. I still find it hard to comprehend how the official state allowed this to happen, and how disastrous it easily could have been.

The response to COVID also created increased demands for state intervention and left a burden of debt. When lockdowns happened the state clearly needed to provide some support. But the furlough scheme was set too generously at 80 percent of people's salaries. This had the effect of preserving the economy in aspic, with little incentive for people to respond to the changed world by establishing new and innovative businesses.

I would have preferred a lower level of direct support to individuals that would have protected people from hardship while allowing them to explore new opportunities that might have arisen. The American scheme was better in that it paid money to individuals, not companies. The United States saw a much healthier level of business creation during the pandemic.

The Treasury also squandered money on the "Eat Out to Help Out" scheme—subsidizing people to eat out in restaurants, cafés, and pubs—which could have contributed to the spreading of the virus. There was also the "Bounce Back Loan" scheme that was found to have resulted in a great deal of fraud.

The rise in public spending in 2019 and 2020 was much larger in the UK than in other economies—an 11 percent rise compared to 9 percent in the United States and 5 percent in Germany. This often gets blamed on Boris, but the lead came from the Treasury under Rishi Sunak.

As we came out the other side of COVID, I think there was a missed opportunity to recognize that things needed to change. The massive increase in the size of the state during the crisis and the associated huge costs should have led to an honest conversation with the public about how to move out of our low-growth trajectory. Combined with the opportunities of Brexit, it could have been a real moment to lay out a bold new vision for the future. But just as with Brexit, there was a lack of clarity about what that vision could be.

The failure to seize this opportunity was a frustration for me, but again, it would be too simplistic to point the finger at Boris Johnson. It was in my view a much more systemic problem, the roots of which lay in the fact that the Conservative Party over many years in government had lost its way. If anything, the unique charisma of the prime minister disguised the extent to which he was being frustrated by the situation in which he found himself.

Boris is a great front man and big-picture thinker. As well as having a clear idea of the sort of country he wants the UK to be, he is also a brilliant communicator and campaigner. He can sell an optimistic, upbeat vision of Britain in a way that resonates with voters. But it is too much to expect the front man and ideas person to also have to run the whole show himself. A prime minister has to trust good people around him to act on his behalf to carry out his wishes. Those people are hard to find, and those who end up being appointed don't always have the prime minister's best interests at heart.

The experience of COVID demonstrated the extent to which the official bureaucracy around the prime minister was lacking in capacity. But there were also major problems with the political operation. Boris was frequently ill-advised by those around him, and undoubtedly came to realize this as time went on. But as I was to discover, there is often little opportunity once you are in Number 10 to build the team required. Conservatives in the UK have a major problem with political infrastructure. I look back and regret that fundamental differences of opinion as well as chaotic organization meant we did not achieve the changes the country needed and had voted for.

CHAPTER 7

Liberty, Equality, and Wokery

The United States of America is Britain's proudest creation, albeit an unintentional one. Although we have long since ceased to smart over the rejection of British rule in 1776, in the U.S.A. we see the continuation and perfection of ideas formed in the British Isles. The philosophy that shaped the Constitution of the United States was drawn explicitly from hard-won British constitutional freedoms and the belief that they needed to be advanced.

In the middle of Thetford in my Norfolk constituency, there is a golden statue of Thomas Paine, one of the town's most famous sons. Born there in 1737, he emigrated to Philadelphia in 1774 under the sponsorship of Benjamin Franklin. His writings provided a rallying cry for the American Revolution and were influential in the founding of the new republic.

The United Kingdom and the United States share a unique heritage of freedom. We are exceptional. From Magna Carta to the U.S. Bill of

Rights, there is a clear intellectual and philosophical lineage that binds us together through the spirit of our foundational documents. They embody a fundamental belief in the freedom of our peoples to live in peace, protected by the rule of law and strict limitations on the powers of government.

For centuries, our countries have been beacons of hope for oppressed people across the world. At the same time, our culture of freedom has allowed businesses to flourish and our economies to grow, massively improving living standards for all our people. Free markets have been at the heart of our success and strength.

Our countries have also known the heavy responsibility of global leadership. In the nineteenth century, Britain was the world's richest economy and, thanks to the Royal Navy, had its most powerful military. In the twentieth century, that economic and military preeminence passed to the United States. It should be a matter of pride that both countries combined that raw strength with a persistent belief in democracy and free trade, seeking to advance political and economic freedoms throughout the world.

Of course, neither country has had a perfect history. Aspirations of freedom among many of our people were not fulfilled for far too long. But even as campaigners fought for equal rights, they did so on the basis that we were not living up to our stated values. The moral standard has always been set high for us, even when we have fallen short. That is the fundamental and enduring difference between us and the repressive regimes that oppose such aspirations in principle. It is these ideas that have provided a powerful lodestar for the free world.

Yet these ideas are being increasingly questioned—not just by totalitarian regimes that have never believed in freedom, but within our own societies. People benefiting from free speech and a free media have used these advantages to try and challenge our underlying values.

They reject British and American exceptionalism. In fact, they often claim that Britain and the United States are uniquely bad and that our countries have had a negative influence on the world.

From extremist environmentalists to de-growthers to de-colonizers, they question the very ideas that have underpinned progress. Even scientific facts discovered during the Enlightenment are now debated as if they are matters of opinion and politics. Even the basic tenets of biology. When I entered politics in 2010, I had absolutely no idea that less than a decade later I would become embroiled in a debate about whether a woman could have a penis.

It started with a tweet. Back in April 2018, I tweeted in support of Mumsnet, the online forum for mothers, over their insistence on having a free discussion on transgender policy. I believe in free speech and not shouting down those with opposing opinions. My fundamental view was that adults should be free to live their lives as they want. I was also clear that women were defined as biologically female. I thought nothing of this commonsense position and got back to my day job at the Treasury.

It was just under eighteen months later that I got a call from an aide to the prime minister asking me if I still agreed with my tweet. I knew where this was leading. Amber Rudd had just resigned from the Cabinet as work and pensions secretary, having held the additional role of minister for women and equalities. Sure enough, I was called by the prime minister himself asking me to be equality minister.

In typical Boris fashion, he told me, "Liz, I want you to be a Geoffrey Boycott in this role"—a reference to the famously cautious England cricketer of the 1970s, presumably suggesting he wanted me to play defense on the issue, hose things down, and not create any trouble. That might have suited him, but I don't really see myself as a Geoffrey Boycott figure. I told Boris I preferred Ian Botham, the charismatic attacking cricketer who once grew so frustrated with Boycott's negativity that he conspired with the opposition to dismiss him from the match. Boris countered by suggesting that he saw me as more of a Ben Stokes, the modern-day England star . . . and so it went on. It was somewhat surreal to be conducting a ministerial appointment through the medium of an extended cricketing metaphor, but we eventually agreed I would step up to the crease.

Coincidentally, in my Trade job, I later persuaded Boris to appoint Ian, now Lord, Botham to be his trade envoy to Australia, a country that has generally had the better of its cricket battles with England, but against whom Botham achieved some of his greatest triumphs.

On taking up this additional portfolio, I became responsible for the Government Equalities Office, a rather strange beast in the Whitehall jungle, which sat within the Cabinet Office. I also inherited an LGBTQ action plan that had been drafted by my predecessor-but-one, Penny Mordaunt, and which included a whole pan of hot potatoes, including backing for self-identification for transgender people and a ban on conversion therapy, which had the potential to become very contentious.

While I supported the right of adults to live freely, wearing the clothes they wanted and making the changes to their bodies they wanted, there were three major problems with the proposals.

First, I was concerned about under-eighteens who had not yet developed adult decision-making capabilities. I was clear that it was wrong for them to be allowed, let alone encouraged, to make irreversible decisions about their bodies by taking puberty blockers or undergoing some kind of surgery.

Second, it was important that women's sex-based rights were protected. For generations, we had fought for these rights for safety and fair treatment. It was important that single-sex facilities (such as changing rooms and refuges) and women's sports competitions were protected and maintained.

Finally, there was the issue of free speech. I was not prepared to allow Orwellian Newspeak to push out normal language about women—for example, the mantra that "trans women are women" or the notion being promulgated by the National Health Service that *people* have periods or give birth. Anyone should be able to express themselves freely and honestly about the world around them and not be pilloried. Instead livelihoods have been destroyed over the expression of simple facts.

The first noteworthy case in the UK was that of researcher Maya Forstater, who didn't have her contract renewed at the Centre for Global Development in 2019 after she described transgender women as men. She took her case to an employment tribunal, which concluded she had been a victim of discrimination on the grounds of her beliefs, and she won compensation of nearly £100,000 ($126,600) for loss of earnings, injury to her feelings, and aggravated damages. But that came after three and a half years of legal wrangling.

Her views, shared by me and backed by the vast majority of the British public, put me into direct conflict with the trans rights lobby. I was labeled "evil," "vile," "a bigot," "a homophobe," "a disgusting transphobe," and much else besides.

Stonewall, a UK charity that had previously campaigned for the fair treatment of gay people—a cause I supported—had now become obsessed with the trans debate. They had used their position to put pressure on government departments and public bodies, which, along with large corporations, had been paying Stonewall for their counsel on LGBTQ issues, so their influence was considerable. Anyone who didn't agree with them was regarded as a bigot. I discovered that companies had been encouraged to adopt policies around pronouns and gender-neutral facilities under threat of having their Stonewall approval removed. It was akin to a woke protection racket.

I was more than used to making arguments against the intolerant Left. I was a veteran of these battles, having had fights as a student at Oxford University in the 1990s. I had abhorred the bullying of gay students at my school and opposed Section 28, a ludicrous piece of legislation that effectively stopped schoolteachers from talking to pupils about homosexuality. I also virulently objected whenever I felt that my being a girl meant I was treated differently than my brothers.

What I discovered after being elected to the Oxford University Student Union (OUSU) as their executive officer was that this was not everyone's idea of equality. What the Left wanted was to acknowledge the "oppression" of particular groups and afford them privileges accordingly. Few people, however, seemed willing to take on the Left. So I did. I argued publicly that the position of "Women's Officer" was patronizing and sexist and should be abolished. But the Left didn't want to have a debate about the principle—instead *I* was censured by the OUSU executive for being "sexist." It was an early taste of the sheer intolerance of the Left and their bullying tactics in the face of anyone who didn't agree with them.

On another occasion, I refused to apologize when someone complained after I shouted across the OUSU office for one of the LGB team (no T in those days) to deal with a query from someone who had called the student helpline. That in turn got me censured for being "homophobic." I thought it was bizarre that some of the most privileged, educated people in Britain were determined to cast themselves as victims.

I discovered while taking a course on political sociology that much of the intellectual backing for identity politics came from the postmodernist movement, in particular French philosopher Michel Foucault. His ideas rejected objective truth in favor of societal power structures. This postmodernist philosophy, together with later developments like Critical Race Theory, gave rise to the idea that oppressed groups had to be helped collectively.

Little did I know that these ideas, which struck me as niche at the time, would become so embedded in our politics and societies. I was also surprised to see the same intolerance and victimhood that I had seen at Oxford entering the workplace. I had assumed that as these people grew up, they would become more tolerant and open-minded. Sadly, they did not.

Identity politics and the modern equivalent, "wokeism," have become endemic in our society, our businesses, and the public sector. And, incredibly, much of it began in the beacon of constitutionally protected liberty, the United States of America. The home of Martin Luther King Jr., who in 1963 spoke of his dream that his children would be judged not by the color of their skin but "by the content of their character," now appears to subscribe to the view that the color of your skin *is* more important than the content of your character.

In this looking-glass world, activists advocate that people of different races or sexes should be treated differently, and that they are inherently different. We have heard feminists argue that the reason we had the financial crash was because women weren't running the banks, and that the nuclear bomb would not have been invented if women had been running the world. This cult of female exceptionalism is equally as prejudiced as the male exceptionalism that leads to sexism against women. I find it all utterly tiresome and aggravating.

Women are just as capable of making poor decisions as men, just as they are as capable of making good ones. They have just had less opportunity to do either. Instead of setting one group against another, we should judge people on their individual character and abilities. Dividing people into identity groups and arguing that we need to give them special treatment only embeds inequality.

So I took on the equality brief with a very clear view of what needed to change. I knew that, just as with my skirmishes at OUSU, this would not endear me to those who had drunk the Kool-Aid of the Left's identity politics. It would also be a challenge to many of the civil servants working in the Government Equalities Office, who were very much signed up to the prevailing agenda. This is a symptom of something we have seen happening more and more in government in recent years: if you're an environmentalist, you go and work at the Environment Department, and if you're an equality campaigner, you go and work at the Government Equalities Office. Thus we end up with activists as civil servants, which I don't think happened in the past and which can present real problems.

Some of my Conservative predecessors were content to simply go along with this direction of travel. They seemed to think these social changes were inevitable and that the Conservative Party could not afford to be left behind. This was certainly what I found on the trans and gender self-identification issues. It had become the prevailing view that this was another Section 28 and that we risked making those mistakes again and suffering the consequences of being on the "wrong side of history." Many transgender people who spoke to me told me they were horrified by the way their lives were being weaponized as part of others' agendas. They just wanted the freedom to live their lives.

As well as the trans extremism, the Black Lives Matter movement was also imported from the United States after the murder of George Floyd by a Minneapolis police officer, even though the situation in the UK was completely different. The Labour Party leadership got in on the act by ostentatiously taking the knee, while the Football Association directed the England football team to do likewise. I found this gesture unedifying, not to mention that it created a worrying precedent. It set off a wave of demands for historic statues to be pulled down and for people to apologize for their family's role in slavery.

I think this is completely the wrong path to go down and leads to unraveling rather than progress. We all understand that accepted values have been different at different times in our history. But endless relitigation of the past both omits the strides that have been made and takes our gaze away from the present. What we should be focused on is fair treatment now. I found it incredible that people were highlighting acts of slavery that took place hundreds of years ago but were apparently unbothered about the real slavery taking place in the Xinjiang region of China.

What was worrying about the woke movement was how it had a momentum of its own, despite the views of the vast majority of the public and their elected politicians. Programs and discussions on these subjects became increasingly prevalent in schools, on university campuses, in the NHS, and at companies.

Some schools were teaching that there are multiple genders and insisting children use unisex toilets without any consideration of girls' safety. There were attacks in prisons by male inmates who had designated themselves as transgender. The police were designating biological males who had committed rape as women. The National Health Service put out guidance about "chestfeeding" and allowed people who were not biological women into single-sex hospital wards (a policy that has since been reversed).

Appallingly, all of this was happening under a Conservative government. Whereas I was prepared to have the fight, too many of my Cabinet colleagues wanted to put their heads in the sand. There were even some backbench Tory MPs and advisers in Number 10 who actively supported the self-ID agenda. As I moved forward with my plans to stop self-ID, there was a barrage of leaks to the press. It became a Saturday night tradition that I would receive a WTF text from Boris demanding to know why our plans had been leaked. I had to point out that as the person who wanted to get this done, it was not in my interests for this to be in the public domain. Had he considered that one of his own advisers might have leaked the story?

It felt like we were fighting a battle on the front line from the position of common sense. But the Conservative Party did not philosophically agree, and Number 10 wanted to avoid making a definitive decision.

I eventually got self-ID reversed through a statement I delivered in the House of Commons. There was a lot of support from women's rights activists and the predictable backlash from the Left. Slowly the tide was turning. Eighteen months later, the Scottish government was not able to progress its own woke plans because of a public outcry over the Gender Recognition Reform Bill that contributed to the downfall of Scottish First Minister Nicola Sturgeon. The bill, which was passed by the Scottish Parliament but eventually blocked by the UK government, would have allowed Scottish citizens to legally change their gender at sixteen, without the diagnosis of gender dysphoria by a doctor. More important, they could have made the change after living as their new gender for just three months. The furor over the case of the biologically male double rapist Isla Bryson, who was originally incarcerated in a Scottish women's prison and only transitioned *after* being convicted, shone a light on how dangerous wokeism had become.

As well as the reluctance among some in the government and on the Tory backbenches to take on the woke orthodoxy, we were also hidebound by the failure of the coalition and Conservative governments before us to have changed the underlying legal framework. A lot of the problems we faced were because of the Equality Act 2010, which was passed in the dying days of the last Labour government. This piece of legislation enshrined in law the left-wing concept of identity-based politics.

That whole approach has been at the core of left-wing and Marxist thinking for decades. It embeds collectivism by prioritizing group identity above individuals and their families. That is also why it's so popular with those who like big government: they can take an authoritarian and bureaucratic approach to policing inequality and arbitrate between the competing interests of particular groups. It is one of the biggest successes of the Left in recent years to have had this long-held set of assumptions written into such a totemic piece of legislation, which has governed how the public and corporate sectors now deal with these issues.

I decided that to shift what was happening on the ground in Britain, we needed to take on the Equality Act. I wanted to repeal it and replace it with a new law that would ensure fair treatment for everyone, regardless of their characteristics. In other words, it would be grounded in conservative principles of individual liberty and human dignity and be concerned with equality of opportunity and treatment, not equality of outcome. I wanted a return to liberty and the rule of law.

My proposal to repeal and replace the Equality Act was resisted by Number 10, which felt it would be too controversial. This, in my view, is emblematic of one of the biggest mistakes we made as Conservatives when we took office in 2010: not rolling back the encroachment of left-wing thinking into our laws and institutions. We failed to understand what the Labour government was doing, and too many Conservatives were merely focused on getting into power rather than thinking about how to promote conservative ideas.

Left-wing notions of identity politics have long sat alongside other instincts, including the desire to police language and an intolerance toward contrary views and debate. The moral certainty of the Left leads them to believe that those who hold different views are not just wrong but morally inferior, and therefore deserving of, in the modern parlance, being "canceled."

It is clearly the job of conservatives to stand up to this and call it out. But too often those on the Right are persuaded by the old "right side of history" argument to go along with the fashionable trend and consensus. And that is how the Left wins. It is the reason I was not able to reverse the Equality Act: I was told, "We can't possibly repeal it, because we don't want to look like we're against equality."

Issues like LGBTQ rights and the environment seem progressive and safe—how could any reasonable person possibly be against them? But too often they are used as a Trojan horse for top-down collectivism. We have reached the point where tax cuts are often seen as having negative political connotations because in people's minds they connote a lack of caring. That is a huge win for the Left, which has successfully linked positive associations to their chosen causes, which are actually very damaging to the country.

This has had an impact not only on the Left and the public but even on those who should be challenging it on the Right. Some Conservative MPs now appear to make political judgments based on whether or not they pass the London dinner party test—whether voicing a certain opinion with left-wing friends and friends of friends could result in their being treated as a social pariah.

They might conclude, for example, that they will be condemned as mean if they don't support increases in welfare and public spending, or be branded a reactionary zealot if they voice concerns about Net Zero or trans rights. So they are instead persuaded that they should adopt the prevailing consensus about what is politically acceptable, for fear of being condemned as "nasty."

Modern technology, particularly social media, has not just exposed public figures to greater abuse from trolls and organized campaigns of activists. It has enabled the left-wing guardians of the new political correctness to police views and language. And so people self-censor for fear of being "canceled."

One of the reasons this has become so pernicious and restricting is a lack of competition in these new public spaces. Where once we might have had democracy, now there are oligopolies that make these decisions. So if you are a commentator and you get canceled and de-platformed by the BBC, Sky News, Twitter, and Facebook, you can't get your message across. When other entrants into the market, such as GB News, attempt to challenge the consensus, they face boycotts by the corporate advertising cartels.

The threat presented by the "woke" movement in the United States and Britain (as well as Canada and Australia) has become increasingly clear. There is now a concerted challenge and threat to our core Anglo-American values. It comes as much from within as from without, with left-wing activists crowding our university campuses and public institutions and seeking to embed a narrative that the West is to blame for all the world's wrongs. Anti-capitalist movements combine with radical environmental campaigners, advocates of critical race theory, and gender ideologues to find new ways to attack our traditional way of life and divide our society. Virtually all of the things that have made us strong and prosperous are being systematically undermined by those who seek to impose their woke values and close down debate.

The underlying assumption is that British and American values are fundamentally bad and need to be torn down, while too many politicians have acquiesced in the name of "being on the right side of history." But it is precisely that history that we need to reclaim. The idea that the British Empire was evil and shameful, or that the United States has been a force for oppression, is simplistic and wrong. We should demand that the whole story of our countries—warts and all—be properly told and understood. Not everything in our history was positive, but there was far more good than today's woke revisionists would ever admit. We should say so.

We should always be prepared to be self-critical and question how our societies can be better. Freedom of speech and the ability to challenge our governments and institutions is a fundamental part of our liberal democracy. But in recent times there has been a tendency to see only the negatives and to deny the positive impact of our beliefs. Self-criticism has become self-flagellation.

This is not only damaging to our sense of national identity, but actively plays into the narratives being pushed by our enemies overseas. Those who seek to diminish the importance of Western values will only be encouraged when they see us engaged in ever more agonized repudiations of our past and ever more esoteric culture wars.

We need to respond robustly to this challenge. We need to be proud of our core values and tell the story of freedom again. That means being intolerant of intolerance and speaking out loudly and clearly when opponents of freedom seek to curtail legitimate debate. We should also push back against the rewriting of history that seeks to dismiss the many benefits that our values have brought to the world.

Conservatives cannot afford to be passive in the face of this threat. We need an activist policy to restore our core values and not allow the Left to fill the void. We should be promoting liberty, not wokery. We must focus on individual dignity and humanity, not quotas and targets or equality of outcome.

Much of the problem lies in the power of the administrative state. We need to restore democratic accountability so that activist officials cannot promote their personal views using public money.

There should also be no grants of public funds to organizations promoting positions that fundamentally undermine our values. I defunded Stonewall in the departments in which I operated as a minister. This should be done across the government.

We must give parents much greater choice in schooling and ensure greater transparency over curricula in schools so that they can drive decisions about what their children are taught.

We also need to ensure that interest groups cannot get away with bullying businesses into taking particular actions or stances through explicit or implicit threats.

Many businesses earnestly set out diversity, equity, and inclusion (DEI) or environmental, social, and governance (ESG) policies as a way of virtue-signaling and demonstrating support for the latest fashionable cause. But their actions often end up being discriminatory: think of the so-called "ethical investors" who refuse to buy shares in energy or "sin" industries, or who boycott produce that comes from Israel. There has been a welcome flurry of anti-ESG initiatives in Texas and a number of other U.S. states seeking to prohibit companies that pursue discriminatory ESG policies from benefiting from government investments. In the

UK, we should take a similar approach to prevent such companies from bidding for government contracts, for example.

Finally, there needs to be a determined effort to root out the self-same bias and prejudices too often found among the regulators and arbiters whose job it should be to stand up for freedom of speech and fair play.

It's especially important that this occurs in broadcast media and on social media platforms. The chilling act of de-platforming those with mainstream views, something usually associated with totalitarian regimes, should be deemed beyond the pale in Western democracies. This needs to be done through the development of popular conservative platforms and making sure regulators are properly accountable so that they are not operating in a biased way.

When I put out my tweet in 2018, I wasn't expecting to be called up to fight on the front line of the equality debate. But I am glad I did it. The madness of identity politics and wokery is doing huge damage to our society and our public services, and it needs to be taken on. Conservatives need to dismantle the architecture that has enabled these fringe ideas to flourish and instead restore the primacy of individual liberty, the family, and parental authority. I am not prepared to leave the field until the battle is won.

CHAPTER 8

Out into the World

"Strong Britain, Great Nation" blared out from Boris's iPhone as we drove towards the White House on September 21, 2021. The tune had been written by British primary schoolchildren from Bradford and released earlier that year. Mocked by the *bien pensant*, it reflected the core patriotism that most of our fellow countrymen and women feel. It was Boris's clear belief in Britain and his talking down naysayers that had so connected with people across the United Kingdom in 2019.

For all our disagreements on China and Net Zero, I fundamentally share Boris's love of our nation. Britain is a great country that stands for the right things and has a positive impact on the world. But too many in the British establishment cringe with embarrassment. They are desperate to forget our past and kowtow to the Global Left's agenda.

Just six days earlier, I had been invited to Downing Street, where Boris had assigned me the foreign secretary role. He'd said he wanted me to inject some positivity into our foreign affairs and promote Global Britain and our outward-facing support for free democracies. He praised my stint at International Trade, where I signed trade deals and generated enthusiasm for British exports and investment. He also took the opportunity to tell me that now that I was a senior minister, I should shut up about taxes being too high. I had no intention of doing so.

When I arrived at the Foreign Office, I found a demoralized bunch. My predecessor had been a hard taskmaster! And it's not much fun being in the Foreign Office during COVID when drink receptions are canceled and travel is replaced by Zoom calls. The fallout of Biden's hasty withdrawal from Afghanistan, by which the Foreign Office had been blindsided and disappointed, and their subsequent castigation by the media, weighed heavily on them. Although they had recently regained control of international aid, there was a general sense of declining prestige, as the Foreign Office had lost other key responsibilities like trade policy.

This was a shame. I was immediately impressed by the caliber of many of the officials. There were hidden depths to their work—from those who had supported the Baltic states to overturn Soviet rule in the 1980s to agents who had provided vital intelligence to disrupt authoritarian regimes. I now had responsibility for the Secret Intelligence Service, MI6, including approving their most contentious and risky operations. I have huge admiration for what they do.

Unfortunately, these admirable tendencies were mixed with the modern government culture of risk aversion and HR-ification. The hierarchy had encouraged a focus on the wrong priorities, notably a messianic zeal for Net Zero and hand-wringing do-goodism. There had also been poor leadership from senior ranks in the past. A case in point was Simon McDonald, the former permanent secretary who recently admitted that the day after the Brexit vote in 2016 he had told everyone in the organization that he'd voted Remain and commiserated with them all. This approach encouraged others to allow their personal views to affect their work.

The Foreign Office had been undermined for years by governments that hadn't taken foreign affairs seriously enough, exacerbated by a media that also did not do so. When Labour was in government, the Foreign Office budget was squeezed. They were embarrassed by the existence of our overseas territories, which they thought of as relics of empire, and were generally apologetic about Britain's place in the world.

This attitude has sadly become endemic. Successive prime ministers watched as our crown jewels were sold off to fund a bloated domestic budget, particularly a growing welfare state. When I was chief secretary to the Treasury and Boris was foreign secretary, we fought Chancellor Philip Hammond to keep our Bangkok embassy. But the historic building and its gardens were flogged off to the highest bidder and our diplomats relocated to a tower block. The opulent grounds of the Singapore ambassador's residence were sold off. The residence now sits on a patch of land resembling a postage stamp.

I'd watched in horror from the International Trade Department as the Treasury had tried to sell off the Tokyo embassy. This jewel in the crown of the estate was across the road from the Imperial Palace in Tokyo and an important part of Japanese and British history. I felt so strongly about keeping it that I demanded the sale be stopped in my foreign secretary appointment meeting with Boris. He agreed but feared it might be too late to unpick the deal. In the end, I was able to save the historic embassy building itself with its impressive façade, but a swimming pool and staff quarters were sold. We could have stopped the sale altogether, but Rishi was clear with Boris that the £1 billion ($1.37 billion) would have to be found elsewhere. Boris caved.

Ironically, the one historic embassy the Treasury could not dispose of is the Moscow one—across the river from the Kremlin—as it is on a lease from the Russian government.

This whole exercise in selling off the family silver was driven by the Treasury's usual pettifogging attitude. And for what? The capital receipts from flogging off these sites were perhaps in the region of £2 billion ($2.5 billion) overall. When you consider that the NHS spends that sum every week, it's not exactly a huge amount. Yet those grand historic embassies are gone forever. Britain's history was just thrown away. It's the epitome of knowing the price of everything and the value of nothing.

This abacus accounting is compounded at the Foreign Office by that pervasive sense of embarrassment about the British Empire and our history. You cannot escape that history at the Foreign Office HQ on King Charles Street, previously home not just to the Foreign Office but also to the Colonial Office and the India Office, with its Durbar Court and the Indian Council Chamber. There is even an office that has two matching doors on either side designed so that two Indian princes of equal rank could enter at the same time. Some see the place as a relic. My view is it is part of who we are.

The building has been neglected. While some of the major features have been carefully preserved, there are still large parts of it that are distinctly shabby. The statues on the outside of the building are crumbling. I had an idea that we should renovate it and commission new statues of great British heroes, but I was told that if we wanted to do that we would have to sell off even more overseas embassies! This neglect is in stark contrast to the Treasury building next door, which was given a massive renovation under Gordon Brown, with modern offices constructed and historic features restored.

Such short-term technocratic thinking and degradation of British history have combined to make officials in the Foreign Office the most browbeaten civil servants in Whitehall. They've been told for years they're not as important as the International Development Department, that no one cares about foreign policy, and that international relations can now be run from Number 10. Why do we need all these ambassadors and embassies when we can just do video calls? Who cares if the Bangkok embassy is in a colonial mansion or a rented tower block? Well, as a matter of fact, those countries care. And so should we.

Thankfully, funding for the foreign secretary's official country residence, Chevening House, is not controlled by the Treasury but by the Chevening Trust. It was nevertheless a battle to get my hands on it. It turned out that Boris had tried to soften the blow of my predecessor Dominic Raab's demotion to justice secretary by promising him he could retain the use of Chevening. I wasn't going to accept that. This was partly a matter of practicality—Chevening is used by the foreign secretary to host foreign ministers and visiting delegations from overseas. But it was also a matter of principle—I was the foreign secretary, and the house went with the job. Eventually a compromise was reached in which Raab and I would have access to Chevening on a timeshare basis. It was like an exalted student flatshare. I'd arrive for the weekend and find protein shakes labeled "Raab" in the fridge. It probably wasn't necessary. I was unlikely to have taken them.

When I gave my first all-staff meeting in the Locarno Suite at the Foreign Office, I said I wanted to see pride in our country and our diplomatic service reflected at all levels of the organization. We had to get closer to our friends, developing a "network of liberty" with like-minded allies in the United States, Europe, India, and the Asia-Pacific. And we should be much harder-nosed with totalitarian regimes. Principally China, but also Russia and Iran.

I wanted us to have pride in what Britain is and has been. We've had a tremendously positive impact on the history of the world. We are one of the globe's largest economies, and we stand for free speech, the rule of law, freedom, and democracy. Those values are right, and we should be proud of banging the drum for them. That is what I wanted our diplomats and overseas officials to be thinking, rather than being faintly apologetic just for being there.

I also believed Britain's national interests needed to be put at the heart of everything we did. We needed to be commercial but in a way that supports free enterprise democracies. I found there was a squeamish attitude towards trade and commerce in the Foreign Office. It was as though they considered it a bit dirty and beneath them.

In the British establishment, and hence in the Foreign Office, there is a strange combination of superiority complex and lack of confidence in Britain. They love international institutions like the UN, WTO, OECD, and World Bank. They are generally more pro-Palestine than pro-Israel. They are deferential to the United States, particularly Democrat administrations. They are very pro-EU and admire France and Germany in particular. There is more limited interest in Asia-Pacific nations and Eastern Europe. Their attitude toward Africa and India is paternalistic. This, of course, is not universally true and the extents of these opinions vary, but they are the prevailing ethos. And it can be very time-consuming to change course.

Israel was one of the areas where I was most at odds with the Foreign Office view. Israel is the only free democracy in a difficult neighborhood. It was also under existential threat from Iran. I believed that Trump had made the right decision moving the U.S. embassy to Jerusalem. I wanted the UK to do the same. I also wanted to back Israel more strongly at the UN.

I had a major battle over an anti-Israel motion at the UN Human Rights Council. The motion supported the 2001 Durban Declaration, which singles out Israel as a perpetrator of racism. UK officials were planning to abstain and did not seem to intend to consult me about it. When I inserted myself into the issue, we ended up having a number of phone conferences where I was told that if the UK voted to back Israel, we would be "isolated" (the United States was not a member of the UN Human Rights Council at the time). I challenged the officials and said I didn't care if we were isolated. I got Number 10's support and changed our vote. Both France and Germany then switched their votes to back our position. So much for being isolated. We lost by thirty-two to ten with five abstentions, but I was proud that we had shifted the numbers and done the right thing.

This episode was symptomatic of what had happened for years. Too many decisions were made by unelected officials. The UK was risk-averse and afraid to lead. And those who sought to undermine freedom and democracy were thus ascendant. It also illustrated the sheer energy that had to be expended on what should have been an obvious decision, given stated government policy.

There is also a tendency at the Foreign Office to lecture other countries perceived to be less powerful that don't share approved values. When I visited Singapore, my briefing notes suggested I should ask the minister to end Singapore's policy of capital punishment. I did not take this opportunity. Aside from the fact that it is a conscience issue on which MPs have a free vote in the UK (so there is no approved party line to take), I thought it would be counterproductive and patronizing. What business of ours were Singapore's domestic policies? I also pointed out it was not in my brief when I was due to talk to the United States, even though the death penalty exists in a number of states.

The one country the Foreign Office didn't seem to want to lecture was China. Again, this was an area where my view was very different from received Whitehall wisdom. I already had form with our ambassador to China, having objected to her previous attempt to revive a trade committee with the totalitarian dictatorship. I also blocked TikTok from establishing a global HQ in the UK. I refused to give the HQ a government endorsement because the company is simply an outpost of the Chinese state. They went elsewhere. The ambassador tried to persuade me we could work with China and be both friends and rivals, a bit like France. "Except the French aren't committing genocide," I replied.

Again, pressure from an overmighty Treasury played a role. The number of former Treasury and Foreign Office ministers and officials on China's payroll is shocking. I find it extraordinary given that China is the greatest threat to the future survival of the free world. I cannot imagine that people would have wanted to openly accept funding or jobs from the USSR during the Cold War.

I changed our policy to be more supportive of Taiwan. There was huge resistance; it was like wading through treacle. The Chinese and their stooges were in constant touch, essentially trying to bully the Foreign Office to shift the terms of the debate and make the One China policy even more restrictive. My view is that the West should be pushing back and supporting Taiwan in every possible way. Of course, China doesn't want a free democracy seventy miles offshore showing its people what life could be like without totalitarian rule.

Even getting to the bottom of arrangements with the Taiwanese was difficult. It was brave Eastern Europeans, like Lithuanian foreign minister Gabrielius Landsbergis, who had done the most to challenge China, and I wanted them to have our full support. Likewise our Australian and Japanese friends, being in the neighborhood, understood the risks. The meeting of the G7 foreign ministers that I would host in Liverpool was the first that put out a statement supportive of Taiwan.

My first public outing as foreign secretary was at the UN General Assembly four days into the job. At International Trade most of the discussions were with friends and allies—but at the Foreign Office I also had to deal with the dark side. Officials prepared some platitudinal lines for me to take. They often tried to exclude political advisers for fear I would go off script. But I had my own agenda anyway. Both with and without Boris, I met leaders and foreign ministers.

One memorable moment was when Brazilian president Jair Bolsonaro challenged Boris to a tug-of-war to show who was tougher after going through COVID. Sadly, this epic sporting event never took place. I also had my first meeting with Russian foreign minister Sergey Lavrov, who looked like he had been embalmed. He was surrounded by thuggish-looking apparatchiks—I might have been meeting a gangster. It was here that he issued his invitation for me to visit Moscow.

While the UN General Assembly is a useful way to meet counterparts, a sort of diplomatic speed dating, as an institution it does not work. There is so little that is agreed on that serious progress cannot be made on any issue. The whole UN edifice screams "sick building syndrome," giving off an air of a tired postwar institution that is no longer relevant. The Security Council is a case in point. I sat there with Lavrov, the Americans, the French, and the German minister, with the Chinese foreign minister beamed in from Beijing. How on earth were we supposed to guarantee global security when those who threatened it the most were among us?

It was during the UN General Assembly that Boris and I took the Amtrak from New York to Washington, D.C., to meet President Joe Biden at the White House. Our meeting in the Oval Office lasted around an hour and a half, which was rather longer than we had expected. The British media are obsessed with the timing of these events and drawing spurious conclusions about the state of the "special relationship," but the truth was that it owed more to Biden's penchant for telling extended anecdotes in response to any issue that came up. "Ah, that reminds me . . ." he would say, as his officials looked at each other with knowing smiles. Ten minutes later, the story would end and he would move onto something else. We talked about trade, and I finally managed to get the ban on British lamb into the United States removed. And I again asked the Americans to join the CPTPP to create an economic bulwark to China.

Despite the lack of presidential enthusiasm for any trade deal, the British press would not stop asking about a post-Brexit agreement with the United States. This was obviously not going to happen. Biden did not want to upset the Democrat base. I mentioned that the only conceivable way we might make any progress was if we somehow joined the United States–Mexico–Canada Agreement (USMCA), given this was the only one of Trump's deals that the Biden administration actually liked. Of course, my fleeting suggestion then dominated the media.

It is at the level of the "deep state" that the United States and the United Kingdom are most closely intertwined. The degree of intelligence-sharing and military cooperation between our countries makes the bilateral relationship a particularly important one that endures across changes of government on both sides. This has big advantages to the strategic defense of the West, but I found that the continuity also frequently spills over into the political arena.

In the State Department I could see some of the same problems that we had with our Foreign Office, minus some of the colonial guilt. The close cooperation between our intelligence and defense establishments leads many in the U.S. foreign policy and national security establishment to believe their counterparts in Britain and other countries should fall in step with them on those issues too. They take it for granted we will follow their lead. In this way, British foreign policy risks becoming driven by the same technocracy that has captured it in the United States. The geopolitical impact of this can be significant when, as we were soon to experience, our enemies start to move against us.

I had already expressed my skepticism of the Iran nuclear deal (the Joint Comprehensive Plan of Action, or JCPOA) to Boris in a Cabinet subcommittee when Trump was in office, and I had been slapped down. I thought Trump's tougher approach to Iran was the right one. I now had to deal with Iran directly and was under instructions to back the Biden plans to revive the nuclear deal.

Yet there were British nationals who were sitting in Iranian prisons, including Nazanin Zaghari-Ratcliffe, the mother of a young girl, and

Anoosheh Ashoori. These cases had caused public outcry in Britain, and Nazanin's husband Richard had been running a campaign to get her released. The United States did not want to contemplate demanding action on this until talks had been completed on a renewed nuclear deal. Since I thought this was never going to happen, I was very concerned about the fate of Nazanin and Anoosheh.

I sat down in another soulless UN room with the new Iranian foreign minister, Hossein Amir-Abdollahian, part of the new hard-line government of President Ebrahim Raisi. As is usual for a meeting with a hostile country, most of it was taken up by listing the many issues on which we disagreed and scoring points off of one another, without either side conceding anything. The Iranians were filming the meeting on an iPhone, adding to the tense atmosphere. At one point, Amir-Abdollahian said that women were good at math, which was clearly intended to be a jibe. It was lost in translation.

But Amir-Abdollahian also made a remark suggesting it was in both our interests to resolve a number of "long-standing issues." The one at the top of our list was freeing Anoosheh and Nazanin, who had been detained in Iran for more than four and five years respectively. For Amir-Abdollahian, it was the historic dispute about the debt Iran claimed the UK owed for a canceled tank order from the 1970s.

I was determined to get Nazanin and Anoosheh back home, and I needed no other encouragement to press ahead with doing whatever we could to achieve that. Richard Ratcliffe was one of the first people I spoke to upon taking the role of foreign secretary, and I promised him I would do my utmost to bring his wife home. Understandably there was some skepticism: Why should I be any different from my predecessors? But as I told him, I was willing to do whatever it took.

With this hurdle overcome, we began the difficult business of negotiating with the Iranians. I had lots of calls with the foreign minister, who was clearly no great fan of female politicians. I had also gotten to know a lot of the foreign ministers from the Gulf states, a group of whom I invited to Chevening, where I secured their help in reinforcing our messages to the Iranians. The Omanis in particular were very helpful and would be crucial throughout the process.

I'll never forget that moment, sitting in my office, when I took the call from our woman on the ground, Stephanie al-Qaq, and our ambassador, Simon Shercliff, confirming that the wheels had gone up on the plane returning Nazanin and Anoosheh home to freedom. One of the best feelings I ever had as a minister was watching their plane land at Brize Norton with Richard and seven-year-old Gabriella and Anoosheh's family, as Nazanin and Anoosheh then disembarked to be reunited with their families.

As for our overall approach to Iran, I was not in a position to effect change with the United States, which was so clearly determined to resurrect the nuclear deal. Even if a deal had ever been desirable, it was a waste of time with the Iranians building up their nuclear capability. Just as with Russia and China, we needed to show we were not afraid—appeasement would only lead to worse in the future. I also thought that continuing in an agreement that involved both the Russians and Chinese was asking the world's gangsters to guarantee peace.

The COP26 conference on climate change was another arena where I could not see the point of tying our own hands economically. Why should we let China and Russia and Iran dominate fossil fuels? Before entering politics I had worked for the oil giant Shell in LNG shipping, and I knew how strategic these supplies were.

It was ironic that, after trying to cancel COP26, I should end up being a key host of the event. I was deputed to greet leaders and ministers who had flown in from around the world on gas-guzzling jets to talk earnestly about reducing carbon emissions. I love Glasgow, where the conference was held, and was able to visit my old stomping ground of Paisley nearby as well as my favorite chip shop from my school days, the Hippy Chippy.

COP26 was exactly the hot-air fest that I'd predicted it would be back in 2018, but I was able to pursue my agenda on the margins. I had the job of escorting the then Duchess of Cornwall around the reception at Kelvingrove Art Gallery and Museum. This was a great pleasure, as she is very amusing and popular—so much so that we didn't make it from one side of the room to the other. She was waylaid by a demob-happy Angela Merkel, and I bumped into Joe Biden again. He remembered our meeting at the White House, telling me he'd never forget "those blue eyes," even though we'd both been wearing COVID masks.

We talked about China and Biden told me he had met President Xi repeatedly when they were both vice presidents of their countries. He claimed to have a better insight than most into the Chinese premier's thinking. My impression is that Biden does understand the nature of the Chinese threat better than some in his administration. His stance on Taiwan, for example, is robust, but his public pronouncements on the subject tend to get rowed back by his staff. As with most presidents, he is presiding over a foreign policy establishment that is dominated by technocrats. They see foreign policy as a rational exercise of logic and gamesmanship, failing to understand just how ruthless and malign our enemies are.

The tyranny of the technocracy, of which I now have my own extensive experience in the UK context, is particularly strong in American foreign policy. This has led to some notable miscalculations and failures to confront moral outrages around the world. Because they assume that all players are acting rationally, they struggle to deal with some of the more depraved actions of our enemies. Evil people whose intention is to kill their opponents and dominate by force are not playing by the same rules as us. Appeasement might "avoid escalation" in the short term, but it stores up trouble for later. I found Biden's White House and State Department to be far too wedded to the technocratic mindset.

At the Glasgow summit, we had a session on the variously named Build Back Better World or Global Partnership for Infrastructure Investment, or European Gateway, or our own recently established British International Investment. I had championed working together on this economic outreach. I didn't much care what it was called; I just wanted the West to challenge China's Belt and Road Initiative, through which Beijing has effectively been buying influence through its investment in infrastructure around the world for over a decade.

The West spends more on international development than China spends on Belt and Road. But whereas the Chinese are driven by geopolitical domination, too much of our international development money ends up being spent in a want-to-be-do-gooding unfocused way or, even worse, undermines our values. It seemed crazy to me that we were spending untold millions in international aid—yet most of this was going into a general pot while China was busy tying countries into unpayable debt and taking control of strategic ports, technology, and infrastructure.

It was clear that many of our potential allies in places like the Caribbean and the Pacific were struggling to get financing for their projects or to deal with their security concerns and were turning to China or Russia because there was no alternative. Mia Mottley, the prime minister of Barbados, said Barbados had turned to China for financing as they could not get anything from the World Bank or the free world. The Solomon Islands recently signed a security deal with China. Of course, the Chinese use all kinds of inducements to get countries to sign up.

I was concerned that the World Bank and other international financial institutions on which we were spending vast amounts of money—but over which we had little control—were not helping this geopolitical challenge. I wanted to take our money away from these institutions and instead work with our allies on much more geopolitically focused economic outreach. This should have included trade and investment.

Because of the UK's poor financial position, we had reduced our aid as a proportion of GDP to 0.5 percent from 0.7 percent (as it happens, I am not in favor of these input targets anyway). But unbelievably, we hadn't reduced funding to the World Bank. The UK was its second biggest donor but nowhere near the world's second biggest economy. The Treasury was very resistant to reducing funding. I had a row with Rishi Sunak to get the World Bank contribution to be reduced as much as possible, which I eventually won. The problem is that too many former Treasury officials and ministers go on to work for the World Bank and similar institutions, so they do not want to see it deprived of funds. It's yet another body that does not serve a key purpose.

I thought our approach should be to work directly with our allies, deepening our economic and defense ties and building a network of those countries that back freedom. I believed that India, the world's largest country by population and its largest democracy; Indonesia, the fourth largest by population and a major democracy; and Australia, a long-standing ally of the UK, were key to that push.

I saw the deployment off the coast of India of a Queen Elizabeth–class aircraft carrier, complete with our new F-35 jets, conducting a joint exercise with the Indians. We have since signed a military access agreement with Japan and a cooperation agreement with Indonesia on cybersecurity.

The AUKUS pact with Australia and the United States is another example of the UK demonstrating to our allies that we are prepared to show up. This to me is a much better use of finite resources than putting money into the World Bank's bottomless pit.

With the reset of our foreign policy and the worrying buildup to a war in Ukraine, I had more than enough to get stuck into. Lord Frost had the job of negotiating with the EU on the vexed issue of the Northern Ireland Protocol, which covers a variety of unresolved post-Brexit questions relating to customs and trade with respect to the border between Northern Ireland and the Republic of Ireland. Essentially, under the protocol EU law, not British law, applied in Northern Ireland. In addition, goods that had previously entered the Northern Ireland market freely from the mainland of Great Britain now faced red tape and delays. This is like goods facing additional bureaucracy between California and Hawaii. I was happy to leave the sorting out of this to Lord Frost.

But it was not to be. David Frost resigned on December 15 from his role as chief EU negotiator, leaving a vacant position. Lots of people told me not to touch it with a barge pole—that it was the Gordian Knot of British politics—but I couldn't resist. I put in a call to Boris and expressed my thoughts on what we should do to take on the EU over the unworkable and damaging Northern Ireland Protocol. Sure enough, when we were having an early Christmas lunch with my sister-in-law in Winchester a few days later, a call came through from Boris asking me to take on this new task. I joked with David Frost that it was an early Christmas present.

I wanted to talk frankly with the EU and move away from a public blame game. But I was under no illusions that the negotiations would be easy. The EU wanted Northern Ireland to stay in its regulatory orbit. We wanted to restore the cross-UK economic links and our national sovereignty and territorial integrity. It became clear that my counterpart from the EU, Maroš Šefčovič, did not have the mandate to fix this from his higher-ups. France and Germany still wanted to punish Britain for leaving and were not prepared to allow any flexibility.

Visiting businesses in Northern Ireland, I could see they were being forced to complete lots of pointless forms. At the same time, the unionist community felt disengaged from the rest of the United Kingdom because of the barriers to trade. This put at risk the Good Friday Agreement, which puts equal priority on the East–West relationship between Northern Ireland and the UK and the North–South relationship between Northern Ireland and the Republic of Ireland. Needless to say, there were a lot of unhelpful interventions from U.S. politicians like Nancy Pelosi, Congressman Richie Neal, and Biden himself, who were generally on one side of the argument, doubtless egged on by the Irish embassy in Washington.

After a particularly tense discussion in Brussels, Boris told European Commission president Ursula von der Leyen that the UK was going to act unilaterally, since we were making no progress because of the EU's inflexibility. I told Šefčovič the same, and I then prepared a law to put through Parliament with Attorney General Suella Braverman. This became the Northern Ireland Protocol Bill and used the doctrine of necessity to overcome international law issues. It was resisted by those in Cabinet who wanted to maintain the status quo, namely Rishi Sunak and Michael Gove. Yet Suella Braverman made a powerful case at the subcommittee, and we won through.

The only way we were going to restore the sovereignty and territorial integrity of the United Kingdom and Northern Ireland was to press ahead with the bill. We got it through second reading in June and were prepared to use the Parliament Act to pass it. This essentially meant the House of Commons could overrule the House of Lords after one year if the Lords continued to object to a piece of legislation. Given that the unelected House of Lords was particularly hostile to the bill, this was likely to be necessary.

It never got to that point, as my successor withdrew it. Yet the Windsor Framework that he installed in its place simply does not resolve the issues. Too much was given away to the EU. That is why I could not support it. Not getting it right meant storing up problems for the future by moving the economic gravity towards an all-Ireland economy. We are still in a quagmire. We must have a Northern Ireland that is in regulatory terms separate from the EU and part of the UK. We need another renegotiation to get to that point. The UK is not going to get what we want without a fight.

In taking this on, the Foreign Office needs to move away from its desire to please the EU bureaucracy and the State Department. I was clear as foreign secretary that our sovereign decision-making would always come first.

The time is also ripe for a rethink of how we operate with our friends and foes. While our enemies ruthlessly move against us, we give the impression of wanting to conduct international social work. UK politicians and our allies across the West need the bravery to confront the situation we are in. The WHO, WTO, and UN are past their sell-by dates. We need institutions that recognize we are dealing with an axis of authoritarian states.

After the end of the Cold War, the COCOM, the Coordinating Committee for Multilateral Export Controls on Warsaw Treaty countries and China, was disbanded. This committee comprised the United States, NATO allies, Australia, and Japan. A version of this with an expanded remit covering trade, exports, and investment is what we need now—an economic NATO. We simply cannot afford to leave economic and security outreach to Russia, China, and Iran.

CHAPTER 9

The World at War

My phone rang beside my bed at 3:30 a.m. on a Thursday in late February 2022. It was Nick Catsaras, my private secretary. He told me the event we had all been dreading had come to pass. Vladimir Putin had mounted a full-scale assault on Kyiv. For months we had known this was likely to happen, and it had been growing more certain by the day. Yet to hear it confirmed was terrible. A ground war in Europe for the first time in decades. It shattered all the illusions we had about European security.

Russian forces had been conducting exercises near the border with Ukraine since the spring of 2021, and there had been a further buildup of tanks and troops in the autumn. The United States and the United Kingdom were privy to very specific intelligence that Putin was planning to invade Ukraine more or less immediately after the Beijing Winter Olympics were over—and those games had been formally closed the previous Sunday.

We had spent the autumn and winter doing all we could to deter an invasion and to persuade the Russian regime that it would be a strategic mistake. The problem was that what looks irrational to Western politicians can look logical to a dictator. The UK was a galvanizing force in the G7. We were the first European country to send weapons to Ukraine and led on calls for tough sanctions. We called for the Nord Stream 2 gas pipeline that runs from Russia to Germany to be canceled. We warned the Russians that Ukraine would fight and we spelled out the consequences for the Russian people.

The UK had already been training up the Ukrainian army since 2015, and Boris, Defense Secretary Ben Wallace, and I were determined to help as much as possible. This involved wading through a lot of Whitehall treacle. The machine was risk-averse and cautious. We knew we were racing against time to get the weapons over before Russia attacked.

A lot of the Foreign Office apparatus that focused on Russia had been disbanded after the end of the Cold War. This included the Information Unit, which had countered Soviet propaganda. Russia specialists had been relocated to other growing interests like the Middle East and Asia. Many resources had also been sucked into international development. We immediately redeployed people and reestablished the Information Unit, which had an important role in countering Russian disinformation.

Together with the United States, we deliberately released intelligence to smoke out the Russians and expose their tactics. We needed to convince international doubters what they were up to. This was something of a risky tactic, given the inglorious history of published intelligence in the run-up to the 2003 invasion of Iraq. We knew that Russia was planning all manner of "false flag" operations to give themselves a pretext for the invasion and muddy the picture. By announcing in advance that we knew exactly what they intended, we were able to expose those tactics and prevent their disinformation campaign from getting off the ground.

It was a massive effort to build capacity in the Foreign Office, especially the sanctions team. They were struggling with the sheer bulk of the work thanks to cumbersome legislation. The Sanctions and Anti-Money Laundering Act had been bastardized during its progress through Parliament—another example of our failing to streamline our approach after voting to leave the EU.

Incredibly, some of the legislators who had made these sanctions difficult to apply were actually in the pay of Russian oligarchs. Lord Pannick, for example, had sponsored amendments in the House of Lords that created obstacles to implementing sanctions. Pannick had previously served as a lawyer to the Russian oligarch Arkady Rotenberg, a close friend of Putin. He had helped him fight sanctions from the EU following the Russian annexation of Crimea. I found it extraordinary that this did not receive more scrutiny. Here was a British legislator, who had been employed by Russian oligarchs to fight sanctions, who then sought to water down sanctions legislation.

By November, it was clear that dealing with Russia was our absolute priority and that our Eastern European allies would be critical. They understood the Russian threat best and were the most at risk. I am a long-standing fan of the Baltic states and Poland; I admire their visceral love of freedom and democracy after having spent so many years under communist terror. Visiting during the 1990s, I saw the energy that a free economy and free society can unleash. I wished we had more of that spirit in Britain. As a toddler in 1977, my parents took me to spend a year in communist Poland. I was too young to remember our stay, but maybe it embedded an appreciation for Eastern Europe somewhere deep in my psyche.

These brave countries were on the frontier of freedom, and I wanted to do all I could to back them. In November I headed to Tapa, Estonia, where UK troops were stationed next to the Russian border. After greeting our troops, I got into a tank to go see the border. It was -10 degrees Celsius (14 degrees Fahrenheit) and there was deep snow. I didn't envy those stationed out there. But it was clearly a vital sign of NATO's collective resolve, and I delivered a strong warning to Putin:

> We want a world where freedom and democracy don't just survive, they thrive. To this end, we will stand with our fellow democracies against Russia's malign activity. We will support Ukraine and stability in the Western Balkans, to safeguard their security and build their economic resilience. We have seen this playbook from the Kremlin before when Russia falsely claimed its illegal annexation of Crimea was a response to NATO aggression. NATO is an alliance forged on the principle of defense, not provocation. Any suggestion that NATO is provoking the Russians is clearly false. Any action by Russia to undermine the freedom and democracy that our partners enjoy would be a strategic mistake.

True to form, the British media chose to focus more on the photographs of me riding in a tank than on the imminent prospect of war in Europe.

From there, I headed on to the NATO summit in Riga, followed the very next day by the OSCE (Organization for Security and Co-Operation in Europe) meeting in Stockholm. Tensions between Russia and America were palpable, with U.S. secretary of state Antony Blinken and Russian foreign minister Sergey Lavrov having a set-to at dinner. I had another meeting with Lavrov the next day. It proved to be as fruitless as the last.

As things got worse, I found myself in December hosting the G7 foreign ministers' meeting in Liverpool. I was determined to do all we could to have a common line on sanctions as a warning to Putin. Russia had to believe this would be much more than a slap on the wrist. That meant sanctioning Russian banks and individuals with connections to Putin, seizing their physical assets, and degrading Russia's economic position to make it a pariah state. This was agreed to, and we gave public warning that there would be "severe consequences" if Russia invaded.

Importantly, the Japanese backed the approach, showing this was not just a Euro-Atlantic concern but something of global consequence. Yoshimasa Hayashi, the Japanese foreign minister, also showed his musical prowess during the summit as he played "Imagine" on John Lennon's piano at the Beatles Story museum. I confess to Lennon being my favorite Beatle, although he was clearly a lefty. But for a brief moment that night in Liverpool, we reveled in that message of idealism, escapism, and hope.

The work didn't stop. Our family's first (and last) Christmas at Chevening was interspersed with frequent visits from civil servants and secure phone calls, as well as briefing parliamentarians. Cell phone reception is not great there, and the Foreign Office's portable secure devices are best described as antiquated. I spent much of the Christmas recess hanging out of a bedroom window on the top floor where my brother was staying, trying to hear what Tony Blinken was saying, with two private secretaries crouched next to me.

We were on perpetual tenterhooks throughout January. The long-planned two-plus-two (foreign and defense ministers meeting) in Australia was vital for the progress of AUKUS and our submarine deal with Australia and the United States. However, it was under constant threat of being terminated by panicky officials calling from London.

Regrettably, by this stage, we pretty much knew war was inevitable. We had intelligence that this was not going to be just another assault on the Donbas, the likes of which had been ongoing since Russia invaded

Crimea in 2014. It was going to be a full-blown attack on Kyiv. But my G7 colleagues and I refused to give up hope. We committed to putting as much pressure on Moscow as we could while helping Ukraine prepare.

I visited Moscow on February 9 to urge Russia to pull back from the brink. The trip almost didn't happen. I had been laid low with COVID and had therefore been unable to join Boris's visit to Kyiv the previous week. In fact, I was only given the COVID all-clear at the Northolt Royal Air Force base minutes before we took off.

Moscow was eerily normal. You could have been in any European city with crowded streets and a buzzing nightlife. I spent four hours in the Foreign Ministry with Lavrov, where he spouted the same propaganda about the West and NATO while serving borscht and vodka. And in a sign that Russia hadn't quite extinguished all remaining freedoms, he smoked heavy cigarettes throughout. He continued to deny Russia had any plans whatsoever to invade Ukraine. I challenged him on the sheer scale of their troop buildup near the border, but he merely responded that it was "regrettable" to be asked to withdraw troops from his country's own territory.

We then had a press conference. Its purpose from my point of view was to make sure the Russian people were aware of our concerns and the warnings we were issuing. Of course, the Kremlin propagandists tried to undermine me—and, regrettably, much of the British press were only too happy to oblige them by running stories amplifying Russian propaganda instead of challenging the increasingly absurd denial of reality on the part of the Russians. It was disheartening, to say the least, to see reputable British media outlets lazily repeating the personal attacks Lavrov hurled in my direction. Unfortunately, useful idiots in the Western media do a lot of our enemies' work for them.

I felt it was important to visit Kyiv as well as Moscow to support our allies in their hour of need. This was not welcomed by the powers that be at the UK Ministry of Defense. They did not like the idea of the foreign secretary going into what was likely soon to be a war zone. There had already been a lot of pressure on us by risk-averse officials to move our ambassador out of Kyiv, against which I had held out again and again.

We pushed forward with the Kyiv visit and set out from Brize Norton on February 17 to meet Foreign Minister Dmytro Kuleba. Our plane was an RAF transporter with just a few seats next to the pilot. We were told there was going to be a go or no-go decision as we approached Ukrainian airspace, which was all very dramatic. We reached that point, nothing happened, and we made it through.

The city of Kyiv seemed rather empty. When we got to the Foreign Ministry, I found Dmytro holed up in his office with cigars and Mozart Kugeln, a speciality chocolate from Salzburg. I was struck by his utter resolution. He recalled the Maidan Revolution of 2014, where the Ukrainian people had stood up for freedom against a regime seeking closer ties with Moscow. People had gone to Independence Square in Kyiv knowing that protesters had already been shot dead by riot police. Yet they went anyway in a show of defiance and succeeded in getting the old regime overthrown.

We lit a candle at the Holodomor Victims Memorial in honor of the nearly five million who perished during the terrible famine inflicted by Stalin on the people of Ukraine. Westerners may have forgotten about the hideous crimes of communism, but in Ukraine they had not. I was more convinced than ever that Putin would face unbreakable resistance.

Back at the Foreign Ministry, I gave a brief speech and held an impromptu press conference in the foyer with the assembled international press pack before heading back to London. It was probably the strangest day trip I have ever undertaken.

The next day, I headed to the Munich Security Conference. Ukrainian president Volodymyr Zelenskyy gave a powerful and brilliant address in which he reminded those present that it was at the same event fifteen years earlier that Vladimir Putin had made his expansionist speech attacking NATO and signaling his intention to turn away from the West. The response of world leaders then, Zelenskyy said, had been "appeasement." The direct result, he said, had been the annexation of Crimea and further aggression against Ukraine. It was hard to disagree.

Despite this, some of our allies were still in denial that the Russians would invade Ukraine. More did not believe it would be a full-frontal attack on Kyiv but rather more of the same tactic used in the Donbas region. Again, I collaborated with Eastern European nations such as Poland to get the message across and put the whole of Europe on full alert. The only problem that marred getting around Munich was U.S. vice president Kamala Harris's cavalcade of nearly thirty vehicles. I don't think the Americans understand how much these immense travel-blocking motorcades annoy representatives of other countries. Or maybe they don't care.

The day after the Munich conference closed, Putin made his speech formally recognizing the Russian-occupied parts of Ukraine in the Donbas as sovereign states. This was clearly a precursor to sending in troops, which he announced the following day. Even then, there was a sense of disbelief among our allies—not just because it was too awful to contemplate, but because all rational sense told them it would be a crazy thing for Russia to do. As we soon discovered, that was no barrier to Putin.

Those last few nights in the lead-up to the invasion were tense, as all we could do was wait. Following the invasion in the early hours of February 24, I rushed into the Foreign Office, rolled out the sanctions regime we had spent the last few months putting in place, and made a statement to the House of Commons. I ended the day with a video conference with Ukraine's foreign and defense ministers. Their fortitude had been amazing. None of the Ukrainian cabinet had left the country, despite the United States offering them an escape route.

The next few weeks were round the clock. I was constantly on WhatsApp, making phone calls and holding meetings, coordinating sanctions, statements, votes at the UN—even sourcing ammunition. Despite their earlier skepticism, allies such as France and Germany joined the effort, with Chancellor Olaf Scholz declaring the end of Germany's historic policy of "change through trade" in relation to Russia. In Britain, we sanctioned Russian banks and seized the assets of those with connections to Putin and his regime.

I traveled to Vilnius, numerous NATO meetings in Brussels, the UNHCR in Switzerland, and the ICC in the Netherlands. We visited Warsaw and our aid center in Rzeszów. I also traveled to The Hague and various G7 meetings in Germany, as well as an informal NATO meeting in Berlin. Along with the Americans and Canadians, I even attended a European Union foreign ministers' meeting: our disputes with the EU were overshadowed by this threat to our way of life.

There was less harmony within the Conservative Party back in Britain. In November the so-called "partygate" story had broken in the press. These were accusations surrounding gatherings that had apparently taken place on Boris's watch at 10 Downing Street in breach of COVID regulations on social distancing. An enquiry led by Sue Gray was commissioned. There was a drip, drip, drip of stories in the press. Conservative MPs started to get angsty, and opinion poll ratings slipped. But they were also concerned not to disrupt the UK's leadership on the war in Ukraine.

In the months that followed, Russian troops failed to make the expected progress against the courageous Ukrainian resistance. We and our Western allies stepped up to provide military aid and assistance, and I was constantly advocating that we do more: more weapons, more planes, more tanks . . . whatever it took to defeat Russia and drive them out of Ukraine.

Foreign ministers became a very tight-knit group, especially those of us in the G7 who were coordinating the sanctions and in daily contact. We were constantly fighting with our treasuries to get the toughest possible sanctions packages and pushing to go further and faster. Despite being from different political stripes—including a German Green, a Canadian Liberal, an Italian Five Star populist, and a British Conservative—we were adamant Russia must lose. Europe was casting off its previous appeasement attitudes to Russia, which was particularly tough for the Germans. I greatly admire them for that. There was a strand of idealism and hope. At the apex were the Ukrainians themselves.

In the run-up to and through the early stages of the war, there was still a tendency, personified in particular by French president Macron, to believe we should engage with Putin. Many long phone calls were made. I was determined to prevent another German- and French-brokered Minsk-style agreement, which had led to the disastrous situation we were in. The United Kingdom and the United States had to be involved. We set up a UK negotiations team to back the Ukrainians and sent in our top officials.

I did as much as I could, making a series of speeches to push for further support for Ukraine and to dampen calls for a negotiated settlement. There was also a misguided fear of escalation. On various occasions, I would discover attempts to water down my lines, which I believed to be down to pressure from the U.S. State Department. Foreign Office officials were frequently on the phone to their U.S. counterparts. Sometimes they would tell me this is where the "new language" had come from; sometimes they would not. Yet I remained steadfast in my belief that Russia should be held to account and contained for the future. The Ukrainians should not be forced to give up any territory, including Crimea. And we should supply everything the Ukrainians needed, including tanks and planes. It was clear that if they weren't dealt with, our countries would fall victim. I laid out my approach in a speech at the Mansion House in March:

> Some argue we shouldn't provide heavy weapons for fear of provoking something worse. But my view is that inaction would be the greatest provocation. This is a time for courage, not for caution . . . We are doubling down. We will keep going further and faster to push Russia out of the whole of Ukraine.

Russia's malign influence wasn't just on Ukraine. The Russian-funded mercenary Wagner Group was destabilizing Africa. The Balkans were also under immense pressure from Russian and Chinese influence, as I was to see on a visit to Sarajevo. It seemed that wherever you looked, the West's uneasy policy of appeasement was resulting in instability.

In June and July, I was constantly on the move, jetting from one summit or meeting to another. I was beginning to lose my rag at this stage on account of the constant travel and pressure. On one particularly difficult morning, I was delayed by half an hour for an event with the Australian prime minister and the Spanish president because of roads being closed off for the Biden presidential motorcade. I started to jump out of my car to remonstrate with the Spanish police and had to be dragged back in by Nick, my private secretary. After a cooling-off period at a sherry bar, I then flew to Paris to engage in further talks at the Quai d'Orsay, the French foreign ministry.

Each time I touched down in the United Kingdom, the domestic political situation seemed to have gotten worse. More revelations were emerging about so-called "partygate." Meanwhile, Conservative MP and government whip Chris Pincher had allegedly been caught engaging in drunken unwanted groping, and there were disputes about who knew what about his alleged past behavior at the time Boris had appointed him to the government.

I had been an early supporter of Boris Johnson in both the 2016 and 2019 leadership elections, and continued to believe he was the best leader for the party. While I had been frustrated by his decision to raise taxes, I knew that had been pursued mainly by Rishi Sunak, the chancellor, whose influence was at the root of several other missteps by the government.

What I wanted was for Boris to deliver on the promises of the 2019 manifesto, on which we had won our large majority. I was dismayed when he and the whole government got bogged down in the "party-gate" and Pincher allegations. Yet I still couldn't believe Conservative MPs would be stupid enough to depose Boris, who had achieved such a convincing win in the 2019 general election. I evidently had my head in the sand.

On Monday, July 4, at the start of what turned out to be a critical week, I was in Lugano in Switzerland for the Ukraine Recovery Conference. I was then back in London for just a day and could sense something was wrong as I wandered around Parliament. But I got on with my day and at 6:00 p.m. went to brief the Euroskeptic caucus, the European Research Group, on my negotiations with the EU.

Just as Sir Iain Duncan Smith was kicking off the meeting, everyone started looking at their phones. The health secretary Sajid Javid had resigned, calling on Boris to quit. I looked at Iain and we decided to persevere with the meeting. Ten minutes later, everyone was looking at their phones again. Chancellor Rishi Sunak had now resigned as well. At that point it became clear the meeting was pointless, and MPs scuttled off to try to figure out what was going on.

The atmosphere was febrile and events were moving fast, but I was due to get on a plane early the next morning destined for the G20 foreign ministers' meeting in Indonesia. The question was whether I should still go. To me, it seemed quite clear: the foreign secretary pulling out of a major international summit would signal that the government was not functioning. I had a job to do, and it was my duty to get on with it.

I couldn't have been headed to a more inconvenient location. Bali is an eighteen-hour flight from London, and the government aircraft on which I was traveling had to refuel several times during the journey. The Wi-Fi on board was sporadic, so it was hard to keep track of the rapid developments back home. Every time we touched down to refuel, more hysterical messages arrived on my phone in the wake of further ministerial resignations. I discussed with my team whether we should return home, but opted to keep on to Indonesia.

We eventually arrived in Bali, at what was essentially a holiday resort. I tried to continue with the planned program of bilateral meetings, but events in the UK were a major distraction—and not just to me. The other foreign ministers were all gripped by the headlines coming out of Westminster throughout Wednesday. I have found this to be a common theme during international diplomacy, where discussion of domestic political troubles can provide a form of light relief. At times, it almost resembled a group therapy session, allowing us to share our troubles and complaints. But on this occasion there was not much sharing by the others. They wanted to ask me what on earth was going on back home in the UK.

It was the following morning, UK time, that the news broke that Boris was going to resign. While it had started to look inevitable, I received no advance notice. Because of the seven-hour time difference, it was already the afternoon for me, and in between meetings I received floods of messages from colleagues in London telling me to get back urgently. When I returned to my hotel room that evening, I turned on the TV to see Boris standing in Downing Street, delivering his resignation statement live to the world.

I now knew I had no choice but to return to Britain. With my boss deposed, any remaining credibility I had at the meeting was draining away fast, and I had to look to the future. As one of my foreign minister counterparts at the summit WhatsApped me: "Get back home woman and start hustling!"

This was easier said than done. The problem was that our government plane wasn't ready. The crew needed to complete their mandated rest time, so they would not be able to fly until the next morning. A commercial flight was not immediately available that evening. So I found myself stranded in paradise, with the run of this beautiful romantic beach resort with my civil servants and special adviser, desperate to leave as the starting gun was being fired on the leadership contest seven thousand miles away.

As I walked along the beach in Indonesia, I started crying. Whatever happened, I knew this period of intense teamwork with fellow travelers from across the free world was over. I knew I would be waving goodbye to the Foreign Office and some of the best people I had ever worked with. I would miss them.

I knew the fight for the future of the Conservative Party would be much less idealistic and much murkier. I knew it would be brutal. But I felt compelled to do it.

And yet there was so much unfinished business at the Foreign Office. We had started to question the post–Cold War policy consensus, but we had not followed through on the full logic of our approach to China and Iran.

The speech President Zelenskyy made in Munich on the eve of the war laid this out. That city was the perfect location for him to call out the appeasement by the West of an aggressor with territorial ambitions in Europe. For Britain, the Munich Agreement between Chamberlain and Hitler now stands as a mark of naïveté and weakness. By failing to stand up to Nazi Germany early enough, we invited the horrors of the Second World War. Now, after failing to stand up to Putin's Russia, we were seeing the inevitable results.

A fatal complacency befell the West in the 1990s. We thought the battle for ideas had been won. The failure to push Russia in the right direction has cost us dearly. The lack of a serious and united response by the West to the annexation of Crimea in 2014 was obviously a massive error and a moral failing. Barack Obama and David Cameron did not participate in the Normandy accords, leaving it instead to the Germans and French to negotiate with Russia. The end result, the Minsk Protocol, effectively ceded power to Russia over Ukrainian land.

The constant refrain we have heard from the Western foreign policy establishment is that "engagement" is the key, that closer economic and trading links will inevitably lead to peace and harmony and to Russia's becoming a modern and liberal democracy. I think we can now conclude this was a misplaced hope.

Even after all we have seen, the voices of appeasement remain loud. Because Putin has not been shy about making bellicose threats, many in the foreign policy establishment have taken up the mantra that we must at all costs "avoid escalation" for fear of provoking a direct confrontation between NATO and Russia.

This has clearly hampered the West's response in Ukraine, and Putin has used that to his advantage. He knows that despite our toughest rhetoric, his possession of nuclear weapons makes an overt military engagement by the West unthinkable in the eyes of many.

If we take the view that it is impossible for Western nations to engage militarily with a country because it possesses nuclear weapons, then we should prepare ourselves for plenty more incursions into sovereign territory. The only thing an aggressor like Putin understands is strength, and we cannot be cowed by his threats and nuclear saber-rattling. This is an issue that we in the free world need to confront head-on.

At almost every point in the current conflict, Putin has drawn red lines backed up by apocalyptic threats. He said Sweden and Finland joining NATO was a red line. He said the U.S. supplying tanks to Ukraine was a red line. In all of these cases, he has been proved to be bluffing. All of this rhetoric is designed to scare us off, and it is part of a deliberate strategy. Fundamentally, you have two alternatives when faced with aggressors: you either take them on, or you hold back from confrontation because you're scared of what they will do. However you dress it up, the second option is simply appeasement. If we give into it, then we deserve to be known as the modern Men and Women of Munich.

I fear we are making the same mistakes with China as we did with Russia. Western nations have persisted in the notion that deepening economic ties will lead to better outcomes, ignoring the very real evidence this has not happened. We have not woken up sufficiently to the threat China poses to our interests and values, as starkly demonstrated by its genocide of the Uighurs and treatment of Hong Kong. More worryingly, we have given the impression that we will at least equivocate as to whether to stand in defense of an independent country under threat from a nuclear superpower. Providing arms and financial support only goes so far, and we have shown that the calls to avoid "escalation" will always hold us back from matching the strength of our enemies.

On Iran, waiting for the regime to sign the JCPOA while they were backing terrorists like Hamas—which is committing appalling atrocities in Israel—and developing their own nuclear capability has proved to be a mistake.

Ultimately, appeasement does not work. History has shown this time and time again. The understandable urge to avoid conflict has meant we will too often tolerate outrageous aggression, sell out those we should protect, and hope that by doing so we will contain the problem and preserve peace. The evidence that our enemies are moving against us has been plain for many years. Hostile acts by Russian and Chinese state interests have targeted us, whether in the field of economic or cyber warfare. The threat of military action has also been shown to be all too real.

The West has to get serious about the new cold war in which we find ourselves. Our enemies understand that. Russia, China, and Iran are working together to destabilize the West and undermine our way of life. Yet we are still undercutting each other to trade with them. We are harming our own economic interests to export jobs to China in the name of Net Zero. We have been allowing infiltration and censorship. As I write this, a suspected spy is being investigated after allegedly gaining access to the chairman of the House of Commons foreign affairs select committee.

The escalation of aggression by our foes calls out for renewed leadership. And this has to start with the leader of the free world, the United States of America. As well as assembling an economic NATO to take on China in the same way allies took on the USSR, more has to be done. The United States must be fearless. It must rearm and build defense capabilities.

We also need a new era of European leadership. This means listening to our Eastern European allies. It means rearming and spending more on defense. It means cutting off our economic dependency on China. And it means an end to the appeasement of Iran.

The conflict has already begun. Our enemies are already fighting it. The only question is whether we take them on or allow them to win by default.

CHAPTER 10

The Battle for the Conservative Party

When I arrived back in London after the G20 ministers' meeting in Bali on the Friday following Boris's resignation, my house was already filled with a motley crew of advisers and friends eager to get behind my nascent leadership campaign. We set to work. That weekend we had a lot of MPs over for chats and I recorded my campaign launch video in the back garden.

Why was I standing to be leader? I felt compelled to. I knew that without Boris's charisma or any bold policy changes, we risked pushing our country and our party into a cul-de-sac. I had a very clear idea of what needed to be done. I'd been thinking about these things for over a decade. This was the last chance to change Britain in a positive way before the next general election. I had come to the conclusion that there wasn't anyone else who both shared this vision and could win.

I was also being egged on by my supporters who wanted a champion of Conservative ideas to run. Not everyone was so positive. My husband Hugh said it would be impossible to lead the party, given the level of infighting and nihilism demonstrated by the removal of Boris. The Conservatives were too divided to back any decisive course of action, he said. But even Hugh, who predicted it would all end in tears, accepted that this was the moment I was expected to run and that if I didn't, people would say I had bottled it. Ian Sherwood, my political agent in my Norfolk constituency, also thought I should run—but he thought it would be for the best if I came second.

There is no doubt I was underprepared, both for the contest and the prospect of winning. Unlike some, I had not been spending my time in government plotting a leadership bid. I'd always become engrossed in the job I was doing to the exclusion of almost everything else. This was true whether I was dealing with floods or hammering out trade deals. By this point, as foreign secretary, the job was 24/7, and all the more so since the start of the war in Ukraine. I might occasionally have discussed the political situation with my special advisers or close friends, but the notion of standing for leader had remained a distant prospect.

What I really lacked was any kind of political infrastructure that could help me deliver the radical, transformative program Britain needed. This was partly because the British system tends to underfund and shut out political expertise; the people who shared my beliefs generally did not have government experience or understand how the system operates. And the people who do understand how the system operates generally do not want to change it. So in the absence of such an operation, the enthusiastic group in my house became my core team.

We were playing catch-up on account of my enforced sojourn in Bali. The focus at this stage of the contest was on Conservative MPs, who would whittle down the various candidates to a final two to be put to a vote of several hundred thousand grassroots party members. I gave the team assembled at my house in Greenwich a pep talk. Misquoting

Superintendent Hastings from the BBC police drama *Line of Duty*, I said, "There's only one thing we care about and that's Tory MPs" (Hastings only cares about "bent coppers").

There were 358 Conservative MPs at that time. The leadership candidates would be winnowed down through a series of exhaustive ballots, with the lowest-performing candidate excluded after each round. To guarantee a place among the final two, I would have to secure the support of 120 MPs in the last round. After that, it would go to a nationwide vote of Conservative members who would have the final say on the new leader.

The center of gravity of the Conservative parliamentary party is significantly to the left of party members in the country on pretty much every issue. And during my nearly fourteen years in Parliament, I have noticed a further shift to the left. MPs who used to talk about limited government and cutting regulation have increasingly been championing Net Zero, pushing for gender self-identification, and opposing fracking. Sometimes this is because they haven't told the truth when getting selected by their local parties. While beating their chests and calling for free markets and controlled immigration in the selection meetings, they vote the opposite way when they get to Westminster. These shape-shifters are "conservatives in name only" (CINOs).

It's certainly true that others have gradually moved to the left during their parliamentary careers. Away from normal daily life in Britain and surrounded by pressure groups and lobbyists for causes that more often than not demand more state intervention or higher government spending, their political compasses go faulty. Twitter has shortened attention spans, and MPs are intimidated by social media storms. Operating in the world of Whitehall and quangos where leftism is the prevailing ethos, it can be easy to think this is the way of the world. And with backbench and ministerial positions not being particularly well-paid, the prospect of a well-remunerated corporate job after service in politics is attractive. They are thus influenced to appease or adopt leftist positions.

COVID had meant most MPs were away from the parliamentary estate for much of 2020 and 2021, as a socially distanced chamber could only accommodate a fraction of our number. Hybrid sittings with video links became the temporary norm. This had a particularly disruptive effect on the 106 Conservative MPs who were newly elected in December 2019, many of whom were swept in when we captured the so-called "Red Wall" of seats formerly held by Labour. They were isolated at home and had been given little time prior to the pandemic to get to know and work directly with their new colleagues.

Much of Westminster politics is conducted in the members' tea room and the members' smoking room (although the Labour government's blanket ban on smoking indoors put paid to this ever again being a smoke-filled room). It is in these places that thoughts and ideas are shared, political friendships are developed, and a sense of camaraderie is built. WhatsApp groups, on the other hand, seem to promote mutiny—as we had already seen with the divisive removal of Boris.

British parties are broad coalitions and there have always been Conservative MPs who happily place themselves to the left of the party's center. Margaret Thatcher had to deal with the "wets," and ultimately they removed her from office. They tend to describe themselves as "One Nation" Conservatives and are similar to the "Country Club Republicans" in the United States. They believe in state paternalism rather than full-blown socialism, a tradition embodied by former prime minister Harold Macmillan. There is a strong sense of noblesse oblige about it, and in the modern era, a good dose of liberal guilt too. A common refrain of these Tories is that "we need to be on the right side of history." They are therefore much more willing to defer to supposedly "independent" institutions and accept the prevailing orthodoxy in government and the public sector. From remaining close to the EU to being pro-China, they don't really want any change to the status quo. A less charitable interpretation is they are engaged in appeasing the Left.

There are then Conservative MPs who are on the right on matters like immigration, Net Zero, and wokeism. As the Conservative Party has secured new seats in the North of England, there has been a growing focus on these issues. However, some of these MPs are under the impression that merely tinkering with an already bloated state can help back traditional families or revive industry. Under this belief, having big government isn't necessarily antithetical to being a Conservative; it just needs to be a Conservative big government. This is a forlorn hope. If government grows too big, it inevitably seeks to replace families, parents, free markets, businesses, and communities. And the UK's government is already spending 46 percent of GDP; just how much bigger should it get?

While I share the desire to take on wokeism, redistributionism, and the worst excesses of the environmental movement, I believe fundamentally that this is best driven by individuals and families, not the government. Those of us who believe in Popular Conservatism, or a modernized version of Thatcherism, believe in the nation-state, low taxes, and individual responsibility.

My description above implies there are a number of logical groups among Conservative MPs. Nothing could be further from the truth. The Conservative Party is a constantly swirling constellation affected by current events and electoral geography. Its members differ on key issues like Net Zero, but they also differ on approach: whether or not the governance of Britain needs a shake-up or whether what people want is competent technocracy. Are Britain's institutions part of the solution or part of the problem? The party can also reflect different backgrounds. Those from humbler origins or who are self-made tend to rail more against the corporatist establishment. They feel the hunger to succeed and the pain of the odds being stacked against them by the state, public subsidies, and cronyism.

The battle over popular influence has been raging in Britain since the dawn of democracy. Elements of the establishment have tried to prevent the widening of the political process from including the mass of the population. Victorian grandees such as the Conservative prime minister Lord Salisbury were highly critical of the growth of democracy, arguing that it would lead to chaos and the rule of the mob. Similar arguments were made over extending the franchise to working-class voters.

While it's unacceptable to make such overtly anti-democratic and elitist arguments today, many of the same underlying attitudes persist. The new elites are not just in Parliament but in the permanent administrative state and its associated institutions. Within these, there is an almost contemptuous disregard for party politics and the popular will. We saw this with the Brexit referendum and the election of Donald Trump in the United States. In both cases, a popular uprising was resisted by public officials and the wider political establishment.

Of course, there need to be checks and balances in place in any political system, and civil servants should always be able to offer honest and unvarnished advice to politicians. But there also has to be an understanding that democracy means allowing people to choose the leaders and the policies they wish.

Too many Conservatives understand the need to win popular support for policies in elections but have a distaste for the views of many of their supporters. They see "populism" as a threat that needs to be contained. When it comes to internal party democracy, their attitude toward the views of the Conservative membership is similarly contemptuous. They privately consider it to have been a huge mistake to widen the franchise for the election of the party leader to rank-and-file members.

Much of the leadership election of the summer of 2022 was about this divide. I was of the view that the UK needed significant change and that we needed to be proud of being Conservatives. In particular, I believed the economic orthodoxy of low growth, high taxes, and high spending funded by the government's printing money and artificially suppressing interest rates was unsustainable. It needed to be ended as soon as possible. This would mean challenging the economic establishment, including the Treasury, the Office for Budget Responsibility, and the Bank of England. We also needed to be tougher on China and Russia and play hardball with the EU. I argued that without urgent change we were heading for declining living standards and electoral defeat.

Although my eventual opponent in the runoff, Rishi Sunak, tacked toward my position on a number of issues—namely China and taxes—he was fundamentally the candidate of the status quo. He had run British economic policy for the previous two and a half years. He argued that by continuing with existing policies we could avoid interest rate hikes, runaway inflation, and low growth, and that merely through competent management he could put the Conservatives back on the right path.

Winning over MPs was an uphill struggle. It was a classic exercise in political intrigue and gamesmanship, as the rival campaigns sought to sign up parliamentarians. This involved me in a constant round of meetings and phone calls with colleagues from across the party, seeking their support. I knew this would be the toughest part of the process and that if I could get through it, I would have a very good chance with the membership.

To be self-critical, I think it's fair to say I have perhaps not spent enough time during my career listening to and empathizing with my parliamentary colleagues. And I probably have not done a very good job of hiding what I think about some of them either!

Now I was thrown into a speed-dating exercise, in which I was required to meet and listen to any MP who wanted some of my time. One, for instance, was on the phone with me for half an hour, methodically running through a list of questions, including seeking my view on a certain type of technology. Others wanted to stick with groups of their friends and came to see me together, listing their pet policy issues and making clear that if I satisfied them, they would back me. It was pure political horse-trading.

If that felt grubby and transactional, it was nothing compared to those who nakedly sought to trade their votes for promises of future advancement. Some did this in a roundabout way, telling me, for example, of skills they had recently learned that they felt would make them a good minister. Others were utterly brazen about it. I got a text message from one MP who told me he wanted a particular ministerial job, with a specific list of responsibilities and a seat in the Cabinet. It ended with, "Please confirm you agree to this." I did not.

Amid all this, I was aware my team was playing at a considerable disadvantage compared to our rivals in the Sunak campaign. While my campaign had been thrown together in a hurry and consisted of my handful of special advisers and a few long-standing allies, Sunak had a well-resourced and well-staffed operation from the outset. It was hard not to conclude that his lieutenants had been preparing for this contest for quite some time. Experienced former chief whips and senior ministers and party grandees had been signed up long ago and had been doing the rounds of MPs well in advance of Boris's resignation. This played its part in bringing down the prime minister, with rumors abounding that junior ministers and ministerial aides were being told by figures on the Sunak campaign team in those final couple of days after Rishi had resigned that if they wanted a place on the new team, they would have to join the revolt against Boris and step down at once. Many duly did.

The ruthless tactics that had been used to help bring down Boris were now turned on Sunak's rivals for the leadership. Whilst there was never any suggestion that Rishi himself indulged in such behavior, reports were circulating that MPs were cajoled and pressured by some of his most zealous backers with not particularly subtle threats that if they didn't sign up, they would be permanently out in the cold. I learned it had been the same story in 2005, when the hard-nosed team around David Davis, the early favorite in that year's leadership contest, made similar threats to ambitious colleagues about their future careers if they didn't back their man. He too ended up coming in second.

There was also the suspicion of even less savory activities. A dossier was circulating among journalists containing offensive personal fictions about me, while other malicious gossip began to do the rounds. While the provenance of all of this was shrouded in mystery, my team had to spend precious time responding to even the most ludicrous of these false allegations.

As well as individual meetings, there was a plethora of hustings for different groups of MPs—the European Research Group, the One Nation caucus, the Conservative Environment Network, the Northern Research Group, and so on. Generally speaking, I outperformed expectations here. Spending ten years in government and regularly being sent onto the airwaves to give voice to the line on any number of questions that might arise is useful training for knowing about every policy issue. In particular, I had very clear ideas on how to deal with the EU that appealed to Euroskeptics.

The whole parliamentary hustings process demonstrated just how many factions the parliamentary party had divided into. Many esoteric issues were raised. My overriding focus was on the economic situation, but I got the impression that many MPs simply didn't understand what a mess we were in. As well as matters of policy, some of them were simply interested in knowing how I planned to win the next election—or, more accurately, how I would help them keep their seats.

There were also debates on Channel 4 and ITV, which I found hair-raising. I'd never done a TV debate before in my life and I hadn't had time for enough focused practice beforehand, partly because everything had been so frantic with the endless meetings around Parliament. I hadn't given a second thought to my outfit. Everyone else was slicker and more polished. Afterward, I could tell just by looking at my team's faces that they thought I had bombed.

I was put straight in an urgent boot camp led by Rob Butler, an MP and former broadcaster who was far scarier than anyone who ended up interviewing me for real. The pussy-bow blouse I'd worn for the first debate was banned. Kwasi Kwarteng, a close friend and political ally also from the 2010 intake of MPs, advised having half a glass of wine before going on air. I put in a better performance during the second debate.

The weather during those weeks was stiflingly hot for Britain—up to 40 degrees Celsius, or 104 degrees Fahrenheit—and the lack of air-conditioning meant Parliament was particularly stuffy and airless. It all added to a feeling of claustrophobia and simmering tension. This initial stage of the contest took place over the course of a week, with five ballots of MPs between July 13 and 20. At each stage, the lowest-scoring candidate was eliminated, and there followed further machinations between the remaining candidates to secure their support and the votes of their supporters. It was all very tense and, as ever, there were some very Machiavellian tactics being employed.

On the final MPs' ballot, Rishi secured the most votes with 137, while I narrowly secured second place with 113 to Penny Mordaunt's 105. This was rather closer than I had anticipated from our private tallies of supporters, proving the eternal truth of Tory leadership contests: Conservative MPs comprise the most duplicitous electorate in Christendom.

My support therefore equated to slightly less than one-third of the parliamentary party. Some backed me because they firmly believed in my agenda, others because they liked me personally—and some because they disliked Sunak and his team. It was enough to get me onto the final ballot, but it was a rather fragile coalition on which to rely. This was later to become a significant problem.

I was relieved to have made it through this tortuous Westminster ordeal and to be able to take my case to party members in the country. I was confident I would beat Sunak, and opinion polls of members quickly showed I was the firm favorite. My biggest worry had been about getting through the parliamentary stage of the contest, where I knew my support was weaker. Now I felt much more confident of victory.

The campaign moved outside Westminster, with six weeks of hustings and events around the country, including two more television debates to add to those that had taken place during the parliamentary rounds. There were far too many such events scheduled, with the party organization having gone completely overboard. It became something of a circus, particularly with the debates.

In the meantime, the problems were piling up in the Downing Street in tray and storm clouds were gathering over the British economy. And, of course, the public was being viscerally exposed to all the splits within the Conservative Party. I thought the length of the process and the exposed public nature of it was extremely damaging. Alongside the defenestration of Boris, this prolonged period of infighting irreparably damaged the party in the polls.

The debates were the worst part. I'm always happy to debate policy, but the one-on-one format was terrible and encouraged "blue-on-blue" attacks. I found it a complete ordeal and had to be pumped up in the green room beforehand, often with a soundtrack of Queen and Whitney Houston hits. The debates seemed more about character analysis than serious policy. One topic that came up was the fact that I get my earrings at Claire's Accessories, a budget high street jewelry shop beloved of teenagers. This was interpreted as an attempt by me to be a woman of the people. In fact, it's simply because I hate the idea of getting my ears pierced.

I may have been dreading the debates, but one person who fared even worse was Kate McCann, who hosted the debate on TalkTV. While I was answering a question on live television, she fainted on the podium. The debate was immediately abandoned with huge concern over what had happened to her. Mercifully she was fine, but the whole episode—which took place on my birthday—only added to the surreal nature of the contest.

Throughout the campaign, I found the personal attacks hard to stomach, as well as completely unnecessary. I am used to being shot at by the Labour Party and by commentators. But to hear colleagues I had worked with for years describe me variously as "immoral" or "an electoral suicide note" was very upsetting. I shut myself off from the media because I just couldn't take it. Whereas in previous contests there had been efforts to avoid trashing the party's brand, the assault on my policies was personal and no-holds-barred.

The best bits of the campaign were when I spoke to party members in gardens, football clubs, church halls, and pubs. I felt liberated to rip up the government "lines to take" document and say what I really thought for the first time in years. The positive response showed that the grassroots and I were in tune with each other. On everything from solar farms (I hate them) to women not having penises to quangos being too powerful to taxes being too high, we were on the same page. In town after town, I found Conservative members rooted in their local areas understanding what needed to be done far better than the party HQ's focus groups.

A particular highlight was the GB News event at the Bedford Sports and Social Club in Leigh hosted by veteran broadcaster Alastair Stewart. Leigh, a northern industrial town on the outskirts of Manchester, was one of the new seats we had gained in the 2019 election for the first time ever, and my policies got a great response from the invited audience, comprised mainly of local Conservative members. It gave me hope that this policy agenda had public appeal.

I was clearly winning the argument with the members, but the campaign itself was not all plain sailing. My campaign team was run by Mark Fullbrook and my long-serving adviser Ruth Porter, along with a collection of my other special advisers and allies. Without time to prepare, everything had to be done on the hoof. We were building the car at the same time we were driving along. I was never in the campaign HQ myself, as I was constantly on the road going from event to event, accompanied by aides, most of whom I had only just met.

I felt like I was not in control and just had to trust them to get on with it. This led to some missteps, most notably when a press release was sent out without my knowledge raising the prospect of regional pay bargaining in the public sector, which caused a furor and had to be awkwardly disavowed. That was perhaps the trickiest moment, and the Sunak team inevitably made hay with the error.

Compared to my opponent's slick operation, we had had less time to prepare detailed briefs. That was fine in one sense. Because I had spent years thinking about this agenda and had long been making these arguments in private, it all came off naturally. But it left me feeling like a one-man band—the policy person, the front man, and the organizer. I was often working off the cuff. It was a frustrating and isolating experience.

To make it worse, while I was traversing the United Kingdom, Hugh, Frances, and Liberty were enjoying the holiday I had booked and organized in Florida. They sent me daily pictures of themselves relaxing on the beach, riding rollercoasters, or eating unfeasibly large stacks of pancakes.

Until the final hustings event was done, I couldn't properly relax, despite the polls continuing to give me a solid lead. Only as we entered the last couple of weeks was I able to turn my attention to planning for the likely prospect of victory. I was staying at Chevening during those closing stages, and it was there that we started a round of discreet meetings with senior civil servants to prepare for the transition to power. I spent hours talking through plans with my senior aides and close allies like Thérèse Coffey and Kwasi Kwarteng, who were set to become my deputy prime minister and chancellor, respectively.

On Monday, September 5, I waited with my team in one of the many concrete rooms of the Queen Elizabeth II Conference Center in the heart of Westminster. Rishi Sunak and his team were also there. Sir Graham Brady, the chairman of the 1922 Committee who was acting as returning officer, asked Sunak and me to each bring one person to hear the result. I brought Hugh and Sunak brought Oliver Dowden, the MP chairing his leadership campaign.

Brady told us I had won the leadership contest by 81,326 votes to Sunak's 60,399. I commiserated with Sunak and he congratulated me. I was very pleased to win, and it was a huge relief just to have ended the uncertainty. But as always, my mind raced ahead to what I would have to do next. I was to make a speech to the large audience of MPs and party members who were waiting downstairs. I knew that every word I uttered and every move I made would be under the microscope.

We all went downstairs to a packed hall for the official announcement. Once the result had been publicly revealed, I took to the stage to make my acceptance speech and declared:

> I know that our beliefs resonate with the British people—our beliefs in freedom, in the ability to control your own life, in low taxes, in personal responsibility—and I know that's why people voted for us in such numbers in 2019. And as your party leader, I intend to deliver what we promised those voters right across our great country.

During this leadership campaign, I campaigned as a
Conservative and I will govern as a Conservative. My friends,
we need to show that we will deliver over the next two years.
I will deliver a bold plan to cut taxes and grow our economy.

I was hugely proud to have been elected leader of the oldest and
most successful political party in the Western world. But I knew there
would be battles ahead. In choosing me as leader, the Conservative
Party had voted for bold action and a clear direction. My campaign
might have been messy, but it had chimed with the instincts of the
membership. They had ultimately rejected technocracy.

The Conservative rank and file might have placed their faith in me,
but my colleagues in Westminster were another story. A majority of
them had supported my rivals in the final MPs' ballot, and a significant
number of them remained actively opposed to me. It seemed that even
though the votes had been counted, significant elements of the Sunak
leadership campaign had not given up.

I had difficult decisions to make about appointing a Cabinet and the
wider team of almost one hundred other ministers. There were a lot of
people who considered themselves to be current Cabinet ministers: all
the existing ones plus those who had resigned from Cabinet jobs very
recently. There were also the other contenders in the leadership election, all of whom had put in a good performance and were impressive
people. Add to that the fact that during thirteen years in government,
many MPs had felt they were unfairly passed over for a promotion or
unfairly sacked. It was impossible to please them all.

During the bruising leadership campaign, I had frankly lost trust in
many of my erstwhile ministerial colleagues who were supporting my
opponent. They had spent the last six weeks not just attacking me but
seeking to undermine my plans, saying my agenda was unworkable.
Even after it was clear their candidate wasn't going to win, they carried

on trashing me and the Conservative brand. Rishi himself had made it clear he didn't want a role. I was very doubtful that I could trust some of the others on his team, or that they would be prepared to implement the Conservative agenda on which I had been elected. Their outright hostility had made it almost impossible for me to appoint them.

So I put together a team of trusted allies, including some who had been rivals in the leadership election like Penny Mordaunt and Kemi Badenoch, and also some Sunak supporters who I believed were capable and willing to serve conscientiously in my administration. Frankly, I never want to see another reshuffle board again in my life—yes, the British government really is appointed with the aid of a whiteboard and dozens of Post-it notes. Of course, it was impossible to include everyone, and no doubt there were good people I left out. There were others who were going to be a problem inside or outside the tent. I knew they would cause me trouble from the backbenches, but I thought I wouldn't be able to get anything done with them inside the government.

So it was that I would now embark on my ambitious agenda as prime minister with a starkly divided party. I had gotten through the leadership election with a hastily assembled team who had delivered an impressive victory against the establishment favorite. We were a small band of insurgents with big ideas for change. With a mandate from the membership, I was now going to set about implementing my agenda. Even if my parliamentary colleagues had reservations about it, I expected them to at least respect my right to deliver what I'd promised.

The campaign had ultimately been a success, but for me it had highlighted some of the major issues facing the Conservative Party. The fact that my agenda was seen as controversial by a number of its leading figures was profoundly worrying. For years, I have been concerned that in both the United Kingdom and the United States the Conservative and Republican parties have lost their way and been outgunned by the Left.

Sound principles of smaller government and lower taxes seem to have fallen out of fashion. Too often the Left has been appeased.

How has this happened, and what can we do about it? Both parties urgently need to find their way back to a position where they can recapture the kind of electoral support they enjoyed in the 1980s. It seems to me that on both sides of the Atlantic, a good place to start is by rediscovering the winning economic formula that drove success over the course of that decade. That was what I was trying to prompt the Conservative Party to do in 2022. What the leadership contest revealed, however, was how out of step many in Parliament were with the views of the wider membership. In the battle between democrats and technocrats, the democrats seemed to have won. But as I was to discover, the technocrats had the full force of the administrative state on their side.

CHAPTER 11

Downing Street

In my acceptance speech on being elected as Conservative leader, I ended with the declaration "We will deliver, we will deliver, and we will deliver." Having won power, I was determined to implement what I had promised. But from the outset, delivery turned out to be a problem.

This was literally true, as Hugh discovered when he attempted to get our usual supermarket grocery order delivered to us in our new home. First of all, he had to convince Ocado it wasn't a hoax and that, yes, he really did want it delivered to 10 Downing Street. Then he had to work out where they could drop it off, whether the police would let them bring it inside the security cordon, if someone would then be able to sign for it, and so on. When the shopping didn't arrive, he called Ocado, only to be told that the order had actually been received some time ago. It seemed that Number 10 officials had indeed taken delivery of it but did not want to disturb the prime minister!

It was an early example of how isolating it is for a prime minister to live "above the shop" in Downing Street. Although our tenure was short, it was quite long enough to experience the pros and cons of the arrangement. I'm not sure it would be rated well on Airbnb.

Like every prime minister since Tony Blair, we actually occupied the apartment above Number 11, which is bigger than the one above Number 10. Arranged on several floors, it was in fact larger in terms of floor space than our existing family home, more like a house than a flat. Surprisingly spacious though it was, overall it felt a bit soulless.

With the Johnsons having taken their furniture with them, the Civil Service had equipped our new quarters with various bits of John Lewis furniture seized from around the government estate. We ordered some of our own, but in any event we were evicted before it could be delivered.

Although there were some fancy curtains, disappointingly there was no gold wallpaper, contrary to press reports about Boris and his wife Carrie's redecoration. Even less welcome, the place was infested with fleas. Although some claimed that this was down to Boris and Carrie's dog, Dilyn, there was no conclusive evidence. In any case the entire place had to be sprayed with flea killer. I spent several weeks itching.

It was also really noisy. Being in Central London, there were the expected sounds of traffic, police sirens, and so on. But in addition there was an almost constant backdrop of chanting and shouting through megaphones from the variety of protesters camped out on Whitehall opposite the gates of Downing Street. Then there was the clock on nearby Horse Guards, which chimed every quarter of an hour. If you were lying awake unable to sleep at night, you could time exactly how long your insomnia lasted. And I did.

The saving grace at Number 10 was Larry the cat. He is a lovely character and seems to take a liking and disliking to all the right people.

The most difficult thing to get used to, however, was just being stuck there. During my year as foreign secretary I had become used to having personal security protection, which meant being accompanied wherever I went by armed Special Branch police officers. But I had largely continued to follow my usual routine, which often included popping out of the side door of the Foreign Office to go for a walk in St. James's Park or to go and have lunch in Honi Poke, my favorite Hawaiian joint. I was occasionally spotted by photographers and the police were always following close behind, but I still had some freedom of movement.

As prime minister, such spontaneous excursions were now all but impossible. I was effectively a prisoner in Downing Street. If I wanted to go anywhere I would have to be driven, and plans had to be put in place in advance to ensure the route and venue were secure. As someone who likes to go out for fresh air and exercise, this was a huge restriction. I particularly missed being able to get my own coffee, and instead had to tell someone else what I wanted from Pret.

If I insisted on going for a run or a walk, arrangements were made for me to be driven to a quiet bit of Hyde Park or to a private garden somewhere. But even this just felt like I was being allowed out into the prison exercise yard. After some brief respite in the open air, I would be bundled into the armored car and taken back inside the ring of steel. As a way of life, the experience was intensely claustrophobic.

It had an immediate practical impact on my ability to keep in touch with those outside the walls and gates. I felt cut off from anyone beyond my immediate circle of advisers and officials, which was exacerbated by the fact that my mobile had apparently been compromised during the leadership campaign and I'd had to change my number. Even if this hadn't happened, the pace of events and pressure of the work meant I would not have been able to keep up with the flood of texts from people wanting to press their cause or offer unsolicited advice. There is often talk of a "bunker mentality" in Number 10, and it is easy to see how it comes about. You are reliant on the small number of people with whom you spend your day, and outsiders cannot easily reach you. Despite being at the apex of government and the subject of intense focus from huge numbers of people, it is a surprisingly isolated position.

Since leaving, I have lost count of the number of former colleagues and friends who have said, "Liz, if only you'd called me, I could have helped." But the reality is they couldn't have. They weren't in Number 10, and the system does a very good job of keeping outsiders at bay. It's also less advice that's required and more implementation. This has been a problem I've experienced in every ministerial job I've done, from the very start of my time in government. The system is incredibly nonporous.

When I was looking to reform justice or sell a trade deal, I might have wanted to consult outside views, but the barriers to doing that are significant. There are constant questions about who you've met and why, and every contact has to be recorded and scrutinized. Every meeting is treated with suspicion, and the Freedom of Information Act (FOI) means that innocent meetings are privy to the press and often deliberately misconstrued—yet another problem created by Tony Blair (although in the case of FOI he has at least since admitted his error).

The result is that ministers' offices become a closed loop in which you are reliant on a few people you can trust who filter all the information you receive. It's even harder to bring outsiders into the Civil Service, whatever their expertise. In Number 10, I faced the same problem but on steroids. I am someone who likes to shoot the breeze and bat ideas back and forth, but as prime minister there was precious little opportunity to do that, even if I could have found the time.

My most trusted confidant is Hugh. I first met Hugh at the Conservative Party Conference in Blackpool in 1997—just after the

Conservatives had suffered a monumental defeat. I was just as politically obsessed then. We discovered we were both political activists living around the corner from each other in Greenwich. When we got married in 2000, Hugh said in his wedding speech that he knew what he was letting himself in for with a deeply politically ambitious wife.

I'm not sure even he, with an uncanny habit of predicting the future, could have realized just how insane things would become. If it was a rollercoaster ride for me, it was even more discombobulating for our family. Frances and Liberty—ages sixteen and fourteen at the time—had been to Number 10 a few times before but had never visited the flat. They were given helpful advice by previous occupants, but nothing could have prepared them for the sheer craziness.

Before we were able to move into Number 10, we had traveled from Chevening to a government flat in the Admiralty Buildings, a stone's throw from Downing Street. Much as we would have liked to have gone back to Greenwich, it was completely unrealistic. The place was swarming with media. So the weekend just before they were due to start the new school term, with Frances starting her A-Levels, they moved to Westminster. The day I entered Number 10 they were driven off to school.

During the time I was in Number 10, I saw quite a lot of them, but frankly I was pretty distracted. There were the constant comings and goings of Downing Street aides, civil servants, special advisers, and my hairdresser, Paul. We never had time to talk about the massive life change it was. They also had to keep running errands for me because it was easier for them to leave the buildings without being spotted than it was for me. I'm pleased that they managed to fit in a sleepover with their friends. And they did get to visit the nuclear bunker.

I am very proud of the way Frances and Liberty dealt with what happened. They insisted on standing alongside Hugh in Downing Street when I gave my valedictory statement. My greatest fear was that the whole thing would have some kind of negative effect on them. My biggest worry was that I had let them down.

Most children find out about the fallibilities of their parents over a number of years. Mine saw all of mine publicly exposed in very short order.

On entering the day-to-day working part of Number 10, the first thing to strike me was just how small the operation was. When I walked into the Ministry of Justice, the Department of International Trade, or the Foreign Office, there were literally thousands of people there running the administration and providing support to me as the secretary of state in charge of the department. By contrast, in Number 10, there were perhaps just over one hundred staff working directly for the Prime Minister's Office. The building itself still feels more like the Georgian terraced townhouse that it is rather than a modern government headquarters.

This partly reflects the fact that the prime minister was historically more like the chairman of the board than a hands-on chief executive. Secretaries of state were expected to get on with the business of government, with the prime minister providing strategic direction from the center and focusing on the big decisions. But over many years, the expectation has grown that Number 10 would be much more directly involved in every aspect of government. I thought that was a mistake and had told MPs during the leadership campaign that I wanted to do things differently.

I had lots of thoughts about how to change the real facts on the ground: not pandering to the twenty-four-hour media cycle, involving the Whips' Office directly in decision-making, not having a parallel operation in Number 10. It's fair to say these attempted changes fell flat.

I wanted Cabinet ministers to be empowered to make decisions in their departments and be responsible for doing so. I would appoint them and give them clear objectives but would not seek to micromanage. This strategy did not work. The centralization of power in Number 10 has become so ingrained that it was very hard to break. I was astonished to find, for example, that at the time of the party conference nearly a month after I took office, one of the most senior members of the Cabinet still hadn't got a media special adviser. It turned out that the appointment had not yet been "signed off by Number 10." In my view, Cabinet ministers should be able to appoint people to such roles without having to jump through the hoops of getting approval from Downing Street.

The prime minister has the power to block things, but it is much harder to instigate them. This becomes a recipe for inaction.

It's a small example, but it was symptomatic of the way Number 10 had become ever more focused on the minutiae, seeking to run the entire government itself rather than concentrating on political strategy. The apparent need to be across everything was driven in part by the increased pressure from the news media, which has come to expect and even demand that each and every news story requires a response from Number 10. I wanted to get away from that, but it proved extremely difficult to change the culture. In the short term, however, my determination to try a new approach led me to put perhaps too much trust in the Treasury to manage the run-up to the mini-budget. But more on that later.

The centralization of power in Number 10 has been a long-term trend and was accelerated by Margaret Thatcher and then Tony Blair during their lengthy tenures in office. They had large majorities and were in dominant political positions in any case. But the expectation has now become baked into the system, so that even prime ministers in a relatively weak position are subject to the expectation that they can run the whole show from the center.

We have created a system where the prime minister is treated like a president but has nothing like the kind of institutional support for the office that we would expect in a presidential system. The civil servants and political staff do their best, but they end up having to cobble together very limited resources while barely managing to cope with the intense demands.

I simply didn't have enough trusted senior people on the political side who could immediately get to grips with the immense challenges of running a government. Here, I think there is a real systemic problem of a lack of supply. The reason we don't have them is clear. In government departments, Cabinet ministers are now able to recruit two or three special advisers as political appointees, but the nature of the job and the pay means these are invariably younger, politically committed people in their twenties and thirties. There simply aren't the resources to hire more experienced hands in their forties and fifties with substantial career experience.

Special advisers then spend a few years doing the job before realizing the hours are ludicrous and the rewards limited, and then they cash in by going to work in PR or lobbying for more money and an easier life. Those who want to remain in politics and progress in their careers only have the option of entering elected politics themselves and trying to become MPs.

This once again comes back to the issue of the permanent Civil Service and the fact that the most senior officials in government are entirely drawn from its ranks. That is where staffers can truly climb the ladder and earn big salaries, but in order to do so they must take a Trappist vow never to sully themselves with party politics. Anyone with any political ambitions or overt affiliations is required to renounce them or leave. In reality, of course, those who spend their lives handling policy and working in government do have political opinions. We just require them to keep quiet.

This dam is increasingly breaking. There is a growing culture of leaks. I found after many of the meetings I had with officials and ministers that misreporting would appear in the papers within hours. This makes it an extremely difficult environment in which to work. Having so little control over who was working with me and their ultimately not reporting to me or my colleagues was a major problem.

Increasingly, officials also want to have a public voice after life in government. With Sue Gray now working for the Labour Party, former permanent secretary at the Department for Education Jonathan Slater making outspoken remarks about schools, and numerous former Treasury permanent secretaries expressing their opinions publicly, it is becoming increasingly ludicrous to claim the system is working.

Special advisers and other political appointees are a tiny minority, and they inevitably get drawn into handling media issues and short-term political problems. What we are lacking is the ability for ministers to make appointments of the senior figures who will actually lead the implementation of their policies and run the parts of government for which they will then be held responsible. This lack of political infrastructure is a much greater problem for Conservatives, as government officials tend towards the left.

I think it would be much fairer and more honest for ministers to decide which senior officials to appoint directly. In the United States, the system includes a much greater role for political appointees at the top of government departments, while also retaining a large number of nonpartisan career officials who serve as administrators at the lower and mid-ranking levels. With the growing power and reach of the administrative state, there are problems getting things done in the United States, especially for conservatives. The UK is even worse.

As it stands, the British prime minister has to operate with a limited number of political advisers grafted onto the official Civil Service machine. I was able to bring with me some media SpAds, policy people, and a political team under a chief of staff, Mark Fullbrook, who was well respected as a political strategist. But none of them had experience working at the top of government, and in the particularly hostile environment I encountered, that made their jobs difficult.

In finding capable people to fill these roles, I was also hampered by the fact that after twelve years of Conservative governments, many of the likely candidates had either moved on or had been working for my opponent in the leadership race. I was very grateful to all of those who came in to help, some of whom had worked for me loyally for years, but they faced an uphill battle from the outset. When things got tough, the limitations of this operation became all too clear.

There were many superstars working in my private office, but they didn't necessarily have the levers or reach to make things happen. The Cabinet secretary in some ways acts as the prime minister's senior official, but has wider responsibilities for the running of the whole Civil Service. Within Number 10 itself, the prime minister's private office is led by the principal private secretary, as is the case in other government departments. The whole structure was very confusing.

It was not just the lack of experienced political operatives and confused official leadership that caused me frustration. I found the lack of personal support for the prime minister pretty shocking too. As I recounted at the start of the chapter, Hugh spent a lot of time sorting out basic logistics so we could eat, among other things, while also doing a full-time job. I also spent a lot of time on quite basic tasks: despite now being one of the most photographed people in the country, I had to spend time organizing my own hair and makeup appointments. Don't get me wrong, there were great people like Clare Evans, who had worked with me at the Foreign Office on events and had come to Number 10, who supported me on this. But it wasn't exactly in her job description!

There was also no medical support, as I have already pointed out in reference to how badly COVID affected Boris. On one occasion when I had a cough, my diary secretary had to go out in the middle of the night to buy me some medicine. This clearly wasn't her job, but there was no one else to ask.

As well as being personally inconvenient, all of these things took precious bandwidth away from me. Here I was as prime minister of a major G7 country, grappling with affairs of state, and I was having to spend time worrying about when I was going to be able to get my hair done. It all added to a sense that the support systems were just not there to allow me to focus on the job I had been elected to do.

* * *

My private secretary was out of breath. It was the evening of October 12, and he had rushed up to the flat to find me with some urgent news. A commercial aircraft flying from Turkey to Manchester was "causing concern" as it headed towards our airspace, and a security alert had been declared. Royal Air Force Typhoon jets had been scrambled to intercept it, and we were awaiting further developments. As prime minister, it would fall to me to authorize the use of force if it proved necessary. I had to remain on standby to give the necessary orders at a moment's notice.

Thankfully, it proved to be a false alarm. Half an hour later the passenger aircraft, escorted by our jets, landed safely at Stansted, where it was isolated and met by police. On investigation, no threat was discovered, and the incident was declared over.

It was a huge relief, but also a reminder of the heavy weight of responsibility that now rested on my shoulders. At any moment a major incident could arise that would require me to take life-or-death decisions. I had to be always prepared for that eventuality.

My experience as foreign secretary meant I had more of an insight into this side of the job than perhaps some other new prime ministers. As well as routinely seeing intelligence reports and overseeing the work of MI6, I had led on our response to Russia's invasion of Ukraine and was across the details of the military and diplomatic support we were giving to Kyiv. I had done the rounds of getting to know G7 leaders and foreign ministers and knew the relevant national security officials both in the UK and among our allies.

Nevertheless, there was a difference between handling such issues as a senior Cabinet minister and doing so as prime minister. I had been involved in some critical defense discussions on a number of issues over the previous year, but the ultimate responsibility was then with Boris. Now the buck stopped with me. This was reinforced when I received the briefing routinely given to new prime ministers on the use of the UK's nuclear deterrent.

The war in Ukraine was also high on my agenda, and President Zelenskyy was the first foreign leader to whom I spoke as prime minister, on my first evening in Downing Street. We spoke for half an hour, and I assured him of our continued steadfast support for him and his country in resisting Russian aggression and pushing Putin's forces back over the border. Usually, new British prime ministers make a point of ensuring that their first conversation with a head of government is with the U.S. president, but in this instance I was clear where the priority lay. President Biden had to wait until later, and much of our conversation when we did speak was, of course, about Ukraine.

I flew to the UN General Assembly straight after the funeral of Her Late Majesty. This was my best visit yet. For starters, I wasn't scheduled to meet the Russians or the Iranians.

After completing my standard lap around Central Park, I arrived at the UN building, where my former foreign minister friends congratulated me on my new job. I also talked to European Commission president Ursula von der Leyen about UK and EU interests.

I met with Biden and others from the United States, including Secretary of State Tony Blinken, for the first time formally as prime minister. We covered all the usual subjects—and Biden regaled me with tales of the Democrat campaign trail, including an incident in which he had fallen over. He said, "I can see them thinking—'You can't get up, Grandpa'—but I got up." I formed the view that he was running again in 2024.

I had a sushi lunch with Prime Minister Kishida of Japan where the legend of the blue Stilton was once again reflected on. I also saw the Israeli prime minister, Yair Lapid, who is a great guy. When I emerged from that meeting, I was shepherded into a laundry lift. Who should be in there but Tony Blair?! He gets everywhere.

I also met Ukrainian First Lady Olena Zelenska at the Ukrainian Institute of America, where there was a very moving display of some of the appalling war crimes that had been committed by Russia. Across the room I saw a blonde lady I recognized. I called out "Hi, Dr. Biden!" to the woman I believed was the U.S. First Lady. As she got closer, I realized it wasn't her at all, but French president Macron's wife, Brigitte. I hope she didn't hear!

In a classic piece of Number 10 staging, I did a round of media interviews near the top of the Empire State Building. Why, oh why? It used up time in our schedule getting up the interminable elevators. And when we finally got to the top, it turned out that a lot of TV interviewers had vertigo. I'm not that great with heights myself, yet again I found myself swept along in the course of events. I guess you can't do it all.

I also discovered that while being prime minister is viewed as important in the UK, you're just another UN delegate in New York. On the way to make a speech to the UN General Assembly that I thought was absolutely crucial, I got stuck behind a municipal garbage truck. I made it just in the nick of time.

During the leadership election, I had been pilloried for my remarks about President Macron. When asked if he was "friend or foe," I had said the jury was out! It had been meant to be a quip. Yet again my irreverence had gotten me into trouble. In fact, I found Macron fine—even fun—though we didn't find common cause politically.

I felt that France had been a major part of the problem with Russia. Macron had been far too keen to have long telephone calls with Putin. He was also too close to the Iranian leadership and President Xi of China, the latter of whom he'd visited with a group of luxury goods manufacturers. Moreover, his insistence on European strategic autonomy and keeping his distance from the United States had in my view weakened NATO and European security.

Macron did have the initiative to set up the European Political Community, a forum for discussion among European nations, after the invasion of Ukraine. I was happy to attend, provided key British interests could be addressed—namely, dealing with the huge flows of illegal immigration and strengthening our response to Russia.

Needless to say, Foreign Office officials and the media establishment were salivating over any sense that we were rebuilding our relationship with Europe. It seemed impossible to have a rational discussion without people wanting to relitigate the EU referendum.

Of course, while everybody else met in the main conference center in Prague, Macron had his own grand side building. I got the message when I met the likes of Dutch prime minister Mark Rutte that everyone was concerned over what was going on in Britain. *Maybe I'm in some serious trouble*, I thought.

It was the Eastern Europeans, as always, who provided succor. The Czech prime minister thought my plans totally reasonable—they had much lower taxes in the Czech Republic and it was already delivering benefits.

In the midst of a serious international outlook and a full domestic agenda, I was keen not to waste precious time on short-term trivialities. Unfortunately, I discovered that some of this was unavoidable. I had certainly not realized the extent to which HR issues and people management would end up on my desk. Whether it was a minister caught up in allegations of misconduct or an adviser caught briefing against a Conservative MP, the need for investigations and other processes took time away from other issues.

Cabinet colleagues and MPs need constant attention. As a Cabinet minister, I had always gotten on with my job as best I could and positively avoided involving Number 10 unless I absolutely had to. I assumed others would do the same, but as prime minister I discovered that they wanted a lot more interaction. There were also many meetings with MPs, and of course as things deteriorated the demand increased. It created a vicious circle as my time was more and more squeezed.

I wanted to focus squarely on the big issues facing the country. This meant consciously moving away from just constantly reacting to headlines. I did not want us to be feeding the journalists of the Westminster lobby system with their preferred diet of triviality and "color" to pad out long-read Sunday newspaper articles. This habit is deeply embedded in our system, but I was determined to try and change the culture. Unfortunately, such was the state of my media operation that I found, to my fury, that even my instruction for trivial process briefings to stop had itself been briefed to the lobby as a process story. Nice one, guys.

The argument I heard from media advisers was that unless we continued to provide this constant diet of trivialities, the lobby would fill the gap with less flattering stories of their own. I found this rather unconvincing and somewhat akin to appeasement. If you go off down that road, ultimately you become obsessed with feeding the media beast, focusing on that to the exclusion of all else.

I wanted us to be different, and to signal my approach I insisted that all the TV screens be turned off in Number 10. I didn't want us to be an extension of a twenty-four-hour news channel, constantly monitoring and reacting to every political squall. I also largely stopped reading the press. This was in part because I had found the personal attacks during the leadership contest painful and upsetting to read.

Inevitably, when you are a senior figure in politics you will attract criticism, but the level of vitriol in some quarters was something else. My way of coping was to filter it out and rely on the media summaries I received from my team for the material I needed to know.

Aside from the personal attacks, I also found the political press utterly depressing. There was often little analysis or attempt to understand complex issues. Instead it was a constant stream of "he said, she said," detailing who said what to whom, who's in trouble, and who's on maneuvers. A huge number of column inches were devoted to what I was wearing—which was generally which clothes were clean that day! It was little more than gossip from the Westminster village and of little consequence to anyone outside it.

Should I, in retrospect, have been warier of such criticism? Given what happened, I can already hear people saying I should have listened more and spent more time keeping the media happy. But this is one of my biggest frustrations with the short-termist, media-driven approach to politics. If you only do the things that are guaranteed to win you favorable headlines and shy away from the more difficult issues that might expose you to criticism, you will never do anything worthwhile. This has been happening in British politics for far too long, and it's why we have many of the problems that we do.

I knew that I faced a particular challenge. The negative stories did not appear out of nowhere, and many of the journalists involved were responding to constant briefings from leading Conservatives who had set themselves in opposition to me.

Unlike previous leaders of the party, I was not given a chance to implement the policies I had been elected on. There was no grace period. Some of my opponents had not given up after the leadership election and were determined to undermine and ridicule me from the outset. I accepted there would always be opposition to bold policies that upset the status quo, and that I would have to be ready for the backlash and abuse from the left-wing media. But what I found infuriating was to know that it was supposed fellow Conservatives who were encouraging some of the worst of it. It also seemed to me to be counterproductive, as they were poisoning the well and further damaging our chances at the next election. Yet there was little I could do about it. I could only trust in what I was doing and hope to prove them wrong in time.

In addition to the personal criticism, there is another type of attack on politicians that has become all too prevalent and which I think speaks volumes about the problems with British political culture. Whenever a prime minister or senior politician is found to have used a private plane to travel to an event, they are routinely attacked by the press and the opposition for a supposed waste of taxpayer money. The same often occurs when MPs receive a pay increase or are revealed to have bought office equipment using their parliamentary allowances.

This has led to a hair-shirt approach to politics in which politicians are expected to put up with a lack of proper support for fear they might be criticized for unreasonable extravagance. This has created some utterly perverse outcomes. For years, the government did not have a dedicated long-haul aircraft for ministers to use for official travel overseas. As a result, they regularly had to charter commercial aircraft at much greater cost, all because politicians did not want to be seen to have commissioned a private jet for their own use. Eventually an RAF Voyager was repurposed to serve this function, but even then there were huge headlines condemning the modest cost of repainting it with the Union Flag on its tail.

This sort of manufactured outrage is absurd. It should not be controversial to suggest that the prime minister's and Cabinet ministers' time is valuable and that they need to be able to travel quickly between meetings at home and abroad. They also need to be able to do so securely, with facilities onboard to allow them to work, and in enough comfort that they are not completely exhausted when they arrive. This costs money, but it is justified by the benefits of enabling them to do their jobs more effectively on behalf of the British people.

It isn't just the thorny issue of private jets. I believe this ingrained self-denial is what has prevented successive prime ministers from pushing for the other resources they need to do the job properly. It has become a political football to the detriment of everyone. If we accept that the prime minister is the most important role in government, with ever-increasing demands being made upon it, we must also accept that it needs to be properly supported. As I discovered, we now have a premiership that is subject to all the pressures and expectations of a presidential system but without the associated infrastructure. That makes it a weak institution, and one that is not serving the public as well as it should be.

The prime minister, Cabinet, and other ministers are significantly underpaid. The prime minister is only paid £75,000 ($95,000) in addition to backbench salary, while other Cabinet ministers are paid less than £68,000 ($86,000). This compares very poorly with quangocrats and ministers in other countries. The net result is these jobs become the preserve of the very wealthy, or of those inclined to make decisions that will be beneficial to a high-paying post-politics career in a field like energy or defense.

The fear of being pilloried by the press and public has had a corrosive effect on our politics. The scrutiny on all politicians, and on the prime minister in particular, is now immense. We are under constant pressure and as a result become less inclined to take risks or rock the boat. This is how we find ourselves with politicians who favor going along with the consensus and seeking easy headlines rather than making the tough choices that are often needed.

As democratic politicians face ever-increasing public opprobrium, it is the technocrats and the supposedly "independent" institutions that are elevated above them and held up as paragons of virtue. There is something rather anti-democratic in this, which I find distinctly troubling, particularly in the light of my own experiences. Motives are attacked and views dismissed simply because they come from a political figure.

Meanwhile, unelected organizations and individuals claiming independent expertise find their pronouncements treated as irrefutable statements of fact. The idea that they might be wrong or pursuing a self-interested agenda is treated as fanciful.

The underlying assumption in all this is that there is something inherently vulgar about politics. This is ingrained in the Civil Service, where I would often hear officials using "political" as a dirty word. This would solicit a long lecture from me about how everything they do is "political" because they work for the government. Politics is how we translate the will of the voters into action. It's democracy.

Against this background, it is no great surprise that democratic politicians as a whole have lost much of their self-confidence and many have begun to defer to the revered cult of the technocrat. That, after all, is usually the path of least resistance. But this equates to being in office but not in power. What is the point?

I was not interested in being prime minister just to govern as the benign proxy for the technocratic establishment. For me, it was not about the office but about what I could do with it. Had I believed I could instead secure the outcomes I wanted as home secretary or chancellor, I would have wanted to be in those roles. But I knew it was only as prime minister that I would have the authority to do what was required.

As I discovered on moving into Downing Street, there are a great many downsides to the job. The relentless pressure. The media abuse and political attacks. The loss of personal freedom and intrusions on family life. There wasn't even the much-hyped gold wallpaper in the flat. The gilded cage was just a cage. With fleas.

The only good reason to be in Number 10 and put up with all of the downsides was for what I could get done while I was there. I might have secured a longer tenancy had I been content to put off the big decisions and scale back my ambition. But I was impatient and had work to do. I wanted to deliver.

CHAPTER 12

Going for Growth

We had done it. After all the policy papers, two books, a bruising leadership campaign, and the disappointments of successive Conservative governments and chancellors, we had finally delivered a Conservative package of tax cuts and supply-side reform that was going to mark a major shift in government policy and signify a new era.

As we were driven down to Ebbsfleet in Kent, just southeast of London, to see new houses being built, I felt a sense of elation. Next to me, the chancellor, Kwasi Kwarteng, was grinning from ear to ear. Kwasi had just announced the Growth Plan—which has since become known as the mini-budget—in the House of Commons.

We had been pushed into the timing of the announcement by events. Because of the hiatus in government caused by the demise of Boris and the long leadership election, the issues in the in tray had been piling up. In particular, energy was a major problem: because of years of short-termist policies, the UK had been left exposed to a massive global spike in energy prices.

We had announced our energy package two days into the government and promised to provide costings with a fiscal event in the ensuing weeks. Then, of course, the Queen had died and the country had gone into a period of mourning. Soon we would be up against party conference season, when politicians desert London for their annual weeks away with their respective party activists in a provincial conference center. We had a narrow window to spell out our economic plans between my return from the UN General Assembly the previous day and the start of the Labour Party Conference on Saturday.

Time was not on our side. I fundamentally believe that elections are won on the basis of what is happening on the ground, not messaging about future prospects. And things were not feeling good. Growth had been stagnant. The average Briton was no better off than they were in 2007, and indeed $10,000 per year worse off than the equivalent American. The state was spending too much—almost half of the country's national income. In order to move things in the right direction, serious action was going to have to be taken that autumn.

This is not to say our economic plans were generated on the hoof. In fact they had long been in gestation. My fellow authors and I had laid out the strategy in our book *Britannia Unchained: Global Lessons for Growth and Prosperity*, published exactly ten years previously in September 2012.

One of those authors was Kwasi himself, and he and I had spent years discussing this agenda. As we put it in the introduction to the book:

> Changing Britain's fortunes needs a relentless energy and determined focus. Vitally we will need to be tougher in taking on vested interests. . . . We have to ensure that the

general climate for business is attractive. This means that we should stop indulging in irrelevant debates about sharing the pie between manufacturing and services, the north and the south, women and men. Instead, we should focus on trying to make it easier for firms to recruit people and ensuring the tax burden is less onerous.

I believed those things were needed then, and if anything I believed them even more after ten years in government. The task was now more urgent. Brexit made it imperative that we should tackle the underlying problems that were stopping Britain from becoming more competitive. Otherwise we were simply accepting decline.

Kwasi and I had both been members of Boris's Cabinet, he as business secretary and me at International Trade. We had sat there in frustration as then chancellor Rishi Sunak raised taxes and blocked serious supply-side reform. We had lobbied Boris not to go ahead with corporation tax rises or windfall taxes but, while claiming to sympathize, he was deeply reluctant to take on the Treasury.

The biggest row was when Rishi had sought to introduce an entirely new tax, the Health and Social Care Levy. There were rumors during the summer of 2021 that National Insurance, a social security entitlement in the UK, was going to be hiked to pay for the NHS. I had been a longtime campaigner against National Insurance. At the first Conservative Party Conference I had attended back in 1997, I had made a platform speech against it, with Margaret Thatcher looking on. It was a fake tax claiming to be an "insurance" against unemployment and sickness. In fact, it was just another way of fleecing the British public, with money going into the public spending black hole.

Ahead of the Cabinet meeting in September 2021, there were lots of attempts by Boris and Dan Rosenfield, his chief of staff, to persuade me not to speak out against the tax rise. It was even hinted by Boris's allies that I wouldn't want to put my potential promotion to foreign secretary in jeopardy. But I insisted on saying my piece. I had not joined the Tory Party and become an MP to raise taxes.

The justification given for creating the new Health and Social Care Levy, according to Rishi, was that it was needed to balance numbers from the Office for Budget Responsibility (OBR), the UK's more unaccountable and powerful equivalent of the Congressional Budget Office. This was a red rag to a bull. I pointed out that OBR forecasts always turned out to be wrong, that we had promised not to raise taxes in our manifesto, and that Conservatives who raise taxes don't win elections. I was backed up by only two other Cabinet members, Lord Frost and Jacob Rees-Mogg. After my comments, Boris said he agreed with me *and* Rishi! Classic.

It was very clear that the answer was not more taxes and bigger government; it was liberating the supply side of the economy to generate more growth and income while holding down government spending. I knew all this would be difficult to implement, because the whole agenda was deeply unfashionable in economic circles. Over time, the lessons of the 1980s and the Thatcherite rolling back of over-taxation and regulation have seemingly been forgotten. The tide had been going out on free market economics. We had bailed out the bankers after the financial crash, which had been used by the Left to discredit free markets. From the Occupy movement to the works of Thomas Piketty, anti-capitalist arguments had been making the running.

The Left used cultural and environmental movements to undermine personal responsibility and capitalist economics. We saw the development of "wokenomics," where big businesses were more focused on so-called environmental, social, and governance objectives than making money. Industry has become increasingly corporatized, going to government for grants and lobbying to retain regulation to keep out competitors.

Instead of taking on the leftists and allowing failing companies to feel the discipline of the market, conservatives had capitulated to them. Central banks from the Federal Reserve to the Bank of England colluded with spendthrift governments, allowing money-printing to pay for the largesse.

Conservatives lost their economic compass and their grasp of basic economic principles, often demanding more regulation and buying into the left-wing spend-and-subsidize model. When I talked about "supply-side reform," it was met with eye rolls from my own parliamentary colleagues. This tendency was exacerbated by the response to the pandemic. UK government spending as a proportion of GDP is now an eye-watering 46 percent.

By the time I won the contest to lead the Conservative Party in the summer of 2022, the chickens were coming home to roost. The United Kingdom was becoming less competitive and relatively poorer. Energy and housing prices were some of the highest in Europe. Roads and rail took longer to build and were more expensive. The High Speed 2 rail line between London and the West Midlands was estimated to have cost ten times its French equivalent. We had not allowed fracking and consequently have energy prices that are twice what they are in the United States. Add to that the fact that (despite my best efforts) our workers face the highest childcare costs in Europe. It had become inordinately difficult to open a bank account.

After some attempts to cut regulation in the early years, red tape had grown under the Conservatives. Successive governments had given in to pressure for more nanny state measures such as sugar taxes, anti-money-laundering rules, data protection regulations, and a host of other measures that have added to the burden. These regulations and costs have had the effect of hampering our manufacturing industry, deterring investment, and driving up the cost of living for ordinary Britons.

The administrative state has accumulated huge amounts of power. The Conservatives' planned bonfire of the quangos (there are over five hundred unelected quangos in Britain) had been snuffed out as long ago as 2011 by lefty claims that we were seeking to abolish forests. Tony Blair and Gordon Brown had imposed a web of legalistic architecture that added process and put more power in the hands of technocrats. We did not reverse any of this legislation. In fact, we added our own.

Brexit offered a huge opportunity to deal with this legacy of red tape. It would clearly be of benefit to the UK economy if regulations like the Working Time Directive were repealed, but we have been too timid in taking that opportunity. The vast majority of EU law remains on the British statute book—it's a bit like getting divorced and then continuing to live in the same house as your ex-husband!

The West had been growing slowly for years, and Britain was among the worst laggards. We urgently needed to change the trajectory if we were to have any chance of seeing results by the time of the next general election. That meant returning to the promises on which we had been elected in 2019, like keeping corporation tax low and reversing the planned increase in National Insurance. It meant getting serious about other supply-side reforms that would boost growth. It meant increasing the productive capacity of the economy and setting the conditions necessary for higher economic growth.

It's a simple enough concept, but achieving it has not always proved so easy. I wanted to defeat the sense that things simply weren't happening in Britain and that we were stuck in a rut. It's why I made the theme of our 2022 party conference "Get Britain Moving."

As well as needing a huge culture shift, our other problem was that the institutional machinery had completely bought into the big-government, high-tax approach that had been cemented during thirty years of economic consensus. I called out the Treasury orthodoxy during the leadership election, and this probably didn't do me any favors with the officials with whom Kwasi and I would have to work.

His Majesty's Treasury is a much more powerful body than its equivalent in other countries because it comprises both the economic and accounting functions of the government. The U.S. equivalent would be having the White House Office of Management and Budget, the U.S. Treasury, and the Congressional Budget Office all rolled into one and headed up by civil servants. This setup has been a problem for years in Britain. Labour prime minister Harold Wilson tried to break it up by establishing a separate Department of Economic Affairs in the 1960s. He failed.

What we now faced was not only that the Treasury orthodoxy had shifted to the left and away from the free-market economics we wished to pursue but that the power of the Treasury orthodoxy had grown. Under Blair and Brown, the Treasury had spread its tentacles over domestic policy. This meant Cabinet ministers not only had a spending cap in their departments but also had to go to the Treasury for permission as to how to spend the money.

They had also given the governor of the Bank of England much greater powers, including making him virtually unsackable during his five-year term of office (since extended by George Osborne to be an eight-year term). Although the Treasury is responsible for setting its mandate for monetary policy, I saw in my time there that talking about it had become a taboo. During the leadership election, I did question the Bank of England's mandate and the period of cheap money that had anesthetized the country. According to some people, this was akin to questioning papal authority. Any attempt to talk about it was considered a challenge to the bank's independence.

If only the words attributed to Mayer Amschel Rothschild of the famous banking family had been heeded: "Permit me to issue and control the money of a nation, and I care not who makes its laws!"

The Office for Budget Responsibility was set up by George Osborne, the chancellor in the coalition government following the 2010 general election. Although it was there to mark the government's forecasting homework, it gradually developed a life of its own and now essentially sets fiscal policy. No other Treasury anywhere in the world had such a rigid and inflexible arrangement.

Both the Bank of England and the OBR are infused with the same Treasury orthodoxy, but as "independent" institutions they are not subject to challenge from elected politicians. Their actions move markets and affect people's lives, but instead of being robustly scrutinized their pronouncements are treated with the same reverence that is given to other technocratic institutions nowadays.

These bodies all instinctively have the same mindset. They were for remaining in the EU and now want to stick as closely to EU law as possible. They are pro-China and generally against using economic measures to shape geopolitics. They are pro-top-down tinkering and more interested in balancing the books than growing the economy. They are also pro-immigration, seeing that as a way of fixing the public finances.

They are fatalistic about Britain's decline, and they don't believe in Britain's manufacturing industry. At one instructive meeting, after we had failed to reach a conclusion on what to do to defend ourselves against unfair trade practices in the steel industry, an exasperated Boris interjected, "Put your hands up, those who want a steel industry in Britain." The Treasury officials who were deputizing for Rishi sat on their hands.

Because they believe the level of economic growth is a given, they underplay the importance of incentives. But incentives matter hugely. Put simply, if we push up taxes to 80 percent, or put so much regulation in place that operating a business becomes almost impossible, fewer people will aspire to earn more or start a new business.

Different incentives have different levels of responsiveness. While most working people are fixed in terms of their ties to a particular place and cannot easily move abroad to a lower-tax country, large businesses and big capital tend to be more mobile. It is much easier for a multinational company like AstraZeneca to relocate and open new facilities in Ireland rather than the UK because Ireland's corporation tax is lower. That is why changes to business taxes, regulation, and the top rates of personal income tax are particularly sensitive.

No one who has not had to deal with the hideous hell of the OBR forecasting process understands just how bad it is. I saw it firsthand as chief secretary and then had the opportunity to look under the hood as prime minister.

The Treasury forecasting process was always overly static. Margaret Thatcher's chancellor Nigel Lawson explained in his memoirs how in the 1980s Treasury ministers took steps to prevent "nonsensical" and "absurd" Treasury forecasts from seeing the light of day, insisting that more realistic figures be published instead. But at least there was an opportunity for internal debate about the impact of taxes and regulation. Now that expertise has been stripped from the Treasury, and the forecasting is carried out in isolation by the policymakers. It takes place at two-week intervals during the run-up to a fiscal event. The Treasury can go from having £20 billion extra to spend or being £20 billion short, simply because some intermediate figure or number has changed.

The OBR's models are static and short-termist. They underestimate the effect that tax and regulation have on people's behavior. And they tend to focus on the one- or two- or at most five-year effects of policy. I call this approach "abacus economics." They tell us who the winners and losers will be from changes to tax rates but do not give sufficient weight to how those changes will boost growth overall. This means, bluntly, that their numbers are frequently wrong.

This had an impact on the debate during the leadership contest. Rishi's team claimed my plans would increase borrowing and add to the national debt. Those attacks were based on flawed OBR modelling. As a former chancellor, Rishi entirely bought into this orthodoxy, while I sought to challenge it.

I agreed we needed to get debt falling in the medium term. But I believed the Treasury plan for doing so was based on a blinkered view of how the fiscal and regulatory framework affects growth. They consistently underestimate the negative effects of taxes and regulations. Squeezing more money out of the economy in the short term with tax rises might seem a prudent way to reduce the budget deficit, but it risks killing the goose that lays the golden egg. You might get decent returns in years one and two, but after that businesses leave, entrepreneurship is choked off, growth stalls, and revenues fall.

In due course we were to hear more about the workings of the OBR. On Wednesday, October 2, Kwasi and I met with the OBR to talk about the medium-term fiscal plan we were developing to ensure debt was falling. The OBR was clear that tax-raising measures were a more certain source of income than cutting government spending, and that government spending had a more direct effect on growth than money in the private sector. In short, it was very Keynesian.

They were not prepared to "score" supply-side measures to any significant level. The plans we had put forward to deregulate and reduce Britain's energy costs would have significantly increased growth, but the OBR did not agree. There was only one supply side measure they thought significantly contributed to the economy: immigration.

I had agreed with Suella Braverman, the home secretary, that we needed to get tough on immigration. Legal migration was far too high—in fact, net migration reached seven hundred thousand in 2022 and six hundred thousand in 2023. Despite immigration and border control being one of the main concerns of voters, the post-Brexit immigration regime was far too generous. Students were allowed to stay for two years after studying in the UK and allowed to bring dependents, including up to four children. Salary thresholds were too low at £26,000—lower than the average British wage. The Home Office was also resistant to differentiating between countries. I wanted to see easier travel in both directions between the UK and both Australia and Japan, which is a very different proposition to a similar arrangement with much less economically developed countries.

The system we had in place was heavily down to pressure from the Treasury and Business departments, which were constantly lobbied by business and universities for cheap labor and a steady supply of international students. The then chancellor, Rishi Sunak, backed his officials' position.

Illegal immigration was also a huge problem. Human traffickers were shipping illegal migrants over the English Channel in small boats. We had a plan to send these migrants to Rwanda, a country with which the UK government had done a deal under previous home secretary Priti Patel. But implementing this deal was continually held up by internal resistance and legal cases in the courts.

I had agreed with Suella that we needed a series of measures to bring the immigration numbers down. She was determined to get it to below one hundred thousand. These measures would include stopping students from bringing dependents and raising the salary thresholds. To tackle illegal immigration we would need to take on the legal establishment. If we were to break this impasse, we would need a notwithstanding clause to disapply elements of the European Convention on Human Rights under the same legal "doctrine of necessity" that we had used for the Northern Ireland Protocol Bill.

The OBR was an obstacle to getting it done. Because of the OBR's faulty numbers, which view immigration as a positive for the public finances (and don't take account of the strain on public services, or indeed the GDP per capita impact), every step to reduce immigration would make their forecasts look worse. And therefore the government would be obliged to cut spending or raise taxes to compensate for reducing immigration! It was literally through-the-looking-glass stuff. If numbers were reduced as Suella had outlined, the OBR claimed this would add £10 billion ($12 billion) to the deficit and therefore necessitate spending cuts or tax raises. These calculations that I believed were wrong were providing the tramlines for government policy.

The arguments Kwasi and I were making were not novel or eccentric. They'd been proved right by the experiences of the 1970s and 1980s, and for a time they were accepted wisdom. But somehow the economic establishment had either forgotten or repudiated them in the years since. Hence we arrived at a situation where my laying out these basic tenets of free market economics during my pitch to become prime minister was painted as some sort of untested heresy.

Despite all these flaws, the prime minister and chancellor essentially have no alternative but the OBR for forecasting. Other government departments are not able to do their own forecasts (as I found when I was international trade secretary). According to the legislation, the OBR has to produce a twice-yearly forecast of the public finances. If the government decided to commission a different body to do a forecast, I suspect it would cause an uproar. As I saw for myself, unelected independent bodies are trusted more than politicians, so that argument would be lost.

Therefore, even though I believed the forecasting process was fundamentally wrong, and even though I believed the numbers were a fiction, I could not denounce them without putting the government in an even trickier position.

But there is a deeper problem than even the flawed forecasting: it is that a media and wider corporate class appear to believe that the future can be predicted this way. They put far too much faith in forecasts. Similar mistakes were made around the modeling for COVID.

I believed in what I was doing from a point of first principles, but very few are prepared to engage in an argument at that level. They prefer instead to engage in monkey tennis around competing predictions of the future. I could not tell you precisely how many jobs would be created in particular parts of the country over the next decade, or what new technologies and products would be developed by businesses during that time. But I do know that a 19 percent rate of corporation tax is much better than one of 25 percent, and that easing the burden of regulation and taxation will result in better growth. Rather than argue about the forecasts, I wanted to get on and prove it.

After years of being thwarted by the processes of officialdom, Kwasi and I knew that the orthodoxy would be a major problem. However, while we were thinking in terms of how to actually make the policies happen, we underestimated the wider fallout about being seen to take on the establishment. That's why all the work we did in the limited preparation time we had was about how to enact the policies and not so much about how to sell them.

In between hustings, I had been rushing back to the foreign secretary's rural retreat of Chevening, where we had a few weeks to work out how to approach all of this. We were there with Treasury officials, many of whom I knew from my time as chief secretary. Supportive Cabinet colleagues Jacob Rees-Mogg and Simon Clarke were also there. Kwasi and I discussed how to navigate the politics of it, both inside and outside government. We agreed there was a triumvirate of problems—the Treasury, the Bank of England, and the OBR—which between them had presided over the drift of economic policy in Britain for thirty years. We knew they represented institutional barriers to our plans.

Of these, we were most familiar with the Treasury. Kwasi had been parliamentary private secretary to Philip Hammond as chancellor when I had been chief secretary, so we both knew how bad the problem was there. We had to work out how we were going to approach this three-headed hydra. One option would have been to go in very hard, abolish the OBR and appoint senior leaders in the Bank of England and Treasury who were prepared to challenge the orthodoxy. That would have been extremely dramatic and amounted to a declaration of war on the economic establishment. It would also have taken time we didn't have.

Instead we decided to pick our battles. We would use the OBR on its twice-yearly cycle and try to work constructively with the governor and the bank. That left the Treasury itself. Kwasi was very keen to replace the incumbent permanent secretary, Tom Scholar, with someone less attached to current thinking. While I didn't have particularly strong views about Scholar, I did believe it was important that the chancellor of the exchequer should be able to choose his most senior official. I therefore agreed that we would thank Scholar for his service on day one and set about appointing a new permanent secretary at the Treasury.

The reaction to this announcement was predictable and telling. Former senior civil servants popped up on the airwaves to vent their outrage, attacking us for compromising Civil Service independence and saying the move would "corrupt our system."

Kwasi had a clear idea whom he wanted to appoint as the new Treasury permanent secretary: an able and long-serving senior civil servant who already had experience running a government department with an economic focus. But by the time we came to consider the appointment some weeks later, events had rather overtaken us. A message was relayed to me from the governor of the Bank of England that the markets might react badly if we installed our preferred candidate, who had not previously worked at the Treasury. Given the extent to which the markets took their cues from the signals given by the bank, it was not wholly clear if the governor's warning was a forecast or a threat. Whichever it was, it sadly had the desired effect. I was prevailed upon to block the appointment. We had struck the first blow against the existing economic establishment, but they had begun to strike back.

In those days at Chevening in late August, in continued scorching hot weather, the core economic ministers and I hammered out the details of the Growth Plan with Treasury officials, with Simon Case also in attendance. We were essentially operating as a government-in-waiting.

There was no word of warning about any likely issues with the bond markets, and no one mentioned the issues surrounding liability-driven investments (LDIs). Simon Clarke, who had been chief secretary to the Treasury for the previous thirteen months and the serving chancellor's effective deputy, had not been made aware of any problems during his tenure.

Although the mini-budget was politically punchy, it was in no way unprecedented in its scale or impact. Kwasi and I had made it clear that we were going to reduce debt and intended to bring forward new fiscal rules and a full spending review later in the autumn. This was a reasonable and credible plan, and it had been well trailed in advance.

The big tax measures were reversing proposed raises in corporation tax and National Insurance. These were not in themselves tax cuts, but rather a freezing of taxes at their current rate. This was not a revolutionary prospectus; it was a return to the Conservative manifesto commitments on which we had won our parliamentary majority.

We also decided to abolish the 45 percent rate of income tax. This tax was essentially an anti-success measure. The highest income tax rate in the United States is 37 percent, and that only takes effect on incomes much higher than those affected by the upper rate in the UK. How were we supposed to remain competitive at 45 percent? The abolition of the 45 percent income tax rate was effectively revenue-neutral, with the Institute for Fiscal Studies describing its effect as "a rounding error in the context of the public finances" and the Centre for Economics and Business Research (Cebr) reporting that cutting the rate would *raise* money over five years.

Jacob Rees-Mogg floated the idea of a flat tax, to which I am instinctively attracted, but we thought it would be a step too far at that point. We also wanted to abolish inheritance tax and were planning that for spring 2023.

The second part of the plan was supply-side reform, including changes to zoning and planning regulations and an energy package.

We planned to set an upper ceiling on the cost of energy for consumers at £6,000 ($7,440), as well as enact measures to support businesses dealing with the immediate issue of the broken UK market. We also planned to open up supply as quickly as possible with more exploration in the North Sea and fracking. I was also in negotiations with the Norwegians about a long-term supply deal.

The Treasury vastly overcosted the package because they based their calculations on the spot price for gas, not the future price curve. Their projection was £58 billion ($72 billion); in reality it cost £25 billion ($31 billion). The Energy Price Guarantee replaced the Rishi/Boris scheme, which paid money out regardless of what the market price was. This failed to provide security but would have been at least as expensive. We replaced what had been a definite cash outlay with a contingent liability.

The Norwegian deal or investing in new energy sources would have been insurance against high prices. In any event, the Norwegians wouldn't give us a good enough deal, so we walked away.

I think it's fair to say that our proactive, creative, commercial approach completely freaked out the Treasury. Treasury officials tried to work with their counterparts in the Energy Department to stop it happening. They tried to persuade the chancellor it was a bad idea.

The third part of the plan was about public spending restraint. We were deliberately careful about discussing public spending, given the very difficult politics of it. We planned to change the trajectory by holding spending down in an inflationary environment. Not reopening the Spending Review represented a tough approach. We also planned to limit the increase of benefits by wages, not prices (although it would turn out that the parliamentary party would not even support this—I fear that MPs have become addicted to spending).

Compared to what the UK is spending now, my plans would have saved £18 billion ($22 billion) in 2023 and 2024 and £17 billion ($21 billion) in 2024 and 2025. Even taking the Treasury's costings of tax cuts, my plans would have added less debt.

All of the tax changes and supply-side reforms in the mini-budget were fully costed by the Treasury over five years, and I have already said I believed the Treasury costings to be over-egged. For example, their costing of the tax measures over five years was £45 billion ($56 billion), whereas independent analysis by Cebr suggested it was £25 billion ($31 billion). And indeed it was shown subsequently that the energy package was half the predicted cost.

But even though I thought the Treasury costings were too high—as subsequent numbers have proved—there was no warning on the part of the Treasury that it would prove too much. Our expectation of receiving a fair hearing was not only reinforced by the Treasury view but by recent experience. There had not been a major market reaction against recent spending commitments, including the furlough scheme, which had cost £70 billion ($87 billion). In the greater scheme of things, the mini-budget's effect on government borrowing was relatively small, even if we took the inflated static-modeling approach of the OBR and the Treasury, which placed its cost at £45 billion ($56 billion) over the first two financial years. This compares to total government spending over two years of £2,000 billion ($2.49 trillion).

I have heard many people say we should have gone slower, delayed the announcements, and "rolled the pitch" better. I accept the communications around it were not as good as they could have been, but I have to ask: What would we have been waiting for? I knew that many of these things would be politically difficult and not immediately popular. The longer you wait in politics, the harder things become, and experience suggests it is better for politicians to strike while the iron is hot and make use of their mandate while it is still fresh. That might have been a miscalculation, but it was not an outlandish strategy.

I came to the table having worked for years in the energy industry, both as an accountant and an economist. Hugh has a degree in mathematical economics from the London School of Economics. This stuff is bread and butter to us, and I talk about it a lot. I am not always good at translating this internal dialogue into something for wider public communication. I assumed people understood what I was trying to do more than they did.

I had been clear that I would cut taxes straight away during the leadership election and had been elected by Conservative members on that platform. If anyone was surprised by the measures in the Growth Plan, they frankly hadn't been paying attention. Or perhaps they had just become used to politicians who talk about wanting tax cuts while putting taxes up. By contrast, I meant what I said.

Others criticized us for not publishing an OBR forecast alongside the plan. But as I have outlined, I had no confidence in the methodology I knew the OBR used and believed its modeling to be fundamentally flawed. And there had been no OBR forecast for many other fiscal announcements, including the aforementioned £70 billion furlough package. The OBR later leaked its calculations purporting to show a £70 billion ($85 billion) hole in the budget and this, once again, proved to be completely wrong.

I don't regret not commissioning a forecast that I knew would be wrong and that would inevitably have undermined our plans from the outset. This led to criticism, but what else could I have done? Given that economic modeling was what I did in my professional career, I suppose I could have cleared a weekend at Chequers to crunch the numbers and write my own detailed forecast. But I hardly think that would have inspired confidence.

The weeks leading up to the launch of the Growth Plan were, of course, not as we had expected. Much of the final preparation took place against the backdrop of national mourning for the Queen. During this period, I was kept busy traveling around the country attending ceremonies with the new King and Queen, but Kwasi and his team were working hard to get the package of measures together. In between my other commitments, I had regular meetings with Kwasi, my own economic adviser Matthew Sinclair, and Treasury officials to go through the details.

Although the prime minister is nominally "First Lord of the Treasury," Treasury officials guard the chancellor closely and were clearly alarmed by my close working relationship with Kwasi. By appointing him chancellor, I knew I had a colleague who was fully signed up to this agenda and who was as keen as I was to deliver it. We knew we had to move fast. The death of Her Majesty meant that we could not stick to our original timetable. But once the mourning period was over, I believed it was right to get on with it.

Throughout this time, I found the Treasury officials directly involved to be diligent and hardworking. They cooperated fully in pulling together the documents, working round the clock to meet the new deadline for what was now being dubbed the mini-budget. The deadline was on Friday, September 23, at the end of a week that would begin with the Queen's state funeral on Monday.

I left for New York for the UN General Assembly immediately after the funeral, going straight to the airport from Windsor Castle. Some of my officials were nervous about my being away in the days immediately before such a significant announcement and thought I ought to have remained at home to oversee things. But I was satisfied with how preparations were going and assured them it would all be fine.

When I got back to the UK on Thursday morning after an overnight flight, the final draft of the Growth Plan was just about ready, and I reviewed the final changes and a memorandum from the chancellor. I signed it off that evening and got an unusually early night.

On the day of the mini-budget itself, I had called a Cabinet meeting at 8:00 a.m. to brief colleagues on the changes we would be outlining.

Kwasi went through the details, which were well received. I then headed to the House of Commons for the statement itself. I felt a huge sense of satisfaction as the chancellor unveiled each of the measures in turn, culminating in the cuts to income tax, before concluding by summing up our new approach:

> Mr. Speaker, for too long in this country, we have indulged in a fight over redistribution. Now, we need to focus on growth, not just how we tax and spend. . . .
>
> The prime minister promised that we would be a tax-cutting government. Today, we have cut stamp duty. We have allowed businesses to keep more of their own money to invest, to innovate, and to grow. We have cut income tax and national insurance for millions of workers.
>
> We are securing our place in a fiercely competitive global economy with lower rates of corporation tax and lower rates of personal tax. We have promised to prioritize growth. We have promised a new approach for a new era. We have promised, Mr. Speaker, to release the enormous potential of this country. Our Growth Plan has delivered all those promises and more, and I commend it to the House.

As he sat down, there were cheers from our supporters on the Conservative benches behind us, but the reaction from some quarters of the party was muted. I was told later that many of the MPs who had backed my opponent in the leadership race remained pointedly silent during the speech and at its conclusion made their disapproval plain to all.

None of that concerned me at the time. After the statement, I headed off to Kent with Kwasi to pay a visit to a housebuilding firm to highlight the positive impact the Growth Plan would have on business. In the car on the way down, we talked enthusiastically about the need to get on with the next round of reforms and to keep up the momentum in the coming months. He was pleased with how the statement had gone, and I was ecstatic to have finally done the things we had talked about and planned for so long. Looking back, that afternoon was probably my happiest moment as prime minister.

We had managed to deliver what we said we would. We had done it in spite of the resistance. Little did I know the establishment was about to use every tool at its disposal to fight back.

CHAPTER 13

End of Days

Your ratings are worse than Mrs. Thatcher's at her most unpopular—but don't worry, we can turn this round!" The cheery tones of Conservative Party chairman Jake Berry hit me as I sat in the car on the way to a business visit ahead of the Conservative Party Conference in Manchester. I had been avoiding the media for days, and now my bubble had been well and truly burst.

It was Friday, September 30, exactly a week since the announcement of the Growth Plan (now universally described as the mini-budget). I had expected difficulties, but the chain of events that had been unleashed had not been predicted by anyone. We had gotten a positive reaction from the supporters of change, but from our opponents we were facing a full-blown feeding frenzy, with a precarious international market, a restive media, agitating politicians, and the establishment all egging each other on.

Contrary to my previous optimism, I now saw that we were operating in an environment that was deeply hostile to the economic policies we were advancing: tax cuts, supply-side reform, and public spending restraint. We simply weren't ready for this level of onslaught. We did not have enough supporters willing to vocally defend our position. Our political infrastructure was weak and very newly established. This was all overlaid with a poisoned political well; a significant number of Conservative MPs remained unhappy with my election to leadership and were not willing to give us a chance.

They objected to the removal of environmental red tape, which allowed us to get on with fracking and build more houses. They objected to the focus on the economy at the expense of subjects like Net Zero. They objected to the speed of implementation. They did not seem to understand that the UK was heading toward an economic cliff with its surging debt and that I was seeking to conduct a handbrake turn to avoid driving off the edge. I could see worse was ahead for the British economy.

Those on my economic team agreed with this prognosis. I had talked the situation through with Simon Clarke, then chief secretary to the Treasury, as we had walked through the woods at Chevening in August making our preparations. Simon, with typical understatement, had suggested that we were in for a "bracing" time. I had said it would be a brutal six months of turbulence and we would have to batten down the hatches. But we agreed it was the only way to get things on the right track. The alternative was an anemic economy, increased taxes, and a likely brutal defeat for the Conservatives at the 2024 election.

I knew the party conference to which I was heading would be difficult. I needed to keep the Cabinet on board, deal with restive MPs, and not show any chinks in the armor into which my opponents would be only too willing to stick the knife.

The backdrop was not promising. Much of the market turmoil had been generated in the United States, which we had not expected or been briefed on. Jerome Powell, chair of the Federal Reserve, had reversed policy in early 2022 after keeping interest rates too low for too long. In March 2022, he started a cycle of interest rate rises, taking the federal funds rate from 0–0.25 percent to 3–3.25 percent by September 2022. The bond market collapsed, and the ten-year U.S. Treasury yield rose from 1.72 percent on March 1, 2022, to 4.01 percent on October 18, barely seven months later. Monetary policy had been reversed, and the annual growth in the main measure of the U.S. money supply (M2) went negative in November 2022 after having had its largest expansion since the American Civil War during 2020. The bond markets had failed to anticipate this and went into a tailspin. The change in interest rate expectations led to a surge in the dollar. All these things caused knock-on effects and chaos in other countries, including in the UK.

As expected, the pound had fallen relative to the dollar following the mini-budget on the Friday, but the fall did not trigger huge alarm since it was within the Treasury's expectations, albeit at the upper end. The pound had also dropped the day before—to its weakest position in thirty-seven years—after the Bank of England had increased interest rates by less than expected. Analysts concluded that the bank had "missed market expectations," and there was increased pressure for further rate rises. The Bank of England had also embarked on a program of quantitative tightening (QT) on the eve of the budget, announcing a plan to sell £40 billion ($49 billion U.S.) of gilts, becoming the first major bank to sell QE bonds. This selling of bonds raised the yields as the supply of bonds was increased, pushing up the cost of government borrowing on the eve of the mini-budget.

Although the dollar was strong following a rate raise by the Federal Reserve, the pound had not been alone: the yen was also suffering.

Yet the fall of the pound was blamed by the media entirely on the mini-budget.

I expected the initial market jitters to settle and was more concerned about convincing malcontents on the Conservative benches that we were now on the right track. This was a battle I believed had to be won and for which I was prepared. What I did not realize was that things were about to get a whole lot worse.

One of my media team mentioned to me that they were having to field questions about the market reaction because the Treasury press team was not stepping up. This worried me because I had been under the impression the Treasury media operation would be in full swing. This, after all, is what they do; they live for budgets (mini or otherwise).

After a calm-ish weekend, during which I had invited my team over to Chevening for a barbecue (Chequers, the prime minister's official country residence in Buckinghamshire, was undergoing some refurbishment), I was hit with news of turbulence in the Asian markets on Monday morning. There had been a further fall in the pound against the dollar overnight and a rise in UK gilt yields. I was surprised this was panicking everyone. As a committed believer in floating currencies, I didn't think the current value of the pound was a central issue. Yet even though the pound had fluctuated wildly over the past year, the media started tracking it as a marker of success.

As I headed back to Downing Street, it became clear more trouble was ahead. Kwasi had done a bullish TV interview on Laura Kuenssberg's BBC show on Sunday but had since shifted into a much more cautious gear. He had apparently been up all night fretting about the market movements.

What neither of us knew was that the UK was sitting on a financial tinderbox. Our pension funds were uniquely exposed to liability-driven investments—the UK had a significant proportion of the world's supply of these products—which meant that every time interest rates went up there would be demands for cash. This then became a vicious circle. The risk was that these pension funds and fund managers would go bust, leading to cataclysmic economic fallout.

During the era of cheap money, pension funds had found it hard to make a return. Therefore they essentially bet on low interest rates. Organizations like BlackRock were particularly exposed. That bet was now looking like a massive mistake because those low interest rates and the cheap money were unsustainable. This was a crisis waiting to happen once the cost of borrowing rose. Interest rates had already started increasing in December 2021, and further rises were inevitable regardless of the mini-budget.

But the market reaction triggered by the Bank of England's inaction on interest rates and quantitative tightening had exposed the problem and brought it to a head. I was astonished to discover no one in the Treasury or the Bank of England had flagged it as a problem, and they had only become aware of it when contacted by nervous pension fund managers that Friday afternoon. In preparing our announcements, the Treasury had been blindsided by this major structural risk. It really was a tinderbox waiting for a spark—and the market upheaval provided it.

One of the reasons we failed to communicate this to the media is we didn't fully understand what was happening ourselves. I hadn't heard of LDIs and neither had most Treasury officials (one of the impacts of removing so much expertise from the Treasury and putting it into the Bank of England and the OBR). We certainly didn't realize it was going to turn into a major issue. We struggled both to understand and to explain what was happening. In a twenty-four-hour news cycle, this is fatal.

When I arrived back in Downing Street on Monday, Kwasi told me the Bank of England felt obliged to make a statement to calm things down. They might even need to "step in" and implement an emergency interest rate rise to restore stability. What few commentators thought to mention amid this speculation was that this course of action—a bigger rise in interest rates—was precisely what the bank had failed to do the previous week alongside the unprecedented quantitative tightening. They were now being urged to correct what the markets saw as their mistake, but the spin was that it was entirely the government's fault.

Because we did not know what was going on—and I personally was one step removed in 10 Downing Street—the Bank of England (and no doubt other parts of the bureaucracy) was able to lay the blame for the market turbulence entirely at the government's door. They got the jump on briefing the press, and various former officials swiftly popped up in the media to lay into the mini-budget.

A media hungry for political drama, with a Boris-shaped hole to fill, eagerly lapped this up. It sells more newspapers and gets more clicks to talk about pesky politicians getting their comeuppance than to do detailed analysis of the regulatory failures of government bureaucrats. Precisely because they are not elected politicians, they escape any reasonable level of challenge or scrutiny.

The other problem was the sheer technical detail involved: a volatile global market spurred by an energy crisis and high levels of government debt, a failure of monetary policy after the financial crises that led to unsustainable printing of money, and a failure to regulate pension funds that led to their near insolvency. It took us days to get to the bottom of it ourselves.

For the media, it was far easier and more rewarding to chase the prime minister and chancellor around pointing the finger and demanding an apology. To date, aside from a report from the House of Commons Work and Pensions Select Committee in June 2023, which was virtually ignored by the media, there has not been a serious inquiry into what happened over the failure of the Bank of England or Pensions Regulator to properly regulate LDIs, even though this was at the heart of the crisis.

The pound recovered throughout Monday, making back its overnight losses and emerging above its closing position the previous Friday. This fact was conveniently ignored amid the frenzied chatter.

I met Kwasi to discuss the market situation. I was initially opposed to making a statement, which I thought would only show weakness and make matters worse. Eventually, after a further meeting that afternoon, I agreed the Treasury should announce the date of our planned medium-term fiscal plan, including details of how we intended to get debt falling as a share of GDP. Under pressure, and against my instincts, I also agreed we would commit to publish a forecast by the Office for Budget Responsibility alongside it.

Shortly afterwards, the bank governor, Andrew Bailey, put out a statement saying the Monetary Policy Committee (MPC), which sets interest rates, would "not hesitate" to increase interest rates as necessary to tackle inflation. This despite the fact that the week before the Bank of England had failed to follow central banks across the world by not raising interest rates enough and implementing QT. While his statement welcomed the government's commitment to economic growth, it also deliberately cast us adrift, stating that the MPC would make a "full assessment" of the effect of our announcements at its next scheduled meeting. The response from market analysts was hostile, with many expressing disappointment that the bank had not intervened immediately. The pound slipped again, which would be blamed on the government.

It's worth stating that of course Treasury officials and Kwasi himself were talking regularly to the Bank of England—and the vast majority of the measures we'd taken had been front and center in my summer campaign—so Governor Bailey's claim that he was "blindsided" by the mini-budget simply didn't stack up.

It had been a turbulent day, and I was frustrated at the apparent inability of the Treasury and the Bank of England to provide reassurance to the markets. They had not forecast the scale of the reaction nor had they taken sufficient action to avert it. That, in my view, was a failure to do their job. But given the lukewarm nature of their public statements, which implicitly accepted the criticisms of our opponents, it is unsurprising that the markets were unconvinced. They could see the governor and the Treasury establishment did not believe in our policies.

This threatened to turn a market squall into a full-blown financial crisis, and it was obvious that an urgent intervention would be required to avert the disaster of collapsing pension funds. On Wednesday, the governor announced that the bank was setting aside £65 billion ($79 billion) to buy up bonds to ease pressure on pension funds and insurance companies. This was more than a complete reversal of the £40 billion quantitative tightening he had announced on the eve of the mini-budget. Even if you accept the conventional wisdom, this QT program was almost twenty times more impactful than the 45 percent tax cut. Yet it was barely mentioned in the media. However, the governor set a time limit of thirteen days on this action, which was profoundly unhelpful, effectively creating another cliff edge to the risk. His argument was that he wanted to avoid creating a moral hazard by signaling the bank would bail out bad investments, but it created further problems. This deadline would in due course become crucial.

The bank's action averted a financial meltdown. But why had the LDI problem arisen in the first place?

Liability-driven investments were the 2022 version of credit default swaps: a product that aimed to reduce risk but actually left its holders open to different, bigger risks down the road. Large investors like BlackRock had bought heavily into them as a way of making money when interest rates were low and pension funds were limited in the products in which they could invest. Even the Bank of England's own pension fund had bought into LDIs.

The overreliance on these products was due partly to poor regulation and oversight by the Bank of England and financial authorities and a lack of awareness by the Treasury. But fundamentally it was the consequence of artificially low interest rates, which had been in place since the 2008 financial crash. Since it was harder to get a decent return on investments in those circumstances, risky schemes like these were dreamed up. This was a problem that would have doubtless faced a reckoning at some point, given the inevitable rise in interest rates. But it was our misfortune to be the ones who entered a room full of petrol while carrying a candle.

As that week ended, things did begin to calm at least slightly following the bank's intervention. But why was it that the guns had been turned on the mini-budget rather than the Bank of England? And why was the fiscal package that was relatively modest compared with previous announcements, such as the cost of the furlough scheme during the pandemic, jumped on with such horror? Furlough cost £70 billion, which was greater than either the energy or tax package. This, I think, is the key to understanding why I was ultimately unable to deliver on my mandate and why my premiership ended the way it did. I came to realize there is no such thing as "the market" in this sense.

Rather, there are groups of influential individuals in the financial establishment, all of whom know and speak to one another in a closed feedback loop. The Treasury, the Bank of England, and the OBR are deeply embedded in these social and professional networks and share the same belief in the established economic orthodoxy. It is a classic example of groupthink. Over time, this group has moved to the left, adopting Net Zero goals and diversity targets while arguably neglecting many of their core duties, such as the Bank of England's responsibility to keep down inflation and maintain financial stability.

The actions of much of the banking industry have become more politically driven. For example, the interpretation of money-laundering regulations has made it harder for right-of-center politicians and organizations to get bank accounts. In 2023, Nigel Farage, the former leader of the Brexit Party, had his bank account at the exclusive Coutts Bank withdrawn. An investigation revealed that this was due to his having what the bank deemed unacceptable views. The subsequent leaking of his account details to journalists by Dame Alison Rose, chief executive of the NatWest Group, which owns Coutts, led to her resignation. Extraordinarily, the financial services regulator, the FCA, failed to find any problem with this.

Both the policymakers within government and the broader ecosystem they regulate have a similar worldview and too much vested interest in protecting the status quo. Their concerns are very different from those of the average British citizen. They are global-left in outlook and pro-China. They intrinsically believe in big government, high taxes, and bloated spending, as they benefit from a large administrative state. Unlike elected politicians, they rarely have to account for these views.

Taken at face value, our plan was a modest fiscal event, particularly given that it was the precursor to a planned spending review and a firm commitment to get debt falling in the medium term, as promised in my leadership campaign. So why was there such an extreme reaction? The obvious answer is that the Treasury establishment and the Bank of England were not on my side. On a personal note, the bank governor himself was clearly annoyed that during the leadership election I had questioned the bank's mandate and said I would look to review it. Under the Bank of England Act, it is perfectly acceptable for Parliament to examine the bank's mandate, but this was painted as an unacceptable attack on an independent institution, as were my criticisms of the OBR and Treasury orthodoxy.

I knew the economic establishment would resent being challenged and that I would have to win the argument against them. But I had not appreciated just how ruthless they would be in pushing back by all means at their disposal. As uniquely influential figures, their signals to the market took on immense significance. It was once said that all the governor of the Bank of England had to do was raise an eyebrow to bring errant financial institutions back into line. While that form of informal regulation is widely believed to have been consigned to history, the "governor's eyebrow" retains the power to shape opinion and move markets.

In our case, it was not just the raising of an eyebrow, but a sustained whispering campaign by the economic establishment, encouraged and fueled by my political opponents in the Conservative Party who refused to accept my mandate to lead. The signal was given that my agenda was a dangerous heresy that could not be allowed to succeed. I had been prepared for a political battle on the merits of our approach, but what I had not accounted for was the strength of the institutional resistance we faced from the outset. It became a question of who had more power over economic and fiscal policy, the elected politicians or the unelected technocrats. As I soon discovered, the answer was worryingly clear: it was them.

The resistance of the economic establishment was a crucial factor in our failure to implement the mini-budget. But it did not take place in a vacuum. Fundamentally, not enough Conservative MPs supported my agenda, and even those who did were not necessarily prepared to do what it took to get the measures through.

In fact, over the course of the previous thirteen years, big-government Conservatives were ascendant. Many of them were well connected in the media and spent their time briefing influential journalists, which shaped opinion as much as the parallel operation by the economic establishment.

From the day of the mini-budget, those Conservatives focused their ire on the abolition of the 45 percent top rate of income tax. I was surprised to find that Conservative MPs should be so resolute in their opposition to a tax cut, of all things, and especially a cut to an anti-success tax that raised little money and had been deliberately introduced by Labour's Gordon Brown to stoke the politics of envy.

This fact pointed to a broader problem with the Conservative Party and what it had come to represent. Ten years earlier, the Conservative Party had supported the reduction of the top tax rate from 50 percent to 45 percent without any problems and more revenue had been generated. If anything can be said to demonstrate the extent to which left-wing orthodoxy had infused British political culture, this was the most striking example.

A narrative developed about unfunded tax cuts. Even excluding the Laffer curve effect, these tax cuts were less than the spending increases that have since taken place. This, I'm afraid, shows how much ground the Left has seized—there is never talk of unfunded spending commitments.

Kwasi and I probably should have realized how this would be spun by our opponents, but we were spending all our time thinking about reviving the ailing economy. In retrospect, the timing of the announcement was a problem. By unveiling the plan on the Friday, it gave MPs a whole weekend to coordinate their opposition, briefing the press and stirring up trouble. Doing so on the eve of the Labour Party Conference also proved troublesome, with the opposition making hay by denouncing the income tax cut and pledging to reverse it. This allowed Conservative critics to claim it had been a political mistake, a theme readily picked up by the commentariat. The "optics" were bad, they said. Frankly, I was sick of hearing about "optics."

Since the leadership election, I had made a concerted effort to avoid becoming overly concerned with "optics." I had made clear I would be pursuing what I thought was right for the country, even if it was not immediately popular. As prime minister, I knew I had to remain focused on that mission. My approach was to perform as best I could in public while making the right decisions in private. I wanted to avoid the trap of becoming obsessed with media coverage. That way lay madness.

It was simply not right or possible for me to spend my time personally overseeing and directing the government's media strategy. That was what our professional media strategists and press officers were for. Here, however, I accept there was a problem of capacity. The Civil Service media operation, particularly in the Treasury, did not perform as well as it should have in laying the groundwork for the mini-budget. I am still not quite sure why. At the same time, the media team in Number 10 were still finding their feet. They did a heroic job but were battling through an unusually hostile environment.

A senior journalist has since told me that part of the problem we faced was a distinct shortage of expert voices supporting our agenda. Broadcasters and press alike struggled to find economists and commentators who could explain what we were trying to do. This was a sign not only of how unfashionable this agenda had become but of how unfamiliar journalists and MPs themselves were with it.

In an ideal world, we would have spent more time providing our allies with materials, lining up supporters, and making the case. But the plain reality was that the time and resources had not been available to us.

One of my team reported having to explain to a confused journalist the idea that excessively high tax rates can reduce rather than increase revenues. The concept of the Laffer curve is a pretty simple one and had been common currency in political discourse during the 1970s and 1980s. But here we were having to explain it as though it were a novel idea. At least that journalist was trying to understand what we were doing. Too many of the others seemed not even to want to bother.

While I was frustrated by the Westminster media lobby's refusal to engage seriously with our arguments, they were to a large extent reflecting the prevailing culture at Westminster. Ideas and serious policy nowadays take a back seat to gossip, plots, and intrigue, and there was no shortage of that during this period. Most prime ministers upon taking office can expect a political honeymoon during which their position in their party is at its strongest. For me, there was no such window of opportunity.

The parliamentary party was deeply divided and had acquired the habits of rebellion and regicide against its leaders. In the space of three years, Theresa May and then Boris Johnson had been brought down by their own MPs, making the position of Conservative Party leader more precarious than it had previously appeared. MPs who had remained loyal resented those who had ousted them and vice versa. We had then been through a bruising leadership contest that further fractured party unity and poisoned personal relationships—and in which more than half the parliamentary party had supported my opponents. Many of them actively wanted to bring me down and, having seen the fate of my predecessors, had high hopes of doing so.

Some might say the Conservative Party resembles an underperforming football team that keeps replacing its manager; at some point, it is going to have to consider whether there is a more fundamental problem. One of my Cabinet colleagues reflected during the turmoil that "the parliamentary party is unmanageable." They say British politics follows American politics, but sometimes the opposite occurs. I remember thinking of this remark when I read about the chaos that engulfed the U.S. House of Representatives when it couldn't elect a Speaker.

I am gregarious and I like people, but even my best friends wouldn't describe me as a great people manager. That responsibility lay principally with the chief whip, and I had appointed Wendy Morton to that role, having been pleased with how she had performed in whipping supporters for my leadership campaign. I believed she and Thérèse Coffey, my deputy prime minister, would be able to engage with the newer MPs, keep open the lines of communication with the parliamentary party, and help smooth over things where necessary. They and all the whips did their very best, but from the outset they faced quite appalling behavior from some of our own MPs.

Life was made absolute hell for Wendy and her deputy, Craig Whittaker. For example, there was bullying by one colleague over his not being invited to the Queen's state funeral, which resulted in a formal complaint and in due course a formal apology. But that was only the tip of the iceberg. The abuse they and others suffered from day one inevitably had a corrosive effect. I found myself having to spend an increasing amount of time giving pep talks to try and lift their flagging spirits. It helped that I am naturally an uber-optimist, but even I found this a strain.

By the time I got to Birmingham for the party conference, rebel MPs were pouring kerosene on the market jitters and my poor opinion poll ratings. They fomented a revolt about the 45 percent tax rate and then moved on to our proposed restraint on the welfare budget.

I was stuck in my suite on the top floor of the hotel, with people constantly coming and going, while having to endure the familiar strains of protesters with loudspeakers outside. It was like a mini–Downing Street. I was occasionally let out for a walk. Otherwise, I was isolated up there with my practice podium for rehearsing my big speech and an endless supply of American pancakes and maple syrup.

The conference was one of the few occasions when Frances and Liberty were able to join us. They were smuggled in under the guise of being Welsh Young Conservatives. Little did the lobby journalists getting into the elevators with Rosie and Molly from Cardiff North know they were my daughters incognito. Suffice it to say, they had more fun than I did.

Up in my suite, I received a number of delegations of colleagues pressing for various policies to be reversed, in particular the abolition of the 45 percent income tax rate. The identity of some of them was

not a great surprise, but it steadily became clear that even my own supporters had been spooked by the media circus that now surrounded the
issue and were not prepared to back it. On that basis, we were unlikely
to get the abolition through a vote in Parliament. I thought that rather
than let the conference be dominated by this issue, it would be better
to lance the boil there and then and back down.

Late that Sunday night, Kwasi and I and advisers met in my room.
He was due to give his main conference speech as chancellor the following day, and it was clear we had to clarify our position before that.
We discussed it and agreed that if the policy was dead, we needed to
take the hit now so that we could move on. If we didn't, the whole
conference would descend into open warfare. We announced the climb-
down and Kwasi went off to rewrite his speech.

I also reflected on what a bizarre turn of events it was for a
Conservative leader to face a rebellion *against* a proposed tax cut,
when so often in the past the pressure from MPs in leadership was for
them to promise even more tax cuts.

Backing down on the 45 percent rate eased some of the pressure,
but critics moved on to complaining about my plans to restrict entitlements and stop Britain's welfare bill from rising so fast. The 45 percent
rate cut had been economically beneficial but politically contentious,
so given the tricky situation I was prepared to scrap it. But the policy
to restrict the growth in benefits—to match the average rise in wages
rather than inflation—was both politically popular and economically
beneficial, and I was determined to stick with it. It seemed to me wrong
that somebody on welfare would get a bigger raise than someone in
work. And I couldn't for the life of me understand why Conservatives
were opposing it. Even Cabinet ministers felt free to air their misgivings
about the possibility that we might not commit to the extra spending.

As this all rumbled on, I was on a merry-go-round of receptions and
events. The least enjoyable of these was an almost entire day of media

interviews, which was even less of an attractive proposition following the U-turn. But it had to be done. More to my taste was the round of parties and receptions, where I got an enthusiastic welcome from the grassroots party members. It was a telling reminder of the disconnect between the MPs in Parliament and the party in the country that had just elected me as their leader.

On Wednesday, I made my keynote speech to the conference, renewing my commitment to focus unrelentingly on economic growth and attacking the vested interests of what I called "the anti-growth coalition." Somewhat helpfully, some of that coalition decided to show up in person, as I was interrupted by environmental protesters from Greenpeace. As usually happens after such incidents, it helped rally the audience behind me, with loud cheers as they were led away.

Despite having to acknowledge the 45 percent rate U-turn, I was determined not to dilute my message on the merits of tax cuts. As I put it:

> Cutting taxes is the right thing to do morally and economically. Morally, because the state does not spend its own money. It spends the people's money. Economically, because if people keep more of their own money, they are inspired to do more of what they do best. This is what grows the economy.
>
> When the government plays too big a role, people feel smaller. High taxes mean you feel it's less worthwhile working that extra hour, going for a better job or setting up your own business. That, my friends, is why we are cutting taxes. . . . We need to be internationally competitive, with all our tax rates attracting the best talent. Cutting taxes helps us face this global economic crisis, putting up a sign that Britain is open for business.

It was satisfying after a difficult ten days to be able to set out my stall as prime minister, making the case for the things I believed in and which I knew were right for the country. I ended on a note of determination:

> This mission will be difficult but it is necessary. We have no alternative if we want to get our economy moving again. I am ready to make hard choices. You can trust me to do what it takes. The status quo is not an option. That is why we cannot give in to the voices of decline. We cannot give in to those who say Britain can't grow faster. We cannot give in to those who say we can't do better. We must stay the course.

This was the central message I wanted my party to hear and understand. With just two years until the next general election, we simply had to knuckle down and get serious about the hard work required to turn the economy around. It was warmly received in the hall, and I hoped it had served its purpose in demonstrating to my colleagues that I was determined to carry on with the job I had been elected to do.

By the end of the conference, I felt cautiously optimistic that we might have weathered the worst of the storm and that the political situation had stabilized somewhat. The day after the conference concluded, I headed off to Prague for the first meeting of the European Political Community (EPC). The round of meetings with other heads of government and discussions on Ukraine and other pressing international issues rather put the domestic political scene into perspective.

When I returned on Friday, a new front had opened up in our battle with the economic establishment. The OBR took its revenge for being sidelined over the mini-budget, sending an email to the chancellor warning of a £72 billion ($87 billion) gap in the public finances on the basis of its latest analysis. This was immediately leaked and briefed to sympathetic journalists, with a former deputy governor of the Bank of England and OBR member trotted out to reinforce the message. The culture of leaking and negative briefing was by now out of control and, frankly, appalling. Here was a supposedly "independent" public body engaging in a deliberate abuse of market-sensitive information in order to undermine confidence in the government. I was furious at their behavior and still am.

I believed the numbers in their analysis were wrong, and so it has since proved. In March 2023, less than four months after the Autumn Statement, the OBR announced it had overestimated its key metric, public borrowing in five years' time, by a staggering £28.4 billion. Subsequent figures have shown the OBR to be even more adrift.

But in the short term, it had the desired effect. It sparked a further round of meetings in which we were pressed by Treasury officials to make further changes to our plans to reassure markets that we would be able to close this gap through spending reductions or other means. The implication was clear: they believed we should reverse course on the mini-budget. Having failed to stop it in advance, the economic establishment was now seeking to do so after the event.

That night, the family and I headed off for our first weekend at Chequers, the prime minister's official country residence. The staff were very welcoming, but it was hard to relax. Chequers was at one stage owned by Oliver Cromwell's descendants, and on the upper floor the Cromwell corridor was replete with memorabilia. I wasn't in the best frame of mind to enjoy reminders of the English Civil War.

On Sunday, Kwasi arrived to join my discussions with the political team about how we should proceed in the week ahead. The House of Commons was due to reassemble after the conference recess, and it was clear we would need to mount a charm offensive with the parliamentary party. The issue of benefits uprating was set to become the next major headache, with scores of MPs now saying they would force a vote and oppose any attempt to peg the increase to earnings rather than prices.

Any hope of getting back on the front foot was short-lived. On Monday morning, the Bank of England announced an increase in the scope of its measures to prop up LDI investments and stop pension funds from going bust. This was made necessary because of nervousness among investors about what would happen at the end of the week when the bank had said its support would end. That drop-off had proved something of a ticking time bomb as far as the markets were concerned.

As a further measure to reassure the markets, Kwasi announced with my agreement that he would bring forward his medium-term fiscal plan from the planned date of November 23 to October 31, Halloween. This was starting to look like a horror story, given that the OBR forecast we had pledged to publish alongside it would now undercut our planned approach to cutting debt. We were now being forced to choose between all manner of unpalatable options on public spending or reversing all the tax announcements from the mini-budget, just to make the numbers fit a forecast we believed to be comprehensively wrong.

It was also at this point that we announced the appointment of James Bowler as the new permanent secretary to the Treasury. I was personally fine with the choice, having rated him highly while I was chief secretary. But I still resented the fact that I had been obliged to block the chancellor's preferred candidate at the behest of the bank governor, Andrew Bailey, who warned of an adverse market reaction.

The following day, it was Bailey himself who caused a market reaction by announcing the LDI support scheme would not be extended beyond the end of the week. This led to the pound immediately falling against the dollar and prompted criticism from fund managers who wanted to see support continue at least until the medium-term fiscal plan had been announced at the end of the month.

Bailey made the statement from Washington, D.C., where he was attending the annual meeting of the International Monetary Fund (IMF). Earlier in the day, the IMF itself had used one of its reports to renew its earlier criticism of the mini-budget. The IMF had not, as its remit suggested, focused on the mini-budget's impact on the economy or economic stability. Its criticism of tax cuts had been about distribution, whether the rich would benefit "too much"—surely a domestic question for the UK government.

The pile-on attacking the policy included everybody right up to Joe Biden, the president of the United States of America. "I wasn't the only one that thought it was a mistake," he opined during a visit to, of all places, an ice cream parlor in Portland, Oregon. "I think that the idea of cutting taxes on the super-wealthy at a time when . . . anyway, I just think . . . I disagreed with the policy."

This was utter hypocrisy and ignorance. The top rate of federal income tax in the United States was 37 percent and only charged to people earning $539,901 and above. By contrast, the top rate in the United Kingdom is 45 percent and paid by those on £125,140 ($138,580 U.S.) and above. I was shocked and astounded that Biden would breach protocol by commenting on UK domestic policy. We had been the United States' staunchest allies through thick and thin.

It became clear we were not just challenging UK economic orthodoxy; this groupthink extended to the leading powers of the West. In America, it had become known as "Bidenomics." And what the Biden administration, the EU, and their international allies didn't want was a country demonstrating that things can be done differently, undercutting them in the process.

The supposedly growth-promoting OECD had been encouraged to develop a minimum tax accord, essentially trying to dampen tax competition and making the West less competitive. Regrettably, the UK had gone along with it. Yet again, after the British public had voted to leave the EU and chart our own destiny, politicians had sided with another unelected international body that would constrain us.

Kwasi himself then insisted on heading to Washington to join the IMF conference, ignoring my suggestion that it was not a good time for him to be out of the country. I thought no one in Britain would care that he had missed the IMF conference, and I could see the situation was very fragile. He thought the IMF meeting was more important, and he didn't want to show any panic. The chancellor and the prime minister not being in the same country during such a tumultuous week would turn out to be a serious problem.

That Monday, I went to visit the England women's football team at their training ground in Twickenham. They had liked the bit in my conference speech where I had lamented when I'd been on a plane as a child and been given a junior air hostess badge while my brothers were given junior pilot badges. As female footballers, they too had had to break through a lot of prejudice. They said they couldn't really believe they were playing for England and asked me if I could believe I was prime minister. I said I struggled to comprehend what had happened to me, going from attending a comprehensive school in Leeds to living at 10 Downing Street.

I'd watched them play Germany at Wembley during the summer in the European Cup final. It had been a fantastic break from the campaign as England stormed to victory. It was nail-biting, though, with the score standing at 1–1 going into extra time and the prospect of a penalty shoot-out hanging over us. I marveled at how the team had the mental resilience to score a goal in the final ten minutes. It's all about "psych-ops," they told me, referring to how they had approached the German team. You have to mess with their minds, they said. Regrettably, that's what my colleagues were doing to me back at Westminster.

The next day, I faced an ambush of backbench Tory MPs at a meeting of the 1922 Committee. The ostensible purpose of the meeting was for me to explain my strategy. Yet my political opponents mounted a concerted effort to undermine me, asking a barrage of hostile questions and then briefing the whole thing to the media. Naively, I had not even brought a media adviser to the meeting. It was an ugly scene and left even my staunchest supporters rattled.

As well as dealing with rebellious MPs, there was also the continuing lack of confidence in the markets. The Cabinet Room was constantly filled with Treasury officials bringing their latest portent of doom. I felt isolated in the face of this onslaught, with Kwasi away in D.C.

That Thursday morning, James Bowler came to see me in the Cabinet Room and delivered a stark warning: if we persevered with our plan to cut taxes, the markets would crash. I also received a warning letter from the Cabinet Secretary echoing this point following his conversation with Governor of the Bank of England, Andrew Bailey. With the Bank of England's support for pension funds about to end—and the governor refusing to extend it—investors would begin a fire sale of government bonds. We risked a complete market meltdown that would see the government unable to finance its debts.

To avoid this, I was told, we would have to signal a complete and unambiguous change of direction. That meant a U-turn on corporation tax, reinstating the previously planned increase from 19 percent to 25 percent. The mini-budget would be dead, and my entire economic agenda with it.

I knew they had me at gunpoint. This warning was in fact an ultimatum. If I refused to change course, the financial catastrophe they predicted would undoubtedly occur. The culture of leaking and briefing would ensure the markets knew exactly what the bank and the Treasury establishment had advised me, and any remaining confidence in the government would evaporate. By presenting the advice in this way, they ensured I had no option but to take it.

Throughout the day, I tried to reach Kwasi to discuss what had now become an existential crisis for the government. Still in Washington at the IMF meeting, he proved difficult to pin down. When I did speak to him, he didn't appreciate the scale of what was happening. He spoke about not panicking and just holding our nerve. It didn't help that he wasn't in the country. Things always look less bad when you are almost four thousand miles away. "Kwasi," I told him, "I'm being threatened with a market meltdown. This is f***ing serious."

Everyone else on my team had already been convinced to surrender. I had been the last holdout, but I now realized it was a hopeless position. Faced with the prospect of a catastrophic economic meltdown, I had an overriding duty as prime minister to do what was necessary to avoid it. However painful it was to abandon policies I believed in and knew to be right, that duty came first.

With the decision made, I went into full damage-limitation mode, operating almost on autopilot. I had to consider what else would be required to steady the ship. There had already been extensive calls for Kwasi to be removed, and I couldn't see how he could now credibly present such a major policy reversal himself. Reluctantly, I concluded that to restore confidence, we needed a new chancellor who could steady the ship. Appointing another true believer in my agenda would not have cut the mustard.

That night, I could hardly sleep. The Horse Guards clock chimed every fifteen minutes, counting down to the hideous day ahead. I ran through in my mind everything that had happened and was going to happen. My attempts to turn around British economic policy and get the country on the right path had been comprehensively trashed. Ever the optimist, I had been hoping there would be a more positive turn of events after the relentless stream of bad luck and negativity. But I knew

I was running out of road. It was like a game of Tetris when you start losing control and the pieces are getting closer and closer to the top.

On Friday morning, as Kwasi was flying back to London, I called Jeremy Hunt, the former Cabinet minister Boris had beaten for the party leadership in 2019. He was in Brussels and initially rejected the call, not recognizing the number. When I finally spoke to him and asked him to take over as chancellor, he was somewhat taken aback to say the least. We do not share the same political views, but I had always got on well with him and I believed he would be able to do what was now required.

As Jeremy returned from Brussels, Kwasi was flying back from D.C. Yet again I was appalled by a press leak: Kwasi learned of his apparent sacking while scrolling through his Twitter feed on his phone while traveling in the car back to central London from the airport. This was deeply regrettable, and I would have much preferred if, just this one time, the incessant urge to leak had been resisted.

It was a difficult meeting. We had been friends and political colleagues for more than a decade and had developed our political agenda together. We had planned this bold economic approach and both still believed in it. Now it was coming to a painful end. I still don't think he realized how bad things had become during his absence. I laid it out for him, stressing that I simply could not risk the British government going bankrupt. "I'm sorry Kwasi, but I have to do what I can to stabilize things. And that means you going."

He was understandably annoyed, and I don't blame him. He said that sacking him wouldn't save me and that they would come for me next. I conceded he was probably right, but I now had an obligation to at least try to steady the ship in the short term.

That afternoon I gave a short press conference to announce the U-turn on corporation tax and explain what the new chancellor and I would be doing to ensure economic stability. I faced the media frenzy alone. It was a pretty ghastly experience, which felt a lot like officiating at my own funeral. I was absolutely clear that my economic policy was dead, and most people thought my premiership was too.

That weekend, we invited Jeremy Hunt and his family to Chequers for Sunday lunch before he and I sat down to go over the announcements that he would make in the Commons the following day. He had very quickly gotten a handle on the situation and was fully across the details of what needed to be done to calm the markets and provide the necessary reassurance. He had taken to the Treasury very easily, and they to him. That was, of course, the purpose of his appointment. The Treasury establishment had defeated me, so now I had appointed a classic Treasury man as chancellor. I was no longer in control of economic policy.

While our children were playing in the Chequers swimming pool and I was having some time out, I chatted to Hugh on the lawn. He posed the question I hadn't wanted to think about: Given that I had been forced to abandon the policies I had been elected to deliver, what was the point of my remaining prime minister?

That Monday afternoon, I sat in the House of Commons as Jeremy Hunt made his first statement as chancellor, effectively burying the mini-budget. The remaining tax cuts that had not already been reversed were abandoned, including the cut to the basic rate of income tax, reductions in dividend taxes, and freezes on alcohol duties. Sitting alongside him on the front bench in the Commons was something of an out-of-body experience, as I listened to him shredding the platform on which I had won the leadership election. It was uniquely painful.

Immediately beforehand I had been updated on the mood of the Conservative backbenches. It didn't take a genius to work out that it was not good. That evening, I sat down to record an interview with the BBC's political editor, Chris Mason, in which I conceded I had gone "too far and too fast" with the changes I had sought to make. I repeated this admission in private in meetings with MPs and the Cabinet.

There were further such meetings on Tuesday, including one with the anti-EU European Research Group of MPs, who were all very supportive, which was a welcome boost. All the while, people were getting in touch to offer advice on what I should do to reset the government and move on, including whom I should appoint to the Cabinet and whom I should fire. Few of these suggestions were remotely practical, even if I had been minded to agree with them. And none of them was likely to have had any impact on the situation by that point.

If I or any of my team held out hope, then Wednesday, October 19, put paid to it. It began constructively enough with preparation for Prime Minister's Questions, which took up most of the morning. Just before midday, I went over to the House of Commons and went into the chamber for the session. As was now becoming habit, I began by repeating that I was sorry and that I acknowledged I had made mistakes. But in response to Labour taunts, I reminded the House that I had still delivered on reducing energy bills and canceling the rise in National Insurance rates. It was predictably rowdy, but I thought it went as well as could have been expected given the circumstances.

Then, in the afternoon, events took another bizarre turn. I was informed that the home secretary, Suella Braverman, had leaked a sensitive draft ministerial statement to a backbench MP in a serious breach of the Ministerial Code. After a discussion with the Cabinet secretary, I concluded I would have to ask her to step down and called her to my office to tell her in person. In her place, I appointed Grant Shapps, who had a reputation as a competent media performer and who I suspected would not turn down the opportunity. I was right.

This unexpected additional drama meant I had not spent much time thinking about that evening's vote on an opposition motion on fracking. The first I knew there might be a problem was when I was told by the whips that—unusually for a sitting prime minister—they really needed me there to vote myself, as it looked like a revolt by Conservative MPs would leave it too close for comfort. After attending my weekly audience with the King, I headed from Buckingham Palace to the Commons for the vote, which we won comfortably. However, it soon emerged that there had been angry scenes during the vote, with our whips openly arguing with MPs and tempers running high all round.

I was then told that Wendy Morton and Craig Whittaker—the chief whip and her deputy—had both resigned, saying they were unable to put up with the abuse they were getting. I spoke to Wendy and Craig in my office and urged them not to resign; it was clear that it would only exacerbate the house of cards falling down. They were very emotional and there had clearly been much confusion, including trouble stirred up by our opponents. I eventually persuaded them, but they insisted on a statement going out. It was surreal. With my team, I headed over to the Whips' Office and found it in utter chaos. Seeing the looks of despair on the faces of colleagues all around the Commons that night, I just thought to myself: *This is done. This is terminal.*

We went back to Number 10, where we then had to deal with the fallout from the vote and confirm that Wendy and Craig had now un-resigned. Once all that was finally sorted, I went up to the flat. By that time, I had more or less decided that my only option was to resign. I had already done what was needed to avoid an economic meltdown, but the political meltdown of the Conservative Party now appeared unstoppable.

I didn't sleep much that night either, and in the morning I still felt the situation was impossible. I went down to the Cabinet Room and spoke to my chief of staff, Mark Fullbrook, and Nick Catsaras, my private secretary. Both of them reluctantly agreed that my time was up. I went back up to the flat to speak to Hugh, who told me I would have regretted never running for leader and trying to do the things in which I believed, but that I wouldn't regret leaving now that it had proved impossible. He was right.

I went back down to the Cabinet Room for a meeting with Jeremy Hunt. In a last twist of the knife from the market-whisperers, the chancellor told me that my going was now "the price the markets wanted." It didn't matter. I didn't need another push. I was going. The only questions were around timing and the arrangements for choosing my successor, which I started to discuss with the team. I asked Sir Graham Brady, the chairman of the 1922 Committee of Conservative MPs, to come over, and I told him my decision. He said a new leader of the Conservative Party could be chosen and in place by the end of the following week. Only until then would I remain prime minister.

The decision made, I telephoned His Majesty the King to inform him personally. He was as kind and sympathetic as ever. Then the Cabinet Room started to fill up as close colleagues joined my senior officials and the political team. Hugh came down and spoke to them all as we worked on drafting my public statement. There was much agreement that the situation had become inevitable and that the party had become ungovernable. Hugh helpfully reminded me that he had said in July that leading the Conservative Party was an impossible job that no one would want to do.

A last-minute phone call came in from Liberty, calling on me not to resign from the middle of her school playing field. I had to say it was too late.

At 1:30 p.m., I went out to the lectern outside Number 10 and announced my resignation as leader of the Conservative Party. I reiterated that I had been elected with a mandate from the party to change the direction of the government and deliver economic growth. Given I could no longer fulfill that mandate, it was right for me to go.

I was angry and frustrated that it had come to this. But by that stage the overriding feeling was one of relief. The whole experience as prime minister had been quite surreal, and my resignation seemed like just another dramatic moment in a very strange film in which I had somehow been cast.

We spent a last weekend at Chequers, where we gave a farewell party for friends. The following Tuesday, I chaired the Cabinet for the last time before leaving Number 10 to see the King and formally tender my resignation as prime minister.

The first leadership hustings had been held at Elland Road, the home ground of Leeds United football club, the local team during my childhood. In my speech there, I made reference to Don Revie, the legendary manager of the 1970s Leeds team that had won the league who then went on to manage England. The team was known as "Dirty Leeds," and opposing fans accused them of violence and cheating. Brian Clough then took over from Revie at the club in 1974. As dramatized in the film *The Damned United*, Clough tried to shake up the team and get them to play better:

> Well, I might as well tell you now. You lot may all be internationals and have won all the domestic honors there are to win under Don Revie. But as far as I'm concerned, the first thing you can do for me is to chuck all your medals and all your caps and all your pots and all your pans into the biggest f***ing dustbin you can find, because you've never won any of them fairly. You've done it all by bloody cheating.

The players rebelled and Clough was sacked after just forty-four days. In the final days of my premiership, I had said to my private secretary, Nick Catsaras: "If the Conservative Party bin me after six weeks and I'm the Brian Clough of prime ministers, then so be it."

I lasted forty-nine days.

* * *

So, what did I learn from my time at Downing Street?

The main lesson I drew is about the sheer power of the administrative state and its influence on the markets and the wider polity. I had not understood until I became prime minister how powerful these people are. The forty-nine days in Downing Street taught me more about that than the previous ten years in government.

I sat in Cabinets under David Cameron, Theresa May, and then Boris Johnson, all the while growing frustrated over how slow progress was, how nothing much seemed to get done. I thought that with a clearer sense of direction and a more assertive attitude, it would be possible to change things, to challenge the prevailing orthodoxy. I now realize that was not the case.

What I now understand is that in government you have a choice: you can either go along with the orthodoxy, or you get booted out. That was essentially what had happened to me at the Ministry of Justice when I'd tried to challenge the established order. The powerful vested interests there pushed back, made my life very difficult, and ultimately got me fired. I had assumed they were only able to do that because I wasn't at the top. What I now realize is that even when you are supposedly at the top, they can still do it. That is, frankly, scary.

What we saw in September and October 2022 was a government that sought to challenge the prevailing economic orthodoxy being prevented from doing so by those who had created and defended that orthodoxy. The economic establishment used its huge and unrivaled influence over the markets to undermine confidence in the elected government, stir up political resistance, and force it to change course.

The only way to counteract this is vast amounts of political capital. That was in short supply when I was elected. I faced a Conservative Party that after twelve years in office was fractious and split. They were not willing or able collectively to back a bold program.

Many of my critics said I presided over instability, and that is of course true. The case I want to make is that in the current British political system, achieving change without instability is nigh on impossible, given the legacy of twenty-five years of economic consensus and the now ossified system protecting it. Maintaining stability means going along with the status quo.

I regret that we have lost out on benefits for the country that could have been delivered. Analysis suggests that if my plans had been kept, GDP growth would be 2 percent higher by 2030. Investment would not have faltered in the North Sea were it not for the windfall tax. We would have gotten moving on fracking and lower energy bills would have been on the horizon. A more competitive rate of corporation tax would have persuaded the likes of AstraZeneca to open new plants in Britain. Instead we are stagnating.

Whether you agree with what we were trying to do or not, the turn of events is worryingly anti-democratic. We now have unaccountable institutions that are more powerful than elected politicians. That poses a fundamental problem for parties across the political spectrum that seek to challenge the status quo.

Despite the political failings to which I own up, we have a fundamental institutional and governance problem—especially over our economic destiny. When we lifted the rock of EU rules, what was underneath was not a pretty sight. Democratically elected politicians are sidelined in a system that is run by a group-thinking orthodoxy. Simply put, there needs to be greater democracy and accountability. And Conservative politicians desperately need to find their economic compass.

If there's one thing I want conservatives to understand from this book, it is that there is no smooth way to achieve the change the country and the wider West needs. No amount of pitch-rolling and messaging can avoid what will be a messy and chaotic battle against some deeply embedded vested interests and those on our own side who seek to appease them. We have to be brave, and we have to take risks in order to win this fight. It will mean taking on powerful institutions that resist every step of the way.

I sometimes wonder if I should have gone with the grain more. Bided my time. But with two years to go until an election, we didn't have time. We had already failed to deliver change for too long. And it wasn't getting any easier; every day that went by made it harder to challenge orthodox thinking.

In reality, the only choice I had was whether to try to stay in office and simply manage as well as I could within the accepted orthodoxy, tweaking things in the right direction, stopping the worst excesses of the woke brigade and the eco-extremists. I wasn't prepared to do that. The West was in trouble, and we had a real opportunity to do something about it. The real calamity would be if I were still in Number 10, going along to get along while Britain descended further into the abyss.

CHAPTER 14

Ten Years to Save the West

In the first quarter of the twenty-first century, the West has taken a turn to the left. As a consequence, we have become weaker, both inside our own countries and abroad. Our foreign policy has appeased totalitarian regimes, which have thus been emboldened. Government, regulations, and money printing have all expanded, leading to an increase in inflation. Elected officials have been overpowered by an increasingly powerful administrative elite. The aftermath of the Cold War, in which free markets triumphed over statist communism, saw a period of terrible complacency by the West.

This complacency has allowed left-wing ideology to fester and grow in the public sector as well as in the corporate sphere. Cultural relativism, which rejects British and American exceptionalism (as well as that of our free world allies), has been embraced by much of the new elite. Extreme environmentalism and other previously fringe movements such as trans activism have been empowered and gained ground.

Immigration is too high. Much of this decay from within has been encouraged and even sponsored by outside forces, many of them linked to the very totalitarian regimes that seek to undermine our way of life.

Government has ballooned in size. The state now accounts for 46 percent of GDP in the United Kingdom and 35 percent of GDP in the United States. At the turn of the twenty-first century, the figures were 36 percent and 29 percent respectively. There has also been a growth in the number and powers of quangos and regulators. The pervasive reach of state officialdom has encroached ever further into people's lives. Parliamentary sovereignty has been diluted with more power accumulated by the quangocracy, an unaccountable judiciary, and undemocratic international institutions. In the United States, constitutional freedoms are under threat from an assertive administrative state.

Too many conservatives, rather than seeking to roll back this encroachment, have tried instead to bring the government machine under conservative control. This is a futile exercise. Whatever some might claim, big government has never been a friend of conservatism. It takes power away from individuals and families; it saps enterprise and it creates hundreds of thousands of jobs for leftists.

The result of this relentless leftward tilt has been declining levels of economic growth and increased alienation through cancel culture and the wokeism that now prevails in everything from the media to the business world. While outpourings of popular discontent have been seen through the Brexit referendum, the election of Donald Trump, and the *gilets jaunes* movement in France, none of these has changed the balance of power in the medium term. The permanent bureaucracy has been very effective at preventing the implementation of policies that the majority of the public supports.

Conservative parties have often triangulated and accepted the direction of travel. Too many conservatives have stopped making the case for conservative policies and instead tried to get elected based on a promise to manage the bloated state bureaucracy more competently.

I started as an MP in 2010, believing this leftist hegemony could be changed. Like most idealistic politicians, I assumed it was simply a matter of political will. I set about putting out ideas, books, and policy papers. Many of my colleagues did the same.

My subsequent experience in government over the ten years after 2012 showed me the true nature of what we are dealing with. When I was appointed a minister, I worked within the system to try to reduce regulations, curb spending, and reform public services. Many of us in government had the same objectives. I found it cumbersome and frustrating, but I assumed this was to do with my lowly rank.

The higher I rose up the ladder, the more I realized that the problems we faced were deep-seated and serious: a Conservative Party that had lost its compass and instead turned on itself, and a bureaucratic state that was becoming increasingly bold in challenging and obstructing elected politicians.

This has made it all but impossible to deliver popular policies that would improve lives across the United Kingdom. I am talking about such things as building more homes and reforming the planning system, rowing back on Net Zero, stopping the boats coming across the Channel and controlling immigration, cutting corporate taxes, reversing burdensome diversity and equality rules, and getting EU law off the statute book and out of Northern Ireland—all of which would make Britain grow faster while embedding confidence in our values and our way of life.

There has been some progress on this agenda. But looking back I see that the changes I helped deliver—such as school reform, the Australia trade deal and accession to the CPTPP, and stopping gender self-ID—all took energy and political capital far disproportionate to what they managed to accomplish. They were all delivered in the face of near hysterical opposition and occupied huge amounts of political bandwidth. Although they were desirable, none of them were game changers for the future of Britain.

The Growth Plan (otherwise known as the mini-budget) was my attempt to break the logjam and start tackling the big problems in Britain. Even getting it formulated and announced was a major achievement. In the Kafkaesque world of Whitehall, second-guessing, inertia, and sheer inaction prevent many good policies from even getting to this stage. But ultimately the twin forces of institutional resistance and a Conservative parliamentary party that was not prepared to have an economic battle killed it.

The Lessons of a Lost Battle

My purpose in writing this book is not to relitigate the battles of the past quarter of a century. It is to learn from them. I want to provide a call to action for fellow conservatives who share my belief in our nation and our way of life, who share my frustration at what has been going wrong with our politics and governance. I want others to heed the warnings of what I saw happening and learn the lessons of the battle I lost.

First, we must acknowledge that Britain and many other countries in the free world have a governance problem. Politicians, particularly conservative politicians, are increasingly unable to deliver on their promises and often get sidetracked or go along with the status quo. At best they content themselves with making small changes that come nowhere near meeting the scope of the challenges before them. I learned this with my very first policy skirmish, childcare deregulation, where ten years later we have still only delivered a fifth of the potential change.

This is a problem across government on issues large and small. There is a conspiracy of silence about it because serving ministers understandably don't want to admit how impotent they really are.

I know it is comforting for many to believe it would have been possible for us to deliver the Growth Plan—tax cuts, spending restraint, and supply-side reform—if only there had been more "pitch-rolling," better communication, and improved timing. It was just the way we went about it, they say.

But having sat in the hot seat, I can tell you that is simply not true. Frankly, if it were just a question of better PR and political tactics, these policies would have been implemented by now, given that it has been obvious to many for some time that they need to happen. The forces obstructing this agenda are much deeper-rooted and thus more intractable.

We can see this in the fact that the Conservative Party has changed its leader four times since 2016 and economic reform still remains out of reach. Yet the only answer that onlookers ever seem to come up with is to put someone new in charge of the broken machine or to have a reshuffle. At some point, they will have to face the fact that the problem is not the latest tenant of Number 10, but the system itself.

There must also be a recognition that it is not possible to deliver these policies without some degree of friction. Inevitably, the vested interests that are threatened will resist and use every tool at their disposal to obstruct change. Too often politics is presented as being a contrast between stability and chaos, with stability prized as an end in itself. But this hides the real choice. "Stability" usually implies acceptance of the status quo, while "chaos" is used as a pejorative term for any disruptive change. This framing means politicians often conclude that the only way to achieve "stability" is not to seek any change at all.

These problems are not limited to the United Kingdom. When we look at the fractures in the U.S. Republican Party, the growth of the administrative state in Washington, and the size of America's national debt, we see these forces are clearly at work across the free world, and perhaps especially in the English-speaking world. We should look to Canada with great interest to see what will happen if the eloquent Conservative leader Pierre Poilievre wins the next election there.

I hope that reading about my experiences will assist other conservatives in Britain and around the world in their own work to deliver change. To me, helping advance that agenda is the most important thing that could come from my time in government and is what I care about above all.

To that end, I believe there are several important lessons for conservatives to learn about how we can win the argument and successfully implement our policies.

Lesson 1: We Must Be Conservatives

None of the issues we face will be solved without robust conservative leadership. This starts with core conservative principles. It means individuals and families controlling their own lives rather than facing ever more intrusion from the government. It means defending property rights, free speech, and the rule of law. It means standing up for sovereignty, the nation-state, and British exceptionalism. And it means rejecting Net Zero zealotry and wokeism.

The road to hell is paved with compromise and triangulation. Too many conservatives have lost the courage of their convictions in the face of the ceaseless onslaught of the leftist agenda. Instead of confronting these damaging and nonsensical ideas, they have sought to reach accommodation with them and accepted the Left's terms of debate. This has led to the internal decay of conservatism and a focus on the superficial rather than what is important. It has in some cases led to venality and nihilism and to the pursuit of power for its own sake.

Whether through misplaced fear of being on the "wrong side of history" or simple naïveté about the implications, conservatives have too often given the benefit of the doubt to our opponents and allowed them to win by default. We should be clear that our enemies want to destroy us and not labor under the misapprehension that they are well-intentioned or neutral players. We should meet the threat in kind, by fighting for our ideas and fighting to win.

Winning the battle of ideas and exposing our opponents' agenda as dangerous is the only way we will prevail as conservatives. In order to overcome the resistance of the orthodoxy, we need to build significant popular support and be properly organized. This will take time and effort. We need to win the argument on university campuses and in schools. We need more conservative media outlets. We need to use consumer power from the public to challenge the leftist drift of large corporations.

We need better conservative political infrastructure. This means building teams of people and structures that are capable of running government departments and Number 10 with a conservative ideology—well in advance of this happening. This will require significantly more funding going into conservative politics and a change in priorities. More should be spent on the long-term future of the conservative movement rather than immediate campaigning.

The Left has mobilized this way for years, and they are now reaping the rewards. In or out of office, their ideas have gradually infused public discourse and limited the scope of conservative policies. It is time to push back and mount an equally robust campaign against them.

In order to do so effectively, conservatives have to know what they believe and be prepared to stand up for it. Local conservative parties need to hold their representatives to account for how they vote, what they say, and the campaigns they support. The party has to focus far more on the principles of conservatism, as well as on the mechanics of campaigning.

Bravery will be required to change the culture, to get off the back foot and start fighting. The instinctive common sense of the public is our biggest potential asset, but it needs to be properly harnessed. We need to show a clear moral purpose and win support on that basis. I watched during the 1980s and 1990s as leftist organizations built up their support. They were committed. Obsessive. Fearless. We need to be the same. Our country needs us.

Lesson 2: We Must Dismantle the Leftist State

Once we have made the decision to fight for our values, we have to be prepared to take the necessary steps to achieve our ultimate goals. This means, first and foremost, an acceptance that we are not going to succeed in implementing conservative policies while the leftist state apparatus remains intact.

As Ronald Reagan said, the most terrifying words in the English language are "I'm from the government and I'm here to help." We need to restore a healthy skepticism of state intervention and stop pretending that big government can be the friend of conservatives. It cannot. We should by now have seen all the evidence we need that over time state bureaucracies inevitably drift to the left, however virtuous and independent they proclaim themselves to be.

As conservatives, we need to be clear about the imperative to reduce the scope of the state and strip away the power of unelected technocrats. This needs to be asserted as a public good in its own right, returning to people more power over their own lives and trusting them to make their own decisions.

We should also systematically roll back the institutional frameworks that sustain a left-wing worldview in our countries. In the United Kingdom, even after fourteen years of Conservative government, we still have most of the legislative treacle that Tony Blair and New Labour created during their time in office, which has gummed up the official machine and left Conservative minsters increasingly stuck. Whether it is the Human Rights Act, the Equality Act, or the Climate Change Act, these measures are totems of left-wing belief which have been too readily accepted by conservatives as immovable. We should be prepared to abolish them.

Lesson 3: We Must Restore Democratic Accountability

For years, we have been caught in a vicious cycle of politicians having less and less power and the public getting more and more angry that things cannot be fixed. As trust in the political system has been eroded, politicians have ceded yet more authority to unelected technocrats, which has exacerbated the problem. We need to stop the downward spiral by restoring democratic accountability to our institutions.

In the United Kingdom, this means making the Bank of England more accountable to elected politicians and abolishing quangos like the OBR. I have seen only too clearly how much power these bodies wield. It is fundamentally undemocratic for a government to be unable to prevail in its economic policy when it challenges the existing orthodoxy. It will require single-minded determination on the part of politicians to wrest back democratic control from unelected officials.

While the problem is most acute in economic policy, the same issue exists across government, with a mass of quangos, independent regulators, official advisory bodies, and assorted public sector organizations constraining and obstructing ministers at every turn. These also need to be cut down to size, with the notion that unelected officials know best replaced by the principle that power should only be exercised by those over whom the public can exercise proper control.

During the COVID pandemic, we saw the epitome of technocratic control, as government scientists and medical advisers increasingly displaced politicians in the driving seat of policy, affecting the daily lives and liberties of millions of people around the world.

Advisers advise, but elected politicians should decide. That basic democratic principle should not be discarded, however complex and difficult a problem or issue might be. Medical and scientific evidence should always be at the center of decision-making on matters of public health, but where there is a need to balance risks against other harms and the consequences of curtailing basic freedoms, the public should see and expect to see those they elect making the ultimate decisions—and accepting the consequences.

Too often nowadays the way our technocracy works is that politicians are expected to follow Civil Service advice or face questioning or condemnation for disregarding it. Whereas once this advice was entirely private, it is being increasingly aired in public either through leaks or inquiries and information requests. This makes the relationship asymmetric, as experts are hardly ever held to account for the consequences of their advice and politicians are instead expected to carry the can for failures.

For democratic accountability to be meaningful, senior politicians need to have a proper say over those who are providing the advice and carrying out the policies. In the United Kingdom, the prime minister and Cabinet ministers should have the power to appoint their senior civil servants. They should also have much greater discretion to choose who heads up their major institutions and agencies that exert so much influence over people's lives.

The judicial system in particular needs to be properly accountable. The Lord Chancellor's role should be restored to its pre-2005 state. It is right that a sitting Cabinet minister appointed by the prime minister is fully responsible for the appointment of the Lord Chief Justice and other senior judicial appointments. It is one of the striking examples of the diminution of the role of politicians that responsibilities that for centuries lay with the executive branch have now been taken away and placed in the hands of the unelected. While no one would seek to compromise the independence of judges in the courts, the overall administration of the judicial system is a legitimate area for policy debate. The public has a right to hold ministers accountable, so those ministers should have the requisite powers.

I was in the job of prime minister at an inauspicious time, but I could see that for both me and my predecessors the demands of the office were not met by the wherewithal to do it. The many problems I faced were hugely aggravated by the lack of some basic forms of support. The prime minister and senior ministers should have the proper apparatus to do their jobs. This should include realistic salaries, travel arrangements, and medical provision. They should also have administrative and personal support that is able to handle the many different aspects of the role. Currently, they do not.

Running a government department with responsibility for billions of pounds of public money and being head of government of a major G7 country are important roles. Leaving aside the lack of job security, they are all-encompassing, 24/7 roles that require a huge amount of work and attract enormous public and media scrutiny.

Despite this, ministers earn less than those in comparable jobs in the commercial sector and less than the permanent officials who answer to them. A secretary of state earns a total of £151,649 ($189,301). That is less than the amount paid to most of the senior directors in their department, and noticeably less than the permanent secretary, who can earn up to £195,000 ($243,415). Even the prime minister's total salary, at £159,584 ($199,206), is dwarfed by the sums paid to such figures as the chief executive of the NHS (£260,000, $324,554) and the "managing director of passenger services" at the Department for Transport (£265,000, $330,795).

These disparities tell us about the relative position of politicians compared to unelected officials. The latter, as well as enjoying higher salaries and job security, are protected by the doctrine of ministerial responsibility, which in practice means that ministers must take the blame for anything that goes wrong in their departments, whether or not they even knew about the decisions that led to them. No wonder being an official is often a more attractive proposition for talented individuals than entering elected politics, with all the abuse and public opprobrium that comes with it. A rebalancing is urgently needed.

For those who do put themselves in the firing line and become ministers, we should ensure they are properly supported. That doesn't just mean policy and administrative support, but adequate personal assistance as well. The "hair shirt" attitude that has become so prevalent nowadays means we have ministers subjected to innumerable inconveniences in their daily lives. Whether it is having to argue with officials to get access to efficient modes of transport or having to sort out their own medical care and personal appointments, these small irritations detract attention from where it should be: the job they are paid to do. The prime minister in particular suffers from a lack of such logistical support, which for a head of government is little short of scandalous. No chief executive of a major company would be left to fend for themselves in this way. We need to adopt a much more robust approach that recognizes that ministers' time is valuable and their personal welfare is important.

It is not just personal support that needs to be beefed up. Other aspects of the role of a front-rank politician also need proper resourcing. The Civil Service's aversion to "political" activity means there are large numbers of tasks, from engagement with MPs to public communication, that are left to a tiny handful of overworked special advisers, many of them young and inexperienced. These roles are important and should be seen to be. The ability to offer better pay to attract more high-caliber people to such roles would enhance the quality of decision-making, particularly when combined with greater control over the appointment of senior permanent officials.

For democratic accountability to be meaningful, we must recognize that everything government does is to some degree political. A grown-up approach would acknowledge this basic fact and give politicians the assistance they need. I don't deny that there are currently difficulties in attracting high-caliber people to take on political roles. But this is the outcome of the problem we have in politics, not the cause.

Lesson 4: Conservatism Must Win across the Free World, Particularly in the United States of America

Perhaps the most immediate challenge facing conservatives is the need to restore conservative leadership to the United States, Canada, Australia, and across the free world. As I have recounted, I've gotten used to attending international summits and realizing I was the only conservative in the room. That cannot continue if we are to roll back the influence of the Left and take the fight to our enemies overseas.

In the United States, while there has been conservative success in some states such as Texas and in winning control of the House of Representatives, the presidency—and with it the executive branch—is under Democrat control. Conservatives in Britain and other Western countries should worry about this. We need our political allies in the United States to take the White House and pursue a bold policy agenda in 2025.

This is an area in which the center-right has been too weak. Domestic politics in our allied countries matters. The Left is much more adept at organizing across the globe and has done so all too effectively to roll back the achievements of conservatives. They have created international alliances on various issues, from economic policy to climate change action to human rights, all underpinned by left-wing ideology.

Conservatives have to mobilize to counter them. We should not be neutral about the increase in left-wing influence in other Western countries, any more than we should be about such increases in our own countries. Too much of the international economic establishment has been captured by those who are unsympathetic or actively hostile to conservative economics and free markets. Just as I faced opposition within the United Kingdom from our own central bank and financial quango, so their equivalents in New York and Washington also fueled the climate of skepticism. They are part of the same problem.

Those of us on the right need allies if we are to change attitudes and win the battle of ideas once again. That means we must back each other and do all we can to ensure the return of conservatives to power across the West.

Lesson 5: We Must Reassert the Nation State

As we regain conservative control of governments in the West, we also need to ensure they have the tools to deliver conservative policies, whether in terms of economic and fiscal policy or on foreign relations and robust defense. This will require leaders in those countries to reassert the power of the nation-state.

Over very many decades, there has been a trend towards the creation of ever more international institutions and structures to coordinate action between governments. This has often been well-intentioned. But as with domestic institutions, there has been a tendency for these bodies to become infused with certain collective ideas over the decades, to grow the size of their bureaucracies and drift towards the left.

International economic institutions such as the World Bank and International Monetary Fund are the most obvious examples of this, with their collective adherence to economic orthodoxy. But other organizations, such as the World Trade Organization, the World Health Organization, and the United Nations, have also become problematic. Amazingly, these global quangos receive £7.5 billion ($9.2 billion) per year from the British government. It is very hard to justify taxpayer money going into these institutions while our opponents are shirking responsibility and at the same time using international funding as leverage. When we have such bodies tolerating egregious abuses by member states such as China, and the absurd sight of Iran being invited to chair the UN's Human Rights Council, it is clear they have outlived their usefulness.

Alongside such institutions, the vast web of international agreements to which our countries are subject is also causing problems. The UN Refugee Convention and the European Convention on Human Rights, both drawn up in the early 1950s, were important statements of moral purpose whose intentions were directed towards a worthy cause. But certainly for us in Britain they are no longer fit for purpose as they stand, and are increasingly being used by our enemies against us. They have also allowed the embedding of a conception of human rights law that has undermined the sovereignty of Parliament.

Instead of seeking to expand the scope of worldwide agreements and global institutions, we should instead reassert the role of the nation-state and the ability of countries to work together as allies. A restoration of British and American exceptionalism is part of this. Those countries that share the same moral values should join with us to develop a coalition of the willing to deal with rogue states. We should not have to put up with the absurdity of seeing Western countries dutifully complying with international obligations while hostile authoritarian states flout them.

An "economic NATO" should be established with Western countries clubbing together to coordinate their approach to trade with hostile countries. During the Cold War, the United States led the Coordinating

Committee for Multilateral Export Controls (COCOM) on Warsaw Treaty countries and China, which coordinated the economic approach to communist regimes. We should adopt a similar alliance for the economies of the free world now.

Lesson 6: We Must End Appeasement

The final and most fundamental lesson that conservatives across the West need to learn, relearn, and continue to abide by is that appeasing our enemies does not work and should never be pursued. This applies in terms of our political opponents domestically, and it most certainly applies in terms of our enemies abroad.

There is no excuse for not having learned this lesson. We know that appeasement is a disastrous approach, as history has shown time and time again. Yet we seem still to be at risk of repeating the mistakes of the 1930s, this time with China, Russia, and Iran. Those countries could hardly be clearer that they see the West in general and the United Kingdom and the United States specifically as their enemies. Despite this, our governments continue with varying degrees of appeasement, whether through trade deals, farcical attempts at "engagement" on climate change, or turning a blind eye to human rights abuses and hostile military incursions.

Instead of continuing this weak-willed and morally bankrupt equivocation, we need to learn from Ronald Reagan's approach to the Soviet Union. He was unflinchingly blunt in calling it out as "an evil empire" and asserting the virtues of the free world as a demonstrably superior system of government. We need to do the same and firmly stake out the moral and political high ground.

This will involve tough action against China in particular. It will mean uniting to deny China our technology and resources. It will mean exposing China's human rights abuses and giving encouragement to dissident movements that seek to break the stranglehold of the Chinese Communist Party over its people. We should deny China access to our markets and seek to cut it off completely from the world trading system. Anybody doing business with China in Western nations should be regarded as a pariah.

We also need to be much tougher on those in our own countries who are supporters of hostile regimes. In 2019, President Trump designated Iran's Islamic Revolutionary Guard Corps (IRGC) a terrorist organization, and other countries in the West should do the same. Denying China the soft power it has in the United Kingdom by closing down the Confucius Institutes is long overdue. We should also become much more vigilant with regard to individuals entering our countries from hostile states. We know that Russia and China in particular are engaged in a relentless campaign of covert espionage and subversion against us. We need to root it out and ensure that their hostile agents have nowhere to hide.

A Call to Action

People ask me what I would do differently if could relive my time in government. My answer is that I would start much earlier. I do not regret trying to turn the country around when I made it to Number 10. I stick by my promises. But trying to implement bold change after your party has been in government for more than a dozen years is an uphill struggle, even without the attendant problems of an overmighty administrative state and too many CINOs (conservatives in name only).

Knowing all I now know from ten years in government, I can see the challenges are so great that they can only be overcome by persistent and concerted effort. That has to take place over many years. I cannot turn back the clock to the start of my ten years in office, but I can look forward to the next ten years and urge those starting out on that journey to heed my warnings.

We have ten years to save the West. We must start now.

Acknowledgments

The last fourteen years, since I became a Member of Parliament, and the ten years during which I served in government have been a kaleidoscope of experiences, as I have sought to do all I could to push forward the conservative agenda. During that time I have gained inspiration from other politicians, members of the public, friends, activists, and my family. I have also seen some brilliant civil servants chiselling away at the coalface. In putting together this book, I am indebted to all of them for their friendship, support, and encouragement.

In particular, thanks are due to my office and particularly Jonathan Isaby, Ian Sherwood, and Mike Hoskin; all my friends at the Legatum Institute, GB News, and 5 Hertford Street; my parliamentary colleagues including Simon Clarke and Kwasi Kwarteng, who have looked over various chapters; those who supported me in the leadership campaign, including Jon Moynihan and Matthew Elliott; all those who worked for me over the years as special advisers and policy advisers; the team at PopCon—including Mark Littlewood and Ed Barker; The Growth Commission, especially Doug McWilliams, Shanker Singham, Lucy Harris, and Catherine McBride; Lance Forman; my Australian and American allies including George Brandis, Tony Abbott, and Nile Gardiner; my friends in Norfolk including Conservative Association chairman Matt Sawyer; my predecessors Christopher Fraser and Gillian Shephard for their sage advice—not enough of which I listened to; as well as to Greville Howard, Matt Ridley, and Dan Hannan for their help.

Thanks to David Cameron, Theresa May, and Boris Johnson for giving me the opportunity.

Thanks are also due to my literary agent Dylan Colligan and all his team at Javelin, and to Tony Lyons, Elizabeth Kantor, and all their colleagues at Skyhorse for taking on this project and embracing it with such zeal. I must also pay tribute to Tom Spence and Harry Crocker for the vital role they played in getting the project off the ground and to Matt Purple and Kathleen Curran for their meticulous edit of the text. It should go without saying, of course, that any errors that remain are my own.

Finally, I must thank my family for their wisdom, love, and understanding.

Notes

Chapter 1: A Leftist Education

1. Polly Toynbee, "Of All the Wild Tory Dogma, This Cut-Price Baby Farming Is the Worst," *The Guardian*, October 18, 2012, https://www.theguardian.com/commentisfree/2012/oct/18/tory-dogma-cut-price-baby-farming.
2. Catherine Gaunt, "Pre-School Learning Alliance Steps Up Campaign against Ratio Changes," *Nursery World*, March 1, 2013, https://www.nurseryworld.co.uk/news/article/pre-school-learning-alliance-steps-up-campaign-against-ratio-changes.
3. Richard J. Arneson, "Foucault and Postmodernism," Britannica, https://www.britannica.com/topic/political-philosophy/Foucault-and-postmodernism.
4. Hermann Kelly, "The Bloody Origins of Modern Trans and Gender Ideology," The Burkean, May 28, 2022, https://www.theburkean.ie/articles/2022/05/28/the-bloody-origins-of-modern-trans-and-gender-ideology.

Chapter 2: A Hostile Environment

1. *Friends of the Earth Limited Report and Accounts for the Year Ended 30 June 2022*, Friends of the Earth UK, https://cdn.friendsoftheearth.uk/sites/default/files/downloads/FOEL_Annual_Accounts_2021-22.pdf; "Join the Political Lobbying Network," Greenpeace, https://www.greenpeace.org.uk/volunteering/join-the-political-lobbying-network/; "Affecting Change in Six Big Areas," Worldwide Fund for Nature, https://www.wwf.org.uk/who-we-are/big-wins.

Index